# THE NON-PERFORMING LOANS DIRECTIVE

ELGAR COMMENTARIES IN FINANCIAL LAW

**Series Editor:** Iris H.-Y. Chiu, *Professor of Corporate Law and Financial Regulation, University College London, UK*

Volumes in this series provide comprehensive commentary and analysis on major instruments across the spectrum of financial law, from both the European and international sphere. The series addresses a wide range of issues associated with financial law, from banking to capital markets, including topics dealing with wholesale and retail markets. With a clear and structured format that mirrors the logic of the instrument itself and facilitates pin-point searches, each *Commentary* examines the context, interpretation and implementation of key instruments governing the complex field of financial law. Featuring the original text of the respective articles, along with detailed lists of relevant cases and associated regulation, the *Commentaries* form valuable reference works for both scholars who want a platform for their research, and practitioners who need clear guidance on interpreting the rules.

For a full list of Edward Elgar published titles, including the titles in this series, visit our website at www.e-elgar.com.

# THE NON-PERFORMING LOANS DIRECTIVE

## A Commentary

*Edited by*

ANDREA MIGLIONICO
*Associate Professor, School of Law, University of Reading, UK*

ELGAR COMMENTARIES IN FINANCIAL LAW

Edward Elgar
PUBLISHING

Cheltenham, UK · Northampton, MA, USA

Published by

Edward Elgar Publishing Limited
The Lypiatts
15 Lansdown Road
Cheltenham
Glos GL50 2JA
UK

Edward Elgar Publishing, Inc.
William Pratt House
9 Dewey Court
Northampton
Massachusetts 01060
USA

Authorised representative in the EU for GPSR queries only: Easy Access System Europe – Mustamäe tee 50, 10621 Tallinn, Estonia, gpsr.requests@easproject.com

A catalogue record for this book is available from the British Library

Library of Congress Control Number: 2025950644

This book is available electronically in the **Elgar**online
Law subject collection
https://doi.org/10.4337/9781035323401

MIX
Paper | Supporting responsible forestry
FSC® C013604

ISBN 978 1 0353 2339 5 (cased)
ISBN 978 1 0353 2340 1 (eBook)
ISBN 978 1 0353 9026 7 (ePub)

Printed and bound by CPI Group (UK) Ltd, Croydon, CR0 4YY

# CONTENTS

# EXTENDED CONTENTS

# CONTRIBUTORS

**Andreas Kokkinis** joined Birmingham Law School as an Associate Professor in 2020 having before worked at the University of Warwick, UCL, and the University of Kent. He holds a PhD from UCL (2014), an LLM from the LSE (2009), and an LLB from the National University of Athens (2008). Dr Kokkinis has published widely in the areas of corporate governance and financial regulation, and engages regularly with policy makers and the media. His work has been published in journals such as the Journal of Corporate Law Studies, Journal of Financial Regulation, Singapore Journal of Legal Studies, Indiana Journal of Global Legal Studies, and Journal of Banking Regulation. Dr Kokkinis has presented his research in several countries including the US, Colombia, Singapore, Malaysia, Norway, Germany, France, Italy, Spain, Poland, and Latvia.

**Andrea Miglionico** is an Associate Professor of Law at the University of Reading. He is Programme Director of Commercial LLM and Deputy Director of the Centre for Commercial Law and Financial Regulation (CCLFR). He was previously an Associate Lecturer and Research Fellow at the Centre for Commercial Law Studies, Queen Mary, University of London. He has taught undergraduate and postgraduate law courses in the United Kingdom and Europe. He holds an LLM Master of Laws from the London School of Economics and a PhD from the Queen Mary, University of London. Dr Miglionico carries out research in the areas of financial markets regulation, banking law and climate finance.

**Georgios Psaroudakis** is Professor of Commercial Law at the Faculty of Law, Aristotle University of Thessaloniki. He has studied at the Universities of Athens, Oxford, and Hamburg. He has published extensively, in particular on company, insolvency, and financial law and he has participated repeatedly at law-drafting committees in the fields of banking and company law. He is a legal advisor to the Bank of Greece; all views expressed here are solely personal.

**Kyriaki Vasileiou** is a Lecturer in Commercial Law at the University of Manchester, is a graduate of the University of Lancaster where she also conducted postgraduate research under Professor David Milman. She teaches and writes in the fields of company law, corporate insolvency and corporate finance law. Dr Vasileiou is a member of the Centre for Law and Business at the University of Manchester and the co-director of Commercial and General LLM.

**Shunqi Yang** holds a PhD in Law from King's College London (2024), an MA in Law from the University of Bristol (2020), an LLB from Southwest University (2018), and a BA in English from Southwest University (2018). Her research focuses on international corporate governance, financial regulation, and law and technology. Her PhD thesis, *The Regulation of Dual-Class Shares and Weighted Voting Rights: Examining Chinese Corporate Practices in the Context of Global Market Law Reforms*, identifies systemic inconsistencies between reform goals and existing regulatory methodologies. It argues that coherent regulatory frameworks, rather than mere strictness, are essential for efficient capital markets. She has published several articles on topics including dual-class shares, UK stewardship, and Chinese financial courts. Dr Yang has collaborated with scholars from the UK and globally, including those from France, Japan, the US, and Brazil.

# INTRODUCTION

The treatment of distressed loans has become a major concern for supervisory authorities and bank regulators. It is commonly considered that a bank loan is defined as non-performing (NPL) when more than 90 days have passed without the borrower paying the agreed instalments or interest. NPLs play a pivotal role in the linkages between poor lending and credit risk, but this has implications for the management of asset quality and for the stability of the firm and the banking sector. A high stock of NPLs is undesirable to investors and can lead to a decrease in the share price of the bank, profitability loss and potentially to a distressed scenario. During the global financial crisis of 2008–9, banks experienced a surge of NPLs in their books when the inability of borrowers to pay back their loans was magnified by the scant attention to sufficiently manage the riskiness of high levels of deteriorated assets.[1]

The European Central Bank (ECB) established a prudential regime to strengthen the capital rules and banking supervision since NPLs represent a major systemic threat that they are facing as they may rapidly lead to bank and borrower insolvencies. The ECB regulatory initiatives have been followed up by the Commission's proposal for a Regulation on a minimum loss coverage for NPEs adopted in March 2018, which complements the Capital Requirements Directive (CRD IV) and establishes a 'case-by-case' approach in the application of the prudential backstop for NPEs.

In March 2018, the Commission adopted a proposal for a directive on credit servicers and credit purchasers as part of its overall strategy to tackle high stocks of NPLs accumulated on EU banks' balance sheets. The proposal aimed to foster the development of secondary markets for NPLs by removing undue obstacles to credit servicing and to the transfer of bank loans to third parties across the EU. Further, the proposal defined the activities carried out by credit servicers, established common standards for their authorisation and

1 Douglas W. Arner, Emilios Avgouleas and Evan C. Gibson, 'COVID-19, Macroeconomic and Sustainability Shocks, Moral Hazard and Resolution of Systemic Banking Crises: Designing Appropriate Systems of Public Support' (2022) 23(4) *European Business Organization Law Review* 939.

cross-border operation, and imposed conduct rules across the EU. The proposal passed through key revisions and a compromise legal draft before entering into force.

The Directive represents a step forward towards the standardisation of rules for credit servicers and credit purchasers across the EU as it facilitates the sales of NPLs, including across national borders, while ensuring that borrowers' rights are not hampered in the process. Ample supervision is mandated to designated authorities in the home Member State which authorise and supervise credit servicers in co-operation with the authorities of other Member States. The Directive introduces a set of articulated disclosure and reporting obligations for banks selling NPLs (e.g. banks will need to use the prescribed templates for the purposes of providing information to purchasers). The main rationale is to ensure that the prospective purchaser can properly assess the risk while the authorities are mandated to disclose and report the NPL sales. Credit purchasers are subject to several obligations and regulatory requirements. For a non-EU credit purchaser, these include the requirement to appoint an EU representative to ensure compliance with the Directive and non-bank purchasers of certain NPLs need to appoint an authorised credit servicer. However, the Directive is not exempt from criticisms raised by policymakers and stakeholders raising perplexity on the complex regulatory framework and areas of uncertainty where the EU legislator did not clarify the applicability of rules.[2] As noted, it is unclear, for example, if the involvement of a single EU bank in the initial lending syndicate will bring the whole loan into scope or only that portion of the loan funded by the EU bank.[3] This legal uncertainty reflects the numerous amendments and changes which characterised the gestation of the Directive. Further, the Loan Market Association observed that there remain some issues regarding the practical application of the Directive to syndicated lending arrangements.[4]

---

2 For an overview see Andrew Bryan, 'The New NPL Directive: An Uncertain Path Ahead' (2021) 36(11) *Butterworths Journal of International Banking and Financial Law* 755. It is argued that

> Rather than structure the market and give it more liquidity, transparency and standardisation, it is possible that requiring detailed disclosure templates to be filled in will discourage or even render impossible the sale of some NPLs if the information isn't available (e.g. because the originating credit institution no longer exists or sold the loan while it was performing and no longer holds the relevant records or has an interest in the on-sale of the loan).

3 Financial Markets Law Committee, 'Letter to the European Banking Authority: E.U. Directive on Credit Servicers and Credit Purchasers' (30 August 2022), https://fmlc.org/publications/letter-to-the-european-banking-authority-e-u-directive-on-credit-servicers-and-credit-purchasers/.

4 See https://www.lma.eu.com/npl.

The NPLs credit servicing directive complemented the set of regulatory measures to monitor and resolve NPEs. Regulation No 630 of 2019 introduced minimum loss coverage layers of capital for NPEs to address newly formed losses, providing that 'a forbearance measure granted to a non-performing exposure should not discontinue the classification of that exposure as non-performing unless certain strict discontinuation criteria are fulfilled'. In parallel, the Directive No 1023 of 2019 provided a degree of harmonisation for restructuring distressed debts while aiming to develop secondary markets where banks can transfer the risk of holding NPLs to non-bank investors.[5] However the slow pace of secondary markets, which seems to be evolving with difficulties in the short–medium term, has called into question the need to find alternative measures for resolving distressed loans, such as the creation of asset management companies with the objective to fill the information asymmetry between buyers and sellers in the NPLs market.[6] The legislation improves the supervisory toolkit and the classification of loan quality: the need to ensure consistency in the resolving mechanisms of defaulted debts and to create a harmonised monitoring regime has been recognised by the EU authorities in the regulatory approach for NPLs.[7] The objective is to reduce the burden of NPLs in the banks' balance sheets by introducing efficient out-of-court procedures to recover value from collateral and to lower the costs for resolving NPLs, making them more competitive in the market.[8]

The ECB focussed on creating a common classification of the asset quality standard that should complement a classification of sources of banks' funding, i.e. equity and debt, and has incentivised ad hoc resolving options to deal with NPLs swiftly, for example securitisation schemes in some EU countries (e.g. Italy and Greece).[9] The out-of-court procedures are a better option than going to court as they might avoid the length of court proceedings as the available

5 Filippo Annunziata, 'Credit Funds Regulation in the EU and the Debate on NPLS and AMCS. The Need for Further Harmonization' (2022) 19(1) *European Company and Financial Law Review* 66–67.

6 Edoardo Gaffeo and Ronny Mazzocchi, '"The price is right": Using Auction Theory to Enhance Competition in the NPL Market' (2019) 20(1) *Journal of Banking Regulation* 104. See also Ying Qian, 'Evaluating the Potential of Asset Management Companies to Relieve Global Debt Distress' (2023) Boston University Global Development Policy Center, GCI Working Paper 028, https://www.bu.edu/gdp/files/2023/04/GCI_WP_028_YQ-AMCs-FIN.pdf.

7 NPL Advisory Panel, 'Monitoring the State of NPL Secondary Markets' (February 2025), 14–15, https://finance.ec.europa.eu/publications/npl-advisory-panel-paper-monitoring-state-non-performing-loans-npl-secondary-markets_en.

8 Jannis Bischof, Nicolas Rudolf and Wilhelm Schmundt, 'How Do Non-Performing Loans Evolve Along the Economic Cycle? The Role of Macroeconomic Conditions and Legal Efficiency' (2022) 31(5) *European Accounting Review* 1149.

9 Ismael Alexander Boudiaf and Fernando Gonzalez Miranda, 'An Empirical Study of Securitisations of Non-Performing Loans' (2022) ECB Occasional Paper No. 2022/292, 16–17.

legal tools in national judicial systems may not be sufficient or may not allow for the timely resolution of bad loans.[10] The establishment of out-of-court procedures, expediting the timeline for debt restructuring, incentivises the NPL sale and reduces creditors' losses.[11]

The implications of NPLs in the financial markets can turn into banking failures and economic losses as experienced in the aftermath of the global financial crisis. This is exacerbated by a lack of harmonised treatment of non-performing exposures and absence of coordination in the resolving policies.[12] The Directive aims to enhance convergence of supervision; common accounting and regulatory practices are necessary to deal with the NPL problem. This lack of consistency creates a grey area in which the public financial support can affect the recovery and restructuring measures of deteriorated loans.

10 Maziar Peihani, 'Resolution of Small and Medium-Sized Deposit-Taking Institutions: Back to Basics?' (2023) 60(2) *American Business Law Journal* 460–1.

11 It is worth noting that the NPLs credit servicing directive complements the 2015 EU Insolvency Regulation and aims to harmonise pre-insolvency restructuring mechanisms for NPLs among Member States.

12 Seraina N. Grunewald and Marije Louisse, 'How Asset Management Companies Can Help Tackle the NPL Crisis – A State Aid Perspective within the Resolution Framework' (2022) European Banking Institute Working Paper Series no. 109, 2022, https://ssrn.com/abstract=3999059.

# ACKNOWLEDGEMENTS

This edited volume is the result of reflections and thoughts shared with authors and contributors on the trajectory of EU legislation on non-performing loans (NPLs). The research findings and commentary of the NPLs Directive have been presented at the Workshop 'Risk Sharing in the Euro Area' at the Aristotle University of Thessaloniki on 29–30 October 2021, which is part of a joint project with the University of Tübingen financed by the Volkswagen Foundation (https://uni-tuebingen.de/en/144816).

The volume has benefitted from insightful comments and observations raised at the workshop from both lawyers and economists, which provided a critical view of the EU directive and regulatory developments of NPLs credit servicers. This event was instrumental for a preliminary assessment on the draft NPL servicing directive, with a particular focus on discussing what discrepancies exist between Member States in this area, how such discrepancies may influence the common market, and how the Directive will contribute to solving such problems.

The editor would like to thank the contributors, reviewers and colleagues in the field for their patient effort and collaboration provided throughout this work.

The editor also owes a debt of gratitude to and acknowledges the welcome assistance of Fiona Todd, the commissioning editor, of Edward Elgar Law; Roisin Sheridan, the project manager; and the assistant commissioning editors, for their perceptive suggestions and advice on an early draft. Their constructive feedback and rigorous competence significantly enhanced the content of this work. Special thanks are due to Sabrina Zaher, the senior development editor; Emily White, the assistant editor; the senior desk editor and the copy editor for reviewing the manuscript. The author would also wish to thank the series editor of the Elgar Commentaries in Financial Law for feedback and comments on the research project.

The editor is particularly grateful to the Centre for Commercial Law and Financial Regulation (CCLFR) at Reading University for the intellectual environment and institutional support. Sincere thanks are also due to the Law School and Law Research Division at Reading for insightful guidance and scholarly methodology.

# ABBREVIATIONS

| **Abbreviation** | **Expansion** |
|---|---|
| ACPR | Autorité de Contrôle Prudentiel et de Résolution |
| AFM | Autoriteit Financiële Markten |
| AIFM | Alternative Investment Fund Manager |
| AIFMD | Alternative Investment Fund Managers Directive |
| AMCs | Asset Management Companies |
| AMF | Autorité des Marchés Financiers |
| BaFin | Bundesanstalt für Finanzdienstleistungsaufsicht |
| BCBS | Basel Committee on Banking Supervision |
| BIS | Bank for International Settlements |
| CCD | Consumer Credit Directive |
| CESEE | Central and Eastern Europe |
| CRD | Capital Requirements Directive |
| CRR | Capital Requirements Regulation |
| CSDR | Central Securities Depositories Regulation |
| DNB | De Nederlandsche Bank |
| EBA | European Banking Authority |
| EC | European Commission |
| ECB | European Central Bank |
| EEA | European Economic Area |
| EIOPA | European Insurance and Occupational Pensions Authority |
| EP | European Parliament |
| ESAs | European Supervisory Authorities |
| ESFS | European System of Financial Supervision |
| ESMA | European Securities and Markets Authority |
| EU | European Union |
| EUCJ | European Union Court of Justice |
| FCA | Financial Conduct Authority |
| FSUG | Financial Services User Group |

| | |
|---|---|
| GDPR | General Data Protection Regulation |
| IAS | International Accounting Standard |
| IFRS | International Financial Reporting Standards |
| IMF | Independent Monetary Fund |
| IRB | Internal ratings-based |
| ITS | Implementing technical standards |
| Kifid | Klachteninstituut Financiële Dienstverlening |
| LEI | Legal entity identifier |
| LMA | Loan Market Association |
| MCD | Mortgage Credit Directive |
| MiFID | Markets in Financial Instruments Directive |
| MS | Member State |
| NCAs | National competent authorities |
| NPA | Non-performing asset |
| NPEs | Non-performing exposures |
| NPLs | Non-performing loans |
| OJEU | Official Journal of the European Union |
| PRA | Prudential Regulation Authority |
| REFIT | Regulatory fitness and performance programme |
| SMEs | Small and medium-sized enterprises |
| SNA | System of National Accounts |
| SSM | Single Supervisory Mechanism |
| TEU | Treaty on European Union |
| TFEU | Treaty on the Functioning of the European Union |
| UCITS | Undertakings for Collective Investment in Transferable Securities |
| UK | United Kingdom |
| UN | United Nations |
| US | United States |
| WB | World Bank |

# TABLE OF CASES

# TABLE OF LEGISLATION

## EUROPEAN UNION

## GREECE



## ITALY

# TITLE I

# SUBJECT MATTER, SCOPE AND DEFINITIONS

# ARTICLE 1

# SUBJECT MATTER

**Andrea Miglionico**

**This Directive lays down a common framework and requirements for:**

1. **credit servicers of a creditor's rights under a non-performing credit agreement, or of the non-performing credit agreement itself, issued by a credit institution established in the Union, who act on behalf of a credit purchaser;**
2. **credit purchasers of a creditor's rights under a non-performing credit agreement, or of the non-performing credit agreement itself, issued by a credit institution established in the Union.**



## A. INTRODUCTION

1.01 This article provides an introductory overview of the scope of the Directive which covers credit servicers and credit purchasers of a creditor's rights in the non-performing loan (NPL) agreement. Specifically, the provision refers to the regulatory requirements for credit institutions operating in the Union. The Directive represents a notable achievement in dealing with deteriorated loans: it introduces a new category of EU service providers and credit servicers with a view to enhance debt collection procedures. The legislation establishes articulated mechanisms to deal with NPLs through credit servicing activities and consumer credit agreements. The directive also aims to create a common framework for expediting debt collection along with the intermediary function of credit servicers. The overall objective is to incentivise the implementation of recovery procedures for resolving NPLs, making them more competitive in the market. This legislative intervention followed Regulation No 630 of 2019, which introduced minimum loss coverage layers of capital for non-performing exposures (NPEs) to address newly formed losses,[1] and Directive No 1023 of 2019, which provided a degree of harmonisation for restructuring distressed debts.[2]

The need to ensure consistency in the resolving tools of bank crisis management, and to foster a harmonised monitoring toolkit represents a challenge for the EU authorities in the context of NPLs. The directive on credit servicers and credit purchasers represents a central part of the "NPL Action Plan" and the Commission's overall strategy to enhance debt recovery frameworks. The reform also incentivises the development of secondary markets for NPLs, which represents a necessary condition to ensure that credit losses are sufficiently covered, making their resolution or sale easier.[3] The secondary markets for distressed assets are complemented with the implementation of national asset management companies (AMCs) and the market for credit servicers and credit purchasers to manage NPLs in the Eurozone. These measures should be combined with an EU network of cooperation among AMCs and national insolvency regimes. **1.02**

## B. THE REGULATORY FRAMEWORK

The Directive intends to adopt an overall strategy to address undesirable stocks of NPLs through secondary markets and out-of-court resolving mechanisms which should expedite the transfer of bank loans to third parties while, at the same time, removing undue obstacles to credit servicing.[4] It establishes out-of-court settlement mechanisms through the implementation of a distinct common accelerated extrajudicial collateral enforcement system. The reform responds to the surge of impaired assets on banks' balance sheets accumulated in the aftermath of the 2008–9 global financial crisis which has led to several regulatory interventions to create a prudential regime for NPLs. The **1.03**

1 Regulation (EU) 2019/630 of the European Parliament and of the Council of 17 April 2019 amending Regulation (EU) No 575/2013 as regards minimum loss coverage for non-performing exposures (OJ L 111/2019, p. 4).

2 Directive (EU) 2019/1023 of the European Parliament and of the Council of 20 June 2019 on preventive restructuring frameworks, on discharge of debt and disqualifications, and on measures to increase the efficiency of procedures concerning restructuring, insolvency and discharge of debt, and amending Directive (EU) 2017/1132 (OJ L 172/2019, p. 18).

3 Peter Grasmann, Markus Aspegren and Nicolas Willems, 'Tackling Non-performing Loans in Europe' (October 2019) SUERF Policy Note, Issue No 107, https://www.suerf.org/policynotes/8283/tackling-non-performing-loans-in-europe.

4 Johannes Kasinger et al., 'Nonperforming Loans – New Risks and Policies? NPL Resolution after COVID-19: Main Differences to Previous Crises' (2021), SAFE White Paper, No. 84, http://hdl.handle.net/10419/232027.

European Central Bank (ECB) supervisory regime and the European Banking Authority's (EBA) prudential approach to support the capital rules represent the regulatory framework along with the directive on credit servicers.

**1.04** NPLs represent a major systemic threat that they are facing as they may rapidly lead to bank insolvencies. In the aftermath of the financial crisis, the banking sector experienced a rapid rise in loan delinquencies and defaults driven by the limitations of the Basel rules and the adequacy of capital requirements.[5] The crisis amplified the crucial role of NPLs in the linkages between frictions on credit markets and macroeconomic vulnerabilities.[6] The overall regulatory response to the deterioration of loans was characterised by the transition from a backward-looking regime to a forward-looking approach in which credit events are identified before they occur, preparing banks for losses when they were realised.[7] The main issue in the previous regime was the inherent pro-cyclicality of loan performance expectations by banks, meaning that credit institutions underestimated the risk of instability.

**1.05** The financial crisis also revealed that the normative framework of NPLs was defective as it gave firms a high degree of discretion in supervision and enforcement mechanisms. In terms of the prudential regime of NPLs, the main problem was the lack of harmonised rules to assess obligors' ability to repay and the timeframe of non-performing.[8] Various factors determine the assessment of asset quality, namely whether collateral, guarantees, and other forms of security are mirrored in the asset quality classification; whether the full outstanding value or only part of a loan is reported as non-performing; and how to treat restructured loans. The definition of bank capital under the Basel rules has provided further clarity in the assessment of loans, although less attention has been paid to harmonising the classification of assets in the balance sheet.[9] The absence of a common level playing field for NPLs made any meaningful comparison of banks' assets difficult for investors and regulators.

---

5 Aurelio Gurrea-Martínez and Nydia Remolina, 'The Dark Side of Implementing Basel Capital Requirements: Theory, Evidence, and Policy' (2019) 22 *Journal of International Economic Law* 125.

6 Mwanza Nkusu, 'Nonperforming Loans and Macrofinancial Vulnerabilities in Advanced Economies' (2011), IMF Working Paper, 4.

7 Samuel Knott, Peter Richardson, Katie Rismanchi and Kallol Sen, 'Understanding the Fair Value of Banks' Loans' (2014), Bank of England Financial Stability Paper No. 31, p. 7, https://www.bankofengland.co.uk/-/media/boe/files/financial-stability-paper/2014/understanding-the-fair-value-of-banks-loans.

8 Patrizia Baudino and Hyuncheol Yun, 'Resolution of Non-performing Loans – Policy Options' (October 2017) FSI Insights on policy implementation No 3, https://www.bis.org/fsi/publ/insights3.pdf.

9 Basel Committee on Banking Supervision, 'Report on International Convergence of Capital Measurement and Capital Standards' (1988), https://www.bis.org/publ/bcbsc111.pdf.

The Basel Committee on Banking Supervision (BCBS) published guidelines in evaluating credit risk for regulatory purposes:[10] under the Basel II capital framework, the internal ratings-based (IRB) approach required credit firms to provide their own estimations of probability of default, loss given default and exposure at default.[11] A distressed loan is defined as where an obligor is 90 days past due, or is unlikely to pay its credit obligations to the banking group in full, without recourse by the bank to actions such as realising security. The BCBS issued guidance indicating loan classification which recommended banks implement an asset quality system based on credit risk.[12] Further, the BCBS produced guidelines on the prudential treatment of problem assets aiming to set a common definition for the terms 'non-performing loan' and 'forbearance'.[13] This definition applies to all credit exposures from on-balance sheet loans, including debt securities, and off-balance sheet items, such as loan commitments and financial guarantees. The classification of non-performing developed for this purpose combines all exposures defined as in default under the Basel definition which are considered non-performing; exposures determined to be impaired for accounting purposes are defined as non-performing; and loans that are past due by 90 days or where it is determined that full repayment is unlikely[14] are also considered non-performing. The BCBS clarified that collateralisation does not influence past due status and should not be considered in the categorisation of NPEs: in addition, forbearance is defined as "a concession granted by a bank to a counterparty for reasons of financial difficulties that would not be otherwise considered by the lender".[15] Forbearance comprises concessions extended to any exposures in the form of a loan, a debt security or an off-balance-sheet item due to the position of the 1.06

10 Basel Committee on Banking Supervision, 'Sound Practices for Loan Accounting and Disclosure' (1999), Basel Committee on Banking Supervision Paper, 35, para 91.

11 Basel Committee on Banking Supervision, 'International Convergence of Capital Measurement and Capital Standards' (2004) Revised Framework.

12 Basel Committee on Banking Supervision, 'Sound Credit Risk Assessment and Valuation for Loans' (2006), https://www.bis.org/publ/bcbs126.pdf. The purpose of these criteria is to calculate a 'Non-Performing Asset' (NPA) ratio when assessing exposures to other banks.

13 These definitions are intended to complement existing accounting and regulatory measures, and as reference points to promote comparability. See Basel Committee on Banking Supervision, 'Prudential Treatment of Problem Assets – Definitions of Non-performing Exposures and Forbearance' (2017), Guidelines, http://www.bis.org/bcbs/publ/d403.htm.

14 This is similar to the definition developed by the EBA, Final draft implementing technical standards (ITS) on supervisory reporting on forbearance and non-performing exposures under Article 99(4) of Regulation (EU) No 575/2013, EBA/ITS/2013/03/rev1.

15 The Basel Committee on Banking Supervision notes that non-performing status should be applied at the level of the counterparty in the case of exposures to a non-retail counterparty, and at the level of each exposure in the case of exposures to a retail counterparty.

counterparty.[16] It covers exposures of performing and non-performing status before the granting of forbearance measures. The main purpose is to ensure a common approach to the disclosure of modified loans and debt securities due to the case of the borrower's financial difficulties.[17]

**1.07** The crisis amplified the crucial role of NPLs in the linkages between frictions on credit markets and macroeconomic vulnerabilities.[18] The overall regulatory response to the deterioration of loans was characterised by the transition from a backward-looking regime to a forward-looking approach in which credit events are identified before they occur, preparing banks for losses when they are realised.[19] The main issue in the previous regime was the inherent pro-cyclicality of loan performance expectations by banks, meaning that credit institutions underestimated the risk of instability accelerated by a high stock of NPLs.

## C. THE EUROPEAN STRATEGY TO TACKLE NPLs

**1.08** The debate about the implications of NPLs in the financial sector has intensified following the introduction of legislative measures designed to contain the surge of impaired assets on banks' balance sheets. The absence of coordination in the resolving policies exacerbates the lack of consistency in the treatment of deteriorated debts. Employing out-of-court procedures to recover value from collateral and to lower the costs for resolving large exposures, making them more competitive in the market, might avoid protracted judicial proceedings. This expedites the timeline for debt restructuring, incentivises the NPL sale, and reduces creditors' losses. The EU authorities launched several regulatory initiatives to reduce the volume of NPLs, culminating in the approval of the credit servicers directive.[20] This intervention followed Regulation No 630 of

---

16 Forbearance involves granting concessions to borrowers who are unlikely to be able to repay their loans under the current terms and conditions. Its measures can take the form of refinancing or restructuring the loan, or modifying the terms and conditions (including the interest rate and maturity). Such measures should be flagged as forbearance regardless of whether the financial difficulties are structural, such as solvency, or temporary, such as liquidity constraints. See ECB, 'Forbearance: Banks Need to Gear Up' (17 May 2023), https://www.bankingsupervision.europa.eu/press/supervisory-newsletters/newsletter/2023/html/ssm.nl230517_1.en.html.

17 The Basel Committee on Banking Supervision recommends banks not to use forbearance practices to avoid classifying loans as non-performing.

18 Nkusu (n 6).

19 Knott, Richardson, Rismanchi and Sen (n 7).

20 Directive (EU) 2021/2167 of the European Parliament and of the Council of 24 November 2021 on credit servicers and credit purchasers and amending Directives 2008/48/EC and 2014/17/EU (OJ L 438/2021, p. 1).

2019, which introduced minimum loss coverage layers of capital for non-performing exposures (NPEs) to address newly formed losses,[21] and Directive No 1023 of 2019, which provided a degree of harmonisation for restructuring distressed debts.[22] These statutory reforms complemented the prudential regime of the ECB for NPLs – articulated in 'supervisory expectations' of future losses – which strengthened the classification of asset quality and established common practices to prevent a high ratio of distressed exposures to total loans.[23] High volumes of NPEs hinder banks' profitability and credit growth while, in parallel, accelerating the insolvency scenario. The ECB focused on the asset quality standard to improve the identification of sources of banks' funding, i.e., equity and debt, and incentivise ad hoc resolving tools to deal with NPLs, such as publicly-funded securitisation schemes. In this context, the Commission's proposal to create a "bad bank" (i.e., an asset management company) to assist credit institutions in the mutualisation of their legacy assets can be considered an improvement in that it relieves banks from the formation of NPLs.[24] However, this proposal combined with the national provisions to enhance securitisation mechanisms (i.e., asset protection schemes) seems a dangerous return to bail-out packages. Banks should engage in private workouts and credit recovery agreements in order to expedite the resolution of defaulted exposures.[25] Outsourcing debt collection services may create negative externalities, impeding bail-in arrangements and the internalisation of losses. Further, reliance on public recapitalisation measures and government financial support to aid failing banks may affect the development of a secondary market for NPLs.[26]

21 Regulation (EU) 2019/630.

22 Directive (EU) 2019/1023.

23 ECB, 'Addendum to the ECB Guidance to Banks on Non-performing Loans: Supervisory Expectations for Prudential Provisioning of Non-performing Exposures' (March 2018), https://www.bankingsupervision.europa.eu/ecb/pub/pdf/ssm.npl_addendum_201803.en.pdf.

24 European Commission, 'Tackling Non-performing Loans in the Aftermath of the COVID-19 Pandemic' COM (2020) 822 final, 16 December 2020, https://ec.europa.eu/finance/docs/law/201216-communication-non-performing-loans_en.pdf. For a commentary, see Andrea Enria, 'ECB: The EU Needs a Regional "bad bank"' *Financial Times* (26 October 2020), https://www.ft.com/content/cc3a9a51-4d9a-4c73-9ff0-9f623ecf4065.

25 Shekhar Aiyar et al., 'A Strategy for Resolving Europe's Problem Loans' (September 2015) IMF Staff Discussion Note, https://www.imf.org/external/pubs/ft/sdn/2015/sdn1519.pdf.

26 Patrick O'Sullivan, 'State Aid Support to Financial Institutions and the Question of Systemic Importance in the 2008 Financial Crisis: Time for a New Approach?' (2019) 30(5) *European Business Law Review* 721.

# ARTICLE 2

## SCOPE

### Andrea Miglionico

This Directive shall apply to:

(a) credit servicers acting on behalf of a credit purchaser in respect of a creditor's rights under a non-performing credit agreement, or of the non-performing credit agreement itself, issued by a credit institution established in the Union in accordance with applicable Union and national law;

(b) credit purchasers of a creditor's rights under a non-performing credit agreement, or of the non-performing credit agreement itself, issued by a credit institution established in the Union in accordance with applicable Union and national law.

2. With regard to credit agreements falling within its scope, this Directive shall not affect contract law principles nor civil law principles under national law with regard to the transfer of a creditor's rights under a credit agreement, or of the credit agreement itself, nor the protection granted to consumers or borrowers pursuant in particular to Regulations (EC) No 593/2008 and (EU) No 1215/2012, and Directives 93/13/EEC, 2008/48/EC, 2014/17/EU and the national provisions transposing those Directives or other relevant provisions of Union and national law relating to consumer protection and borrowers' rights.

3. This Directive shall not affect the restrictions imposed in Member States' national laws regarding the transfer of a creditor's rights under a non-performing credit agreement, or of the non-performing credit agreement itself, that is not past due, or is less than 90 days past due, or is not terminated in accordance with national civil law.

4. This Directive shall not affect requirements in Member States' national laws regarding the servicing of a creditor's rights under a credit agreement, or of the credit agreement itself, when the credit purchaser is a securitisation special purpose entity as defined in Article 2, point (2), of Regulation (EU) 2017/2402 of the European Parliament and of the Council (20) as long as such national laws:

(a) do not affect the level of consumer protection provided by this Directive;

(b) ensure that competent authorities receive the necessary information from credit servicers.

**5. This Directive shall not apply to the following:**

**(a) the servicing of a creditor's rights under a credit agreement, or of the credit agreement itself, carried out by:**

**(i) a credit institution established in the Union;**

**(ii) an alternative investment fund manager (AIFM) authorised or registered in accordance with Directive 2011/61/EU, or a management company, or an investment company authorised in accordance with Directive 2009/65/EC provided that the investment company has not designated a management company under that Directive, on behalf of the fund it manages;**

**(iii) a non-credit institution subject to supervision by a competent authority of a Member State in accordance with Article 20 of Directive 2008/48/EC or Article 35 of Directive 2014/17/EU when performing activities in that Member State;**

**(b) the servicing of a creditor's rights under a credit agreement, or of the credit agreement itself, that was not issued by a credit institution established in the Union except where the creditor's rights under the credit agreement, or the credit agreement itself, is replaced by a credit agreement issued by such credit institution;**

**(c) the purchase of a creditor's rights under a non-performing credit agreement, or of the non-performing credit agreement itself, by a credit institution established in the Union;**

**(d) the transfer of a creditor's rights under a credit agreement, or of the credit agreement itself, transferred before the date referred to in Article 32(2), first subparagraph.**

**6. Member States may exempt from the application of this Directive the servicing of a creditor's rights under a credit agreement, or of the credit agreement itself, carried out by public notaries and bailiffs as defined by national law or lawyers as defined in Article 1(2), point (a), of Directive 98/5/EC of the European Parliament and of the Council (21) when conducting credit servicing activities as part of their profession.**



## A. THE SCOPE OF THE DIRECTIVE

This article sets the scope of the Directive and regulates credit purchasers' and credit servicers' obligations. The objective is to harmonise the rules for credit servicers and credit purchasers of a creditor's rights under a non-performing credit agreement. The main aim is to facilitate the development of secondary 2.01

markets for NPLs in the EU, while ensuring the sale of such loans does not undermine borrowers' rights. In case a credit purchaser is domiciled or established in the EU, it needs to appoint a credit servicer (or an EU-supervised consumer credit or mortgage creditor) to perform credit servicing activities in respect of NPLs concluded with consumers. The credit servicer will be required to comply with the obligations imposed on the credit purchaser under the Directive. Credit purchasers that are not established in the EU or not domiciled in the EU have to designate an EU-domiciled or EU-established representative responsible for the performance of the obligations of a third-country credit purchaser (the rationale for this is given in recital 41 to the Directive: in this way, the EU legislation ensures that the rights of borrowers can be relied on and that the competent authority can supervise the enforcement of non-performing agreements). The representative will be required to appoint a credit servicer – unless the representative is a credit servicer itself – in respect of NPLs where the borrower is a natural person or small and medium-sized enterprise (SME). The Directive gives EU member states the option of extending this requirement to other credit agreements; hence we may see "gold-plating" by some member states that wish to regulate credit servicing in their jurisdictions more widely. Member states are also required to impose "conduct of business" type obligations on credit purchasers and credit servicers, including a duty to act "in good faith, fairly and professionally", and to provide information to borrowers that is not misleading, unclear, or false. These obligations are new in the credit markets and it remains to be seen how member states will choose to implement them. The Directive also imposes an obligation on EU banks selling NPLs to credit purchasers to disclose certain information regarding the creditor's rights and any collateral using prescribed disclosure templates. Banks selling NPLs to credit purchasers will have to report details of their sales to applicable authorities and regulators, including the legal identifier or representative of the credit purchaser. Credit servicers acting on behalf of a bank or a credit purchaser will, amongst other things, need to be suitably authorised by an EU national competent authority. The regulatory framework also specifies the features of the contractual arrangements between the credit servicer and credit purchaser, rules on outsourcing by credit servicers, requirements on communications with borrowers, and a "passporting" regime to allow provision of cross border services.

**2.02** The article refers to credit agreements which should be regulated under contract law principles or civil law principles under national law. Specifically, the Directive does not affect the national law relating to consumer protection and borrowers' rights, and the discipline contained in the Regulation (EC) No

593/2008 on the law applicable to contractual obligations,[1] the Regulation (EU) No 1215/2012 on jurisdiction and the recognition and enforcement of judgments in civil and commercial matters,[2] the Directive 93/13/EEC on unfair terms in consumer contracts,[3] and the Mortgage Credit Directive.[4] The provision regulates the transfer of the creditor's rights under the non-performing credit agreement to a credit purchaser. Prior to entering into a contract for the transfer, the credit institution provides the prospective credit purchaser with the necessary information concerning the creditor's rights (including any collateral) to enable it to assess the value of the creditor's rights under the non-performing credit agreement, and the likelihood of recovery of the value of the agreement. The credit purchaser needs to ensure the confidentiality of the information provided by the credit institution (including that of the commercial information) to finalise a transfer agreement.

## B. THE REGIME OF EXCLUSIONS

The Directive does not apply to servicing of NPLs not issued by an EU-established credit institution (that is non-bank lenders or non-EU established banks); purchase of NPLs by EU-established credit institutions; transfers of NPLs before the transposition deadline of the Directive; servicing of NPLs by a credit institution established in the EU; an Alternative Investment Fund Manager (AIFM) established under Alternative Investment Fund Managers Directive (AIFMD); an Undertakings for Collective Investment in Transferable Securities (UCITS) management company established under the UCITS Directive (however, there is no express carve-out for investment managers that are Markets in Financial Instruments Directive (MiFID) investment firms, as suggested by some); a non-credit institution subject to supervision under the Mortgage Credit Directive (MCD) or the Consumer Credit Directive (CCD); and servicing by public notaries, bailiffs, and lawyers when conducting credit servicing activities as part of their profession. The Directive also provides that its provisions are not intended to affect national laws concerning the transfer of a creditor's rights under a non-performing **2.03**

1 Regulation (EC) No 593/2008 of the European Parliament and of the Council of 17 June 2008 on the law applicable to contractual obligations (Rome I).

2 Regulation (EU) No 1215/2012 of the European Parliament and of the Council of 12 December 2012 on jurisdiction and the recognition and enforcement of judgments in civil and commercial matters (recast).

3 Council Directive 93/13/EEC of 5 April 1993 on unfair terms in consumer contracts.

4 Directive 2014/17/EU of the European Parliament and of the Council of 4 February 2014 on credit agreements for consumers relating to residential immovable property and amending Directives 2008/48/EC and 2013/36/EU and Regulation (EU) No 1093/2010.

credit agreement/the non-performing credit agreement itself where it is not past due or less than 90 days past due or is not terminated; servicing of credit agreements when the credit purchaser is a securitisation special purpose entity (where laws do not hinder the level of consumer protection provided by the credit servicers and credit purchasers Directive or information provision to competent authorities from credit servicers). This definition focuses on tranching of credit risk and the allocation of losses across tranches although it is not consistent with the definition of securitisation used in most national securitisation laws (e.g., Law 130 in Italy[5] or Law 3156/2003 in Greece[6]). For example, it is possible that a transaction could be structured in compliance with one of those national laws and yet not amount to a securitisation for the purposes of the EU Securitisation Regulation. In such case, it is not clear that satisfaction of the servicer appointment requirements under those national securitisation laws would exclude the operation of the Directive. The second issue is that not all national securitisation laws impose licensing requirements on servicers. It is possible to conceive of transactions where it is permissible under the relevant national securitisation law for the servicer to be an unregulated entity. In that scenario, the requirements set in paragraph 4 of this article might lead to the conclusion that the servicer appointed to such transaction would need to be licensed in accordance with the Directive, notwithstanding the apparent carve-out of securitisations. Accordingly, while 'securitisations' are excluded from the need to comply with the Directive, it is not clear that this exclusion will apply to all transactions which market participants might characterise as securitisations, and it will probably be prudent to ensure that servicers appointed to such securitisations have permission to act as an NPL servicer under the Directive.[7]

## C. THE THRESHOLD OF 90 DAYS PAST DUE

**2.04** At a general level, a NPL is a loan where a borrower is considered unlikely to make repayments in accordance with contractual obligations. In many jurisdictions and for many firms, an NPL is defined as a sum of borrowed money upon which the debtor has not made his or her scheduled payments for at least 90 days. Generally, at some point after the debtor starts making payments

5 Law no. 130 of 1999 (the "Securitisation Law").

6 Law no. 3156 of 2003 (the "Greek Securitisation Law").

7 Jochen Vester and Alan Bainbridge, 'NPLs – EU Directive on Credit Servicers and Credit Purchasers' (February 2023), https://www.financierworldwide.com/npls-eu-directive-on-credit-servicers-and-credit-purchasers.

again on an NPL it becomes a re-performing loan, in some cases even if the debtor has not caught up on all the missed payments. In a sense, an NPL is either in default or close to being in default. The specific criteria for loans to be classified either as 'impaired' or as 'non-performing' vary across jurisdictions and firms, and within firms and across time. As a corollary, the threshold for impairment and provisions is different: in particular, new post-crisis accounting rules on provisioning, whilst welcome in requiring higher overall provision levels, allow a greater degree of management discretion in provision calculations than is currently the case. This matters because it makes meaningfully comparing the quality of different banks' assets more difficult. There are also wider implications. Bad lending is the root of many banking crises. These in turn often induce wider economic contractions. Uncertainty about asset quality, and therefore about whether there is under-provisioning for loan losses, can play a significant role in fomenting crises; and uncertainty about the definition of non-performance can exacerbate them because it makes it difficult for outsiders to decide whether recapitalisation and recovery of the firm can occur. A majority of countries classify loans as non-performing when principal or interest is 90 days or more past due and/or there is "well-defined weakness of loan or borrower".[8] But two issues complicate matters. First, the definition of "well-defined weakness" remains unspecified within and across jurisdictions. In other words, different firms and regulators have different data, and different interpretations of data, used to estimate obligors' ability to repay, and whether it has deteriorated. Second, there are other dimensions besides time (since last repayment) that matter in certain jurisdictions. These include whether collateral, guarantees, or other forms of security are factored into the credit classification process; whether the full outstanding value or only part of a loan is reported as non-performing; and how to treat restructured loans.

Even if repayments are made on time, a loan can go into default if the borrower breaches a contractual covenant, for example, by exceeding a maximum leverage threshold specified in the loan contract. In Central, Eastern, and Southeastern Europe (CESEE) countries, there has been divergence across the region in terms of whether jurisdictions take a 'product' or 'customer' view when determining if loans are performing or not.[9] At issue is the following: suppose an obligor has two or more loans from the same credit institution. If **2.05**

8 Stephan Barisitz, 'Nonperforming Loans in Western Europe – A Selective Comparison of Countries and National Definitions' (2013) Focus on European Economic Integration Q1/13, p. 28.

9 Alexandra Bykova and Olga Pindyuk, 'Non-Performing Loans in Central and Southeast Europe' (2019) wiiw Policy Notes and Reports No. 32, The Vienna Institute for International Economic Studies, wiiw-pol -notes-32.pdf.

the obligor falls behind repayment on one loan but is repaying on the other, there is debate about whether the performing loan should also be classified as non-performing, i.e. adopting a 'customer' view, since the delinquency on one loan implies that the obligor's overall financial state has deteriorated. Convergence around the global statistical definition of NPLs established by the UN System of National Accounts (SNA), and followed by all countries adhering to International Monetary Fund (IMF) or European reporting standards: "a loan is non-performing when payments of interest or principal are past due by 90 days or more, or interest payments equal to 90 days or more have been capitalized, refinanced, or delayed by agreement, or payments are less than 90 days overdue, but there are other good reasons (such as a debtor filing for bankruptcy) to doubt that payments will be made in full".[10] However, loan quality classification schemes range from three to nine categories in some jurisdictions. Furthermore, like the UN statistical definition, which comes with the proviso that the UN "definition of a non-performing loan is to be interpreted flexibly", the drafting of these definitions leaves scope for firm discretion because the meaning of phrases like "other good reasons" are not precisely defined. While there is convergence towards the definition of an NPL as being loans 90 days or more past due, there are differences along quantitative and qualitative dimensions.[11]

**2.06** Quantitatively, the threshold for NPLs ranges from 60 to 270 days, depending in part on the financial product. Commercial banks, for example, defer classifying first lien, residential mortgages as NPLs for some time after 90 days since the last repayment.[12] The same is sometimes the case where the loans are to government or government-backed entities. Credit cards are also sometimes treated differently. Qualitatively, the detail of the definitions, and their substance, also shows variety. For example, some firms take into account the status of the counterparty, particularly whether they have been declared insolvent in the past or at present. Also, some firms explicitly address loan restructuring and concessions to borrowers, while in other instances the issue of loan restructuring, and, by extension, forbearance is not addressed. Another aspect to consider where there are currently differences between jurisdictions is that

---

10 United Nations. Statistical Commission, 2009. System of National Accounts, 2008 (2008 SNA), New York.

11 Yiwei Dou, Stephen G. Ryan and Youli Zou, 'The Effect of Credit Competition on Banks' Loan-Loss Provisions' (2018) 53(3) *Journal of Financial and Quantitative Analysis* 1195.

12 Linda Allen and Anthony Saunders, 'Risk Management in Banking' in Allen N. Berger, Philip Molyneux and John O. S. Wilson (eds), *The Oxford Handbook of Banking* (2nd edn, Oxford: Oxford University Press 2015) ch.7.

of whether or not a loan should be exempt from 'non-performing' status if the value of underlying collateral is sufficient to make good any shortfalls, even where there is poor performance of the underlying loan.[13] The timely recognition of problem loans and credit loss by banks, and proper transparency such that asset positions are well understood by the market, regulators, and the general public, is critical to averting and mitigating crises.[14] Banks can be incentivised by accounting, regulatory and tax considerations in various ways when considering how to identify, and provide against, problem loans. This in turn can result in under-provisioning, particularly when the economic environment is relatively benign. But the early recognition of expected losses in good times is generally agreed by policymakers to contribute to greater bank resilience and mitigate the impact of crises on banks' balance sheets.

13 Javier Suárez and Antonio Sánchez Serrano, 'Approaching Non-performing Loans from a Macroprudential Angle' (September 2018) European Systemic Risk Board, Reports of the Advisory Scientific Committee No. 7, p. 34.

14 Jannis Bischof, Christian Laux and Christian Leuz, 'Accounting for Financial Stability: Bank Disclosure and Loss Recognition in the Financial Crisis' (2021) 141(3) *Journal of Financial Economics* 1188.

# ARTICLE 3

## DEFINITIONS

**Andrea Miglionico**

**For the purposes of this Directive, the following definitions apply:**

**(1) 'credit institution' means a credit institution as defined in Article 4(1), point (1), of Regulation (EU) No 575/2013;**
**(2) 'creditor' means a credit institution that has issued a credit, or a credit purchaser;**
**(3) 'borrower' means a legal or natural person who has concluded a credit agreement with a credit institution, including its legal successor or assignee;**
**(4) 'credit agreement' means an agreement as originally issued, modified or replaced, whereby a credit institution grants a credit in the form of a deferred payment, a loan or other similar financial accommodation;**
**(5) 'credit servicing agreement' means a written contract concluded between a credit purchaser and a credit servicer concerning the services to be provided by the credit servicer on behalf of the credit purchaser;**
**(6) 'credit purchaser' means any natural or legal person, other than a credit institution, that purchases a creditor's rights under a non-performing credit agreement, or the non-performing credit agreement itself, in the course of its trade, business or profession, in accordance with applicable Union and national law;**
**(7) 'credit service provider' means a third party used by a credit servicer to perform any of the credit servicing activities;**
**(8) 'credit servicer' means a legal person that, in the course of its business, manages and enforces the rights and obligations related to a creditor's rights under a non-performing credit agreement, or to the non-performing credit agreement itself, on behalf of a credit purchaser, and carries out at least one or more credit servicing activities;**
**(9) 'credit servicing activities' means one or more of the following activities:**
- **(a) collecting or recovering from the borrower, in accordance with national law, any payments due related to a creditor's rights under a credit agreement or to the credit agreement itself;**
- **(b) renegotiating with the borrower, in accordance with national law, any terms and conditions related to a creditor's rights under a credit agreement, or of the credit agreement itself, in line with the instructions**

**given by the credit purchaser, where the credit servicer is not a credit intermediary as defined in Article 3, point (f), of Directive 2008/48/EC or in Article 4, point (5), of Directive 2014/17/EU;**

**(c) administering any complaints relating to a creditor's rights under a credit agreement or to the credit agreement itself;**

**(d) informing the borrower of any changes in interest rates or charges or of any payments due related to a creditor's rights under a credit agreement or to the credit agreement itself;**

**(10) 'home Member State' means, with respect to a credit servicer, the Member State in which its registered office is situated or, if under its national law it has no registered office, the Member State in which its head office is situated or, with respect to a credit purchaser, the Member State in which the credit purchaser or its representative is domiciled, or its registered office is situated or, if under its national law it has no registered office, the Member State in which its head office is situated;**

**(11) 'host Member State' means the Member State, other than the home Member State, in which a credit servicer has established a branch or where it provides credit servicing activities, and in any event where the borrower is domiciled, or its registered office is situated or, if under its national law it has no registered office, the Member State in which its head office is situated;**

**(12) 'consumer' means a natural person who, in credit agreements covered by this Directive, is acting for purposes which are outside his trade, business or profession;**

**(13) 'non-performing credit agreement' means a credit agreement that is classified as a non-performing exposure in accordance with Article 47a of Regulation (EU) No 575/2013.**



## A. INTRODUCTION

The article defines a credit servicer as a legal person with characteristics to manage and enforce a creditor's rights and obligations under a non-performing credit agreement; and a credit purchaser as a natural or legal person, other than a credit institution, with characteristics to purchase a creditor's rights under a non-performing credit agreement or the agreement itself. The provision states that credit servicers hold obligations related to a creditor's rights under NPLs issued by an EU credit institution on behalf of a credit purchaser (i.e. an entity that purchases an NPL in the course of its trade, business or profession). In this context, EU credit institutions are not 'credit purchasers' under the Credit Servicing Directive. Credit servicers carry out 'credit servicing activities' such **3.01** as collecting or recovering payments due; renegotiating with the borrower the terms of the loan (except where the servicer is a credit intermediary); administering complaints relating to a creditor's rights; and informing the borrower of changes to interest rates or any payments relating to a creditor's rights. Loan servicers are entities that carry out the administration of a loan or portfolio of loans on behalf of banks and loan purchasers (such as NPL investors). They administer the interest payments of debtors, collect the principal, send notices and conduct other activities that affect the recovery value of NPLs. Loan purchasers are entities that buy loans from banks and from other loan purchasers as an investment and usually delegate the servicing of the loans to third-party loan servicers. They are typically investment funds or investment firms.

**3.02** Non-performing agreement is defined as a credit agreement that is classified as a non-performing exposure under Article 47a of the Capital Requirements Regulation (CRR).[1] The criteria set out in the CRR classify a loan as non-performing if it is either 90 days past its due date, or full repayment of the loan without realising collateral is deemed to be unlikely. A credit agreement is an agreement in which a credit institution (as defined in the CRR) grants or promises to grant a credit in the form of "a deferred payment, a loan or other similar financial accommodation".[2] A creditor for the purposes of the directive is a credit institution that has issued a credit or a credit purchaser.

## B. THE CREDIT SERVICING ACTIVITIES

**3.03** A credit service provider is a third party used by a credit servicer to perform any of the credit servicing activities. Third parties (credit purchasers) would be able to purchase NPLs across the EU. Credit purchasers (e.g. investment funds) are not creating new credit, but buying existing NPLs at their own risk. Therefore, they do not need special authorisation but will have to comply with borrower protection rules.

**3.04** A credit servicing activity refers to collecting or recovering from the borrower, according to national law, any payments due related to a creditor's rights under a credit agreement or to the credit agreement itself. It also refers to renegotiating

---

1 Regulation (EU) No 575/2013 of the European Parliament and of the Council of 26 June 2013 on prudential requirements for credit institutions and investment firms and amending Regulation (EU) No 648/2012.

2 The credit agreement is also defined as a loan agreement, the main transaction document for a loan financing between one or more lenders and a borrower. It sets out the terms of the loan; borrowing and repayment procedures; the calculation of interest and fees; and the liabilities and obligations of the parties.

with the borrower any terms and conditions related to a creditor's rights under a credit agreement or of the credit agreement itself in line with the instructions given by the credit purchaser, where the credit servicer is not a credit intermediary as defined in the Consumer Credit Directive or the Mortgage Credit Directive. The activity consists in administering any complaints relating to a creditor's rights under a credit agreement or to the credit agreement itself and informing the borrower of any changes in interest rates or charges or of any payments due related to a creditor's rights under a credit agreement or to the credit agreement itself. The directive does not define credit servicers as financial intermediaries and the credit servicing activities do not include debt collection as a financial service. The lack of a clear definition of the legal nature of credit service providers and debt collectors raises issues for the cross-border nature of collection which may hide unfair and abusive servicer practices.[3] This implies detrimental implications of credit servicing activities for consumers, which also reflects the absence of a level playing field of licensing and authorising requirements. The servicers' performance is regulated through a servicing agreement between servicer and issuer, while the fee expenses are generally associated with the success of operation. The directive prescribes that it is not permitted to outsource all of its activities at the same time; the credit servicer must inform the competent authorities of the relevant Member State prior to outsourcing and the third party it outsources to is not permitted to receive and hold funds from borrowers. The credit servicer remains responsible for compliance with the directive even if its activities are outsourced. Credit servicers must ensure that their management or administrative organs meet the suitability requirements at all times, including where the business activities or the composition of the organ change.[4]

Credit servicers are legal persons acting on behalf of credit purchasers and **3.05** managing rights and obligations under a non-performing credit agreement such as payments collection or renegotiation of terms of the agreement. They would have to obtain authorisation and be subject to supervision by the Member States' competent authorities. Member States should also ensure that there is a publicly accessible up-to-date list or a national register of all credit servicers. In order to protect consumers, all credit purchasers will have an

3 Cătălin-Gabriel Stănescu, 'The Impact of the Credit Servicing Directive on Regulating Abusive Informal Debt Collection in the European Union: A Step Forward or a Missed Opportunity?' (2023) 12(1) *Journal of European Consumer and Market Law* 4–5.

4 EBA, 'Guidelines on the Assessment of Adequate Knowledge and Experience of the Management or Administrative Organ of Credit Servicers' (December 2023), https://www.eba.europa.eu/publications-and-media/press-releases/eba-publishes-guidance-assess-knowledge-and-experience.

obligation to have a credit servicer appointed by a host country for consumer portfolios. In addition, third country credit purchasers also have to appoint a credit servicer for SMEs portfolios to protect entrepreneurs. The protection for borrowers who cannot pay their debts requires credit purchasers and credit servicers to provide accurate information, respect and protect personal information and borrowers' privacy.[5] In advance of the first debt collection, a borrower holds the right to be notified in a clear and understandable manner on paper or another durable medium concerning any transfer of a creditor's rights. The information should include a date of transfer, identification, contact details and authorisation of a new credit servicer or a credit service provider, as well as detailed information on the amounts due by the borrower. The borrower should be informed where they can submit complaints and should not be worse off following the transfer of their credit agreement. Fees and penalties charged by servicers including transfer costs cannot change nor can any additional costs be imposed other than those related to this credit agreement. The contract and obligations between a credit servicer towards a credit purchaser should not be altered by outsourcing of credit servicing. A borrower's individual circumstances such as a mortgage linked to a residential property and ability to repay a loan are taken into consideration while deciding on measures. Such measures may include partial refinancing of a credit agreement, modifying the terms of the agreement, extending the terms of the loan, currency conversions, and other ways to facilitate repayment. Member states may apply measures suitable for borrowers under national regimes but should have an appropriate set of measures at national level.

## C. THE REGULATORY REQUIREMENTS FOR CREDIT SERVICERS

**3.06** The Directive regulates the transfers of credit agreements by establishing a new licensed status for credit servicers. Once they obtain their licence, credit servicers will need to comply with several conduct of business rules towards borrowers (e.g. avoiding any harassment, coercion, or undue influence, acting in good faith, providing clear and truthful information) as well as towards credit purchasers which hire them (e.g. content of management contract, prior notification when relying on credit service providers, recordkeeping). Banks are required to provide all necessary information to credit purchasers to enable them to assess the value of the credit agreement and the likelihood of recovery

5 European Parliament, 'Non-performing Loans: Deal Struck on EU Rules for Selling NPLs to Third Parties' (2021), Press Releases, https://www.europarl.europa.eu/news/en/press-room/20210531IPR05113/non-performing-loans-deal-struck-on-eu-rules-for-selling-npls-to-third-parties.

of value. In addition, any transfer of NPLs will trigger a notification to the borrower, to be done by the credit purchaser or the credit servicer which is appointed. The NPL Directive details the content of such notification: banks must also inform competent authorities about the details of the loans they transferred. The EBA is mandated to implement draft technical standards to standardise a format for this type of reporting. Credit purchasers based in the EU are not required to apply for a specific licence. They should however appoint a bank, a professional performing lending activities or a credit servicer for managing NPLs concluded with consumers. With respect to credit purchasers based in a third country, this appointment requirement also applies for NPLs concluded with any natural person and with small and medium enterprises. If a credit purchaser transfers a credit agreement to another credit purchaser, it must inform the relevant member state's regulatory authority on a biannual basis. A non-EU credit purchaser acquiring EU originated NPLs must designate a representative that is established in the EU. The representative will be responsible for the credit purchaser obligations under the Directive. An authorised servicer will also need to be appointed where there is an EU credit purchaser of consumer NPLs, or non-EU credit purchaser of NPLs granted to any natural person, or micro, small, or medium-sized enterprise. Member states need to be notified of the appointment of a credit servicer. Member states are not allowed to impose additional licensing restrictions except in exceptional circumstances, to encourage growth of the secondary market.

Credit servicers must obtain authorisation from home Member States to carry 3.07
out credit servicing activities and must avoid misleading borrowers. Member States are required to publish a list of authorised credit servicers which will then be able to passport their licence to practise throughout the EU. Credit servicers are responsible for notifying borrowers of an NPL sale and providing specific information ahead of the first debt collection. They must keep records for a period of five years (or up to 10 years, depending on the statutory limitation period of the home Member State) of all correspondence with the credit purchaser and the borrower, all instructions received from the credit purchaser, and instructions provided to the service providers. Credit servicers must enter into a written contract with the credit purchaser. The contract must include prescribed terms reflective of the relevant national law and the directive. Both credit servicers and credit purchasers must comply with overarching standards and principles when engaging with borrowers. For example, to act in good faith, fairly and professionally, and to provide information to borrowers that is not misleading, unclear or false. Credit purchasers must provide information regarding the transfer of NPLs to borrowers, unless the appointed

credit servicer, EU Bank or EU supervised non-credit institution provides such information. Credit purchasers must notify their home Member State EU regulator regarding any NPL transfers and the details of the appointed credit servicer, EU Bank or EU supervised non-credit institution.

# TITLE II

# CREDIT SERVICERS

# CHAPTER 1

# AUTHORISATION OF CREDIT SERVICERS

# ARTICLE 4

# GENERAL REQUIREMENTS

Andrea Miglionico

**1. Member States shall require a credit servicer to obtain an authorisation in a home Member State before commencing its activities within its territory in accordance with the requirements set out in the national provisions transposing this Directive.**
**2. Member States shall confer the power to grant an authorisation referred to in paragraph 1 of this Article upon the competent authorities designated pursuant to Article 21(3).**



## A. INTRODUCTION

4.01 The article provides a general rule on the authorisation process of credit servicers. It sets the discipline on credit servicers and begins Chapter 1 of the directive by prescribing credit servicers to obtain an authorisation in a home Member State before commencing their activities. It is an introductory provision which refers to the dispositions of national laws and procedural requirements of the competent authorities. In order to get authorisation, credit servicers need to demonstrate they meet certain conditions which are grounds for refusal of an application in case of failure to do so. Specifically, credit servicers must be a legal person and have their registered or head office in that EU Member State. The directive prescribes that members of their management or administrative bodies need to be of good repute with a clean police record, have not been declared bankrupt and have the knowledge and experience to act competently and responsibly. They need to employ robust governance and adequate internal controls, follow rules for the protection and fair and diligent treatment of borrowers and for recording and handling their complaints free of charge, apply adequate anti-money laundering and counter-terrorist financing procedures, and be subject to national reporting and public disclosure requirements. This authorisation process aims to harmonise the regulatory framework that will allow credit servicers of NPL portfolios, acting on behalf of purchasers of NPLs, to scale-up their activities in different EU Member States for the first time by using a passport. Those credit servicers will be subject to uniform and harmonised conditions for authorisation, and to harmonised conduct of business rules, across the EU. Each national competent authority will need to maintain a register of authorised credit servicers.[1] Paragraph 2 of the article refers to Article 21(3) which states that Member States shall designate the competent authorities responsible for carrying out the functions and duties under the national provisions transposing this directive.

**4.02** Credit servicers must be authorised in the Member State of their respective registered office (or, if applicable, their respective head office) before they can carry out credit servicing activities within that territory in respect of in-scope NPLs. Usually, the Central Bank as national competent authority provides authorisation to credit servicers. Member States decide whether credit servicers are allowed to receive and hold funds from borrowers and, if they are allowed, then which additional requirements will apply. Once authorised, a credit servicer can provide the services covered by its authorisation anywhere in the EU. This is subject to any additional restrictions or requirements set out in the national law of the host Member State which are required to maintain a publicly accessible online register of credit servicers authorised to provide services within their territory. Member States are required to introduce administrative penalties and remedial measures for breaches of certain requirements

1 The European Banking Authority (EBA) published a set of guidelines on national lists or registers of credit servicers. The guidelines are addressed to competent authorities managing the lists or registers and specify the content of the lists or registers; how they should be made accessible; and the deadlines for updating them. Furthermore, the lists or registers should facilitate borrowers' access to information on complaint handling procedures offered by competent authorities. The guidelines require basic information about credit servicers, such as their name and address and home Member State, as well as other useful information, such as whether the credit servicer is currently authorised to conduct services or to receive and hold funds from borrowers. In addition, the guidelines specify that the lists or registers should be accessible 24 hours a day, 7 days a week, on the website of the competent authority or another electronic tool; that they should not require the user's prior registration as a precondition for access; and that they should be free of charge. The guidelines also set the deadlines by which competent authorities have to update the lists or registers, i.e. one week for regular updates and two working days for critical updates on the withdrawal of authorisation or the banning to receive and hold funds from borrowers. See EBA, 'Guidelines on the Establishment and Maintenance of National Lists or Registers of Credit Servicers under Directive (EU) 2021/2167' (5 March 2024), Final Report, EBA/GL/2024/02, https://www.eba.europa.eu/publications-and-media/press-releases/eba-publishes-its-final-guidelines-national-lists-or.

under the directive in the case of credit servicers, a withdrawal of the authorisation. In the case of credit servicers and credit purchasers (or, where applicable, their EU Representative), an order requiring the relevant credit servicer and credit purchaser (or, where applicable, its EU Representative) to remedy the infringement, and to cease the conduct and to desist from a repetition of that conduct; and administrative pecuniary penalties. Breaches of certain requirements under the directive should not affect, in principle, the validity of the transfers of the NPLs. However, Member States may lay down penalties or include additional restrictions that may negatively affect the validity of the transfer of the NPLs in the event of a breach.[2]

## B. THE ROLE OF NATIONAL COMPETENT AUTHORITIES

Member States must ensure that credit institutions provide information on creditors, non-performing credit agreements and their collateral to prospective credit purchasers. This information will then inform prospective credit purchasers of the associated risks and how likely they are to recover the capital, and must ensure protection of that information.[3] National competent authorities (NCAs) may require this information on a quarterly basis as necessary, or during a period of crisis, where there will be a high volume of transactions. Any information provided under these circumstances must be communicated without delay to the home Member State of the credit purchaser. NCAs need to apply an authorisation procedure for credit servicers requiring them to prove they meet all the conditions, and decide within 90 days whether to grant or refuse authorisation. In terms of regulatory requirements, NCAs have supervisory, investigatory, and sanctioning powers and may, in certain circumstances, withdraw an authorisation; maintain a publicly accessible online register of all credit servicers; allow, subject to certain conditions, credit servicers authorised in one Member State to practise elsewhere in the EU. **4.03**

Member States have very different rules for how credit purchasers are able to acquire credit agreements from credit institutions. Credit purchasers are not **4.04**

2 Allen & Overy, 'Non-Performing Loans. New Framework for Sellers, Credit Purchasers and Credit Servicers' (May 2023), https://www.aohub.com/aohub/publications/non-performing-loans-new-framework-for-sellers-credit-purchasers-and-credit-servicers_1?nav=FRbANEucS95NMLRN47z%2BeeOgEFCt8EGQ71hKXzqW2Ec%3D&key=BcJlhLtdCv6/JTDZxvL23TQa3JHL2AIGr93BnQjo2SkGJpG9xDX7S2thDpAQsCconWHAwe6cJTkzp9TOYg44PH/Cqu0JfTrA&uid=rNi8QInMmsM%3D.

3 Padraic Kenna, 'Public Consultation on Credit Servicers Directive' (7 March 2023), https://www.universityofgalway.ie/media/housinglawrightsandpolicy/Submission-Credit-Servicers-Directive-Public-Consultation-PK-UoG[21].pdf.

regulated in some Member States, while in others they are subject to various requirements, sometimes amounting to a requirement to obtain an authorisation as a credit institution. Those differences between regulatory requirements have resulted in considerable obstacles to legally purchasing credit cross-border in the EU, mainly by increasing the compliance costs faced when seeking to purchase credit portfolios. In order to allow existing credit purchasers and credit servicers to adapt to the requirements of the national provisions transposing the directive and, in particular, to allow credit servicers to be authorised, the directive allows entities that are currently providing credit servicing activities under national law to continue to do so in their home Member State for a period of 6 months after the transposition deadline of this directive. After the expiry of that 6-month period, only credit servicers authorised under the national laws transposing the directive should be permitted to operate on the market.

## C. PROCEDURAL MATTERS

**4.05** Credit servicers that are deemed entitled to receive funds from borrowers (so as to transfer these to credit purchasers) will be subject to extra requirements, such as the requirement to have a separate account in a bank where all funds from borrowers are to be received before being sent to the respective credit purchaser. The directive outlines the procedure for passporting of credit servicing and the conditions that must be fulfilled by the credit servicer. These include providing the home Member State competent authority with details of the host Member State where the credit servicer plans to provide services; and the address of the credit servicer's branch in the host Member State. The directive imposes record-keeping requirements on credit servicers. These include relevant correspondence with both the credit purchaser and the borrower. A credit servicing agreement must include the following requirements: a detailed description of credit servicing activities to be carried out by the credit servicer; the level of remuneration of the credit servicer or how the remuneration is to be calculated; the extent to which the credit servicer can represent the credit purchaser in relation to the borrower; an undertaking by the parties to comply with applicable EU and national law; and a clause requiring the fair and diligent treatment of the borrowers. The directive also sets out additional requirements in relation to the information that a credit purchaser or its credit servicer must provide to a borrower following the sale of an NPL.

# ARTICLE 5

# REQUIREMENTS FOR GRANTING AN AUTHORISATION

**Andrea Miglionico**

**1. Without prejudice to Article 6, Member States shall lay down the following requirements for the granting of an authorisation referred to in Article 4(1):**

**(a) the applicant is a legal person as referred to in Article 54 of the Treaty on the Functioning of the European Union and its registered office or, if under its national law it has no registered office, its head office, is in the Member State in which the applicant is seeking authorisation;**

**(b) the members of the applicant's management or administrative organ are of sufficiently good repute, which is demonstrated by proving that:**

**(i) they have a clean police record or other national equivalent in relation to relevant criminal offences, in particular those relating to property, financial services and activities, money laundering, usury, fraud, tax crimes, violation of professional secrecy or to physical integrity, and also in relation to any other offences under laws relating to companies, bankruptcy, insolvency or consumer protection;**

**(ii) the cumulative effects of minor incidents do not impinge on their good repute;**

**(iii) they have always been transparent, open and cooperative in their past business dealings with supervisory and regulatory authorities;**

**(iv) they are not subject to any ongoing insolvency procedure nor have previously been declared bankrupt unless reinstated in accordance with national law;**

**(c) the applicant's management or administrative organ, as a whole, has adequate knowledge and experience to conduct the business in a competent and responsible manner;**

**(d) the persons who hold qualifying holdings in the applicant within the meaning of Article 4(1), point (36), of Regulation (EU) No 575/2013 are of sufficiently good repute, which is demonstrated by fulfilling the requirements set out in points (b)(i) and (iv) of this paragraph;**

**(e) the applicant has in place robust governance arrangements and adequate internal control mechanisms, including risk management and accounting procedures, which ensure respect for borrower rights and compliance with the laws governing a creditor's rights under a credit agreement, or the credit agreement itself, and with Regulation (EU) 2016/679;**

**(f) the applicant applies an appropriate policy ensuring compliance with rules for the protection, and the fair and diligent treatment, of borrowers, including by taking into account their financial situation and, where available, the need for such borrowers to be referred to debt advice or social services;**

**(g) the applicant has in place adequate and specific internal procedures that ensure the recording and handling of complaints from borrowers;**

**(h) the applicant has in place adequate anti-money laundering and counter terrorist financing procedures where national provisions transposing Directive (EU) 2015/849 designate credit servicers as obliged entities for the purpose of preventing and combating money laundering and terrorist financing;**

**(i) the applicant is subject by virtue of applicable national law to reporting and public disclosure requirements.**

**2. The EBA shall, after consulting all relevant stakeholders and reflecting all interests involved, issue guidelines in accordance with Article 16 of Regulation (EU) No 1093/2010 for the requirements set out in paragraph 1, point (c), of this Article.**

**3. The competent authorities of the home Member State shall refuse an authorisation referred to in Article 4(1) where the applicant does not comply with the requirements set out in paragraph 1 of this Article and, where relevant, in Article 6(2), point (a).**



## A. INTRODUCTION

5.01 The article provides a list of mandatory requirements for credit servicers in order to obtain authorisation to carry out their activities. Paragraph 1 of the provision states that Member States need to lay down required criteria for the applicant which include: rules of conduct for fair and transparent dealings with borrowers; information obligations towards borrowers; new risk management and compliance processes and verification of internal control mechanisms; and reporting obligations to the respective national supervisory body. These requirements aim to ensure transparency and the establishment of a monitoring system of national competent authorities (NCAs) to assess the conduct of business of entities acting as debt collectors operating in the European Union.[1] The applicant must be a legal person with its registered office or head

1 Jean-Baptiste Poulle, Arut Kannan, Nicolas Spitz, Sandra Kahn and Anastasia Sotiropoulou, 'Non-performing Loans Directive' in Poulle et al. (eds), *EU Banking and Financial Regulation* (Edward Elgar 2024) ch.14.

office in the Member State where they seek authorisation; the management or administration of the legal person must be of sufficiently good repute, meaning they must demonstrate they have not been involved in criminal activities, they maintain a "transparent, open and cooperative" relationship with supervisory regimes; and, there is no ongoing insolvency or bankruptcy. Authorised legal persons must ensure that internal mechanisms are in place to respect borrowers' rights. The applicant must provide specific internal measures to record and handle complaints from borrowers, and adequate procedures for the prevention of money laundering and terrorist financing. Paragraph 2 of the article mandates EBA to issue guidelines to assess the adequate knowledge and experience of the management or administrative organ of credit servicers to conduct the business in a competent and responsible manner.

The EBA guidelines specify the notion of adequate collective knowledge and **5.02** experience for the credit servicer's management or administrative organ. They aim at establishing harmonised criteria for the assessment of the adequate knowledge and experience of the individual members of the management or administrative organ of credit servicers, which form the basis for the assessment of their collective suitability and ensure sound assessment processes. The management or administrative organ should collectively possess adequate knowledge and experience to understand the credit servicer's activities and to conduct the business in a competent and responsible manner. This knowledge should be kept up to date, taking into account changes in the nature, scale and complexity of the credit servicer's activities. Adequate knowledge and experience should not be determined by having experience expressed only in terms of a period of time in a certain position or a specific educational degree, but need to be assessed on a case-by-case basis. The guidelines apply to all credit servicers of a creditor's right under a non-performing credit agreement, or of the non-performing credit agreement itself, issued by a credit institution established in the Union. The guidelines apply with regard to the assessment of the adequate knowledge and experience of credit servicers' management or administrative organ, as a whole, to conduct the business in a competent and responsible manner. Where the organ consists of a management and a supervisory function, the guidelines apply to both functions. NCAs should ensure that credit servicers comply with these guidelines. The EBA also provides guidelines on the establishment and maintenance of national lists or registers of credit servicers which specify the types of information that the national lists or registers have to include, with a view to enhance the transparency for credit purchasers and borrowers and to bring about a level playing field across the Union.[2]

## B. THE EBA'S GUIDELINES

**5.03** The EBA is empowered to provide guidance on the adequate knowledge and experience of the management or administrative organ of credit servicers.[3] The guidelines specify common criteria, taking into account the principle of proportionality, to assess the collective adequate knowledge and experience of the management or administrative organ, on the basis of the individual knowledge and experience of the members of these organs. The guidelines apply to competent authorities and credit servicers irrespective of their governance structures without advocating or preferring any specific structure as set out in the defined scope of application. The EBA's role reflects the aim of the directive to create a common framework and requirements for credit servicers of a creditor's right under a non-performing credit agreement issued by a credit institution established in the Union which includes requirements for the qualification of the management or administrative organ as a whole.

**5.04** The EBA guidelines point to the requisite that credit servicers should always act in good faith, treat borrowers fairly, and respect their privacy at the same time as they should effectively service credits. Further, to protect the integrity of the market and to promote trust, it is important to ensure that the management or administrative organ of a credit servicer, as a whole, has adequate knowledge and experience to conduct the business in a competent and responsible manner, according to the activity to be carried out. While some requirements, e.g. on the good repute of the members of the management or administrative organ, are directly encoded within the directive, the requirement that the management or administrative organ as a whole (i.e. that members of such organs collectively) must have adequate knowledge and experience is further specified by the guidelines. The assessment of the adequate collective knowledge and experience is based on the assessment of the individual members. The requirements for authorisation must be complied with at all times. In

2 EBA, 'Final Report on Guidelines on National Lists or Registers of Credit Services' (5 March 2024), https://www.eba.europa.eu/legacy/regulation-and-policy/regulatory-activities/consumer-protection-and-financial-innovation-2.

3 EBA, 'Final Report on the Guidelines on the Assessment of Adequate Knowledge and Experience of the Management or Administrative Organ of Credit Servicers, as a Whole, under Directive (EU) 2021/2167' (15 December 2023), EBA/GL/2023/09.

parallel, credit servicers need to ensure that they meet the suitability requirements, including the requirement of adequate knowledge and experience and good repute, at all times, including where the business activities or the composition of the management or administrative organ change. NCAs have the power to withdraw the authorisation of credit servicers. NCAs supervising credit servicers will also assess as part of their supervisory activities the credit servicers' compliance with the suitability requirements. NCAs will ensure the effective and consistent application of the guidelines in their jurisdiction. NCAs may further clarify the governing bodies and functions on the basis of the definitions provided in the guidelines to which the tasks and responsibilities set forth in the guidelines pertain, when this is appropriate to ensure the proper application of the guidelines according to the governance structures provided for under the national company law.

To ensure proper business conduct, the management or administrative organ should function adequately. This requires that all members of those organs also individually must meet certain knowledge and experience standards to enable effective functioning of the organs, including the ability to discuss strategies and business objectives and to challenge and discuss proposals made by other members. Therefore, the members of the management or administrative organ should have adequate knowledge and experience to fulfil their individual positions. The respective assessment entails whether the inclusion of all individual knowledge and experience results in an organ that has adequate knowledge and experience, as a whole. Whether the individual members of the management or administrative organ, despite their overall responsibility, may have specific roles, the assessment process and criteria can differ to take into account the specific positions held and the principle of proportionality. Despite the directive aiming to establish a common regulatory framework of business conduct requirements for debt collectors, it remains to be seen if EU Member States implement harmonised standards to monitor compliance with the criteria prescribed for obtaining an authorisation. On the application of the proportionality principle, credit servicers should take into account their size, their internal organisation, and the nature, scale, and complexity of their activities when assessing the adequate knowledge and experience of their management and administrative organs, as a whole, and when developing and implementing related policies and processes that ensure that the requirements are met. Credit servicers which service large portfolios of credit or more complex credit should have more sophisticated policies and processes, while smaller credit servicers that service less complex credit may implement simpler policies and processes. 5.05

## C. THE REFUSAL OF AUTHORISATION

**5.06** Paragraph 3 of the article empowers Member States to refuse authorisation if the credit servicers are not compliant with the requirements set in the directive. NCAs should specify the supervisory procedures applicable to the assessment of adequate knowledge and experience of the management or administrative organ, as a whole, of credit servicers and the good repute of its members. They should ensure that a description of supervisory procedures is publicly available to competent authorities by the credit servicer during the course of the authorisation process and is used as appropriate, where possible, for the purpose of the assessment of adequate knowledge and experience. Specifically, the supervisory procedures should take into account situations where credit servicers are also authorised or supervised by non-financial authorities in order to ensure efficient coordination. NCAs should set out a maximum period for their assessment of adequate knowledge and experience of the management or administrative organ, as a whole, of credit servicers and the good repute of its members where such assessments take place after the authorisation of the credit servicer. Where a competent authority establishes that additional documentation and information are needed to complete the assessment, that period may be suspended from the time when the competent authority requests additional documentation and information necessary to complete the assessment until the receipt of that documentation and information. NCAs should inform credit servicers of at least a negative decision on the assessment of suitability as soon as possible. Where provided by national law or defined by the competent authority as part of their supervisory processes, a positive decision may be deemed to be taken by silence when the maximum period for the assessment is completed and the competent authority has not taken a negative decision. NCAs should ensure that their supervisory procedures allow them to address cases of non-compliance with the requirement that the management or administrative organ, as a whole, has adequate knowledge and experience.

# ARTICLE 6

# ABILITY TO HOLD FUNDS

**Andrea Miglionico**

1. **Member States shall determine whether credit servicers, when performing credit servicing activities in their territory, are either:**
   - **(a) allowed to receive and hold funds from borrowers in order to transfer those funds to credit purchasers; or**
   - **(b) prohibited from receiving and holding funds from borrowers.**
2. **In cases where credit servicers are allowed to receive and hold funds from borrowers under paragraph 1, point (a), Member States shall:**
   - **(a) lay down, in addition to the requirements for the granting of an authorisation set out in Article 5(1), a requirement that the applicant has a separate account in a credit institution into which all funds received from borrowers are to be credited and kept until their channelling to the respective credit purchaser, under the conditions agreed with the credit purchaser;**
   - **(b) ensure that those funds are protected in accordance with national law in the interest of the credit purchasers against the claims of the other creditors of the credit servicers, in particular in the event of insolvency;**
   - **(c) determine that, when a borrower makes a payment to a credit servicer in order to, partially or totally, reimburse the amounts due related to a creditor's rights under a non-performing credit agreement, or to the non-performing credit agreement itself, that payment is treated as having been paid to the credit purchaser;**
   - **(d) require a credit servicer to deliver a receipt or a letter of discharge to the borrower, on paper or another durable medium, whenever the credit servicer receives funds from the borrower, acknowledging the amounts received.**
3. **Where a credit servicer does not intend to receive and hold funds from borrowers as part of its business model, the credit servicer shall convey that intention in its application for the authorisation referred to in Article 4(1). In such cases, the requirements laid down in accordance with paragraph 2, point (a), of this Article shall not apply.**

## A. INTRODUCTION

6.01 The article regulates the activity of a credit servicer to receive and hold funds from borrowers in order to transfer those funds to credit purchasers. In the event that a credit servicer receives and holds payments from underlying borrowers, the credit servicer must hold these funds in a segregated account in order to differentiate between the original NPL and the new repayments. The provision sets specific requirements for credit servicers in order to act as a custodian of funds: the applicant has a separate account in a credit institution into which all funds received from borrowers are to be credited and kept until their channelling to the respective credit purchaser under the conditions agreed with the credit purchaser. The applicant needs to ensure that those funds are protected according to the national law in the interest of the credit purchasers against the claims of the other creditors of the credit servicers, in particular in the event of insolvency. Further requirement is to determine that, when a borrower makes a payment to a credit servicer in order to, partially or totally, reimburse the amounts due related to a creditor's rights under a non-performing credit agreement, or to the non-performing credit agreement itself, that payment is treated as having been paid to the credit purchaser. It is also required for a credit servicer to deliver a receipt or a letter of discharge to the borrower, on paper or another durable medium, whenever the credit servicer receives funds from the borrower, acknowledging the amounts received. Member States have the discretion to allow credit servicers in their territory to receive and hold funds from the borrowers. This regulatory regime aligns with the obligations on banks selling NPLs; for example, to provide sufficient information to enable prospective creditor purchasers to diligence the relevant NPLs, to supply data to their Member States on NPL disposals, including providing purchaser details and borrower data.

6.02 The valuation of a portfolio of NPLs involves several actors. Buyers on secondary markets are sophisticated investors, such as loan participating funds. This type of investor does not create new credit, but they are buying existing credit at their own risk and therefore do not cause prudential concerns as their potential contribution to systemic risk is negligible. The directive considers it not to be justified to require those types of investors to apply for authorisation or to set special conditions for them to engage in loan purchasing or acquisition activities. The directive, however, seeks to ensure that consumer protection rules continue to apply, and borrowers' rights continue to be those arising from the initial credit agreement. Recital 52 of the directive states that "in order to ensure a high level of consumer protection, Union and national law provide for a number of rights and safeguards related to credit agreements granted to a consumer". For that reason, the regulatory framework also imposes a number of requirements on credit purchasers (i.e. non-banks) in relation to NPLs issued by EU credit institutions.

## B. THE CREDIT SERVICERS INDUSTRY

Reduced volume of transactions and volatility in the debt market have hindered recoveries and weakened return expectations for NPL portfolios.[1] In response, the market has adopted a more sophisticated and specialised approach to loan portfolios. NPL investors are conducting thorough reviews of their portfolios, focusing on the assets where they have the most expertise, and selling off loans outside those parameters in the secondary market. These deals have been relatively small and low-profile as compared to the banks' bigger NPL disposals. For example, an NPL vendor is more likely to find a specialist buyer for a specific loan exposure than sell a larger, mixed bundle of loans in a big transaction. The NPL market is maturing and becoming more professionalised. Nevertheless, there is still a clear need for professional servicing players and capital. Professional NPL servicers are changing their operating models by no longer deploying their balance sheets for new NPL investments and focusing on consolidation opportunities in the servicing sector, reflecting the increasingly strategic importance of scale in the industry.[2] In turn, NPL investors with capital are exploring selective strategic capital partnerships with NPL servicers to reduce fees and boost net returns. **6.03**

The directive holds NPL servicers to minimum standards and increases transparency in the market. This standardisation and regulation are a positive development for the NPL sector and have been well received by established market players in the financial industry, as well as the introduction of passporting rights, which allow NPL servicers authorised in one Member State to operate across all EU countries.[3] However, the challenging macroeconomic environment has inhibited efforts to boost secondary NPL deals. The European Banking Authority (EBA) reported in November 2024 that EU bank NPL **6.04**

1 Christian Klaus and Michael Mönnich, 'Current Challenges and Strategies in Dealing with Non-performing Loans' (9 January 2025), https://www.bankinghub.eu/finance-risk/non-performing-loans-strategies.

2 White & Case LLP, 'NPL Players Rethink Strategy in a Changing Market' (5 September 2024), https://www.lexology.com/library/detail.aspx?g=7d2f5c9d-7f90-4fee-ba74-bf8ffac24fdd.

3 White & Case LLP, 'Europe's NPL Markets Stall Despite Regulatory Push' (23 December 2024), https://www.lexology.com/library/detail.aspx?g=58a06730-4723-4c7c-b4c7-a68db4bcc986.

stocks reached €373 billion and a 3.4% increase year-on-year.[4] It has been noted that the market is only a fraction of the size it was in 2016 when NPL stocks hit a high-water mark of more than €1 trillion.[5] Moreover, NPL outflows have been flat year-on-year, with only €103 billion recorded in H1 2024, against inflows of more than €113 billion.[6] This reflects the ongoing normalisation and, to a certain extent, the professionalisation of the NPL industry. Even with the year-on-year inflow of new NPLs, there are no signs of a surge of deteriorated loans as bank regulation, management, proactiveness and capital are currently in a much stronger position today than in the aftermath of the global financial crisis.[7] This has resulted in limited transaction flow and, combined with elevated interest rates, has created challenges for traditional buyers of NPL portfolios. Buyers predicated their NPL business models on high deal volumes, winning associated servicer contracts, and the ability to raise cheap financing on capital markets to fund portfolio purchases. With these commercial levers coming under strain, key buyers of bank NPL portfolios have been unable to offer prices that would make NPL disposals worthwhile for banks. This removes capacity and competition from the market. Thus, as banks now enter NPL trades for better capitalisation, they would rather hold underperforming loan books than sell at too-steep a discount.

## C. THE DISCLOSURE REQUIREMENTS

**6.05** The harmonisation and disclosure requirements of the directive have demonstrated to be insufficient to counterbalance the volatility of the market. The directive's additional disclosure and reporting requirements have added complexity and increased compliance costs. They have made it more difficult to operate as an NPL servicer and, to a lesser degree, as a buyer. Eventually, investors, who enter the NPL market at a benign point in the economic cycle, may emerge and value the transparency and disclosure requirements that the directive mandates. However, in the current market, the directive's provisions are unlikely to change the perspective of experienced NPL players. It has been

4 EBA Risk Assessment Report (29 November 2024), https://www.eba.europa.eu/publications-and-media/press-releases/eu-banks-continue-be-robust-although-risks-geopolitical-tensions-and-cyber-threats-remain.

5 European Banking Federation, 'A Closer Look at Non-performing Loans' https://www.ebf.eu/facts-and-figures/non-performing-loans/.

6 Debashis Dey and Dennis Heuer, 'NPL Players Rethink Strategy in a Changing Market' (23 October 2024), https://www.iflr.com/article/2dukn868fy6zmg1p08bgg/banking/npl-players-rethink-strategy-in-a-changing-market.

7 Sherif Elashmawy and Juha-Pekka Kallunki, 'Does Forward-Looking Accounting Improve Bank Asset Quality?' (2025) *Accounting in Europe*, https://doi.org/10.1080/17449480.2025.2470719.

noted that given some of the uncertainties around the scope of the directive, its application should be carefully considered when purchasing portfolios of loans that comprise performing and non-performing loans, when purchasing NPLs that are originated by EU banks but otherwise do not have any nexus to the EU (e.g. non-EU borrowers and non-EU governing law of the finance documents) or when entering into transactions where the credit risk of an NPL is transferred without a transfer of title by the lender of record (e.g. pursuant to a total return swap or sub-participation arrangement).[8]

A credit servicer which is to receive and hold payments from borrowers must **6.06** ensure those funds are credited to and held in a segregated account, until their channelling to the respective credit purchaser. The credit servicer (similar to the credit purchaser) has a range of information and other obligations to the underlying borrowers. It has the ability under the EU regime to passport its authorisation to other Member States, which could create interesting business opportunities for credit servicers. Credit servicers manage the administration of NPLs on behalf of credit purchasers by recovering payments, renegotiating loan terms, and notifying borrowers of any interest rate changes or charges relating to the loans. They notify borrowers of an NPL sale and ahead of the first debt collection, provide specific information, including the date of transfer, identification, contact details, and authorisation of the new credit servicer or credit service provider. The credit servicer should avoid misleading borrowers and keep records for a period of 10 years of all correspondence with the credit purchaser and the borrower, all instructions received from the credit purchaser, and all instructions provided to credit service providers. These obligations do not apply to servicers of NPLs originating from a non-EU bank, or if the credit servicing activities are carried out by an EU credit institution (such as the bank itself), fund managers, UCITS investment companies, or a credit servicer that is supervised by a state authority.

8 Gregg Beechey, Zac Mellor-Clark and Jons Lehmann, 'EU Non-Performing Loans Directive (NPLD) — Implications for Credit Funds?' (6 September 2023), https://www.friedfrank.com/news-and-insights/eu-non-performing-loans-directive-npld-implications-for-credit-funds-11299.

# ARTICLE 7

# PROCEDURE FOR AUTHORISATION OF CREDIT SERVICERS

**Andrea Miglionico**

1. Member States shall establish a procedure for the authorisation of credit servicers that enables an applicant to submit an application and provide all the information necessary for the competent authority of the home Member State to verify that the applicant has satisfied all the conditions laid down in the national provisions transposing Article 5(1), and, where relevant, in Article 6(2), point (a).
2. The application for authorisation of credit servicers referred to in paragraph 1 shall be accompanied by the following:
   (a) evidence of the applicant's legal status and a copy of its act of incorporation and of the company by-laws;
   (b) the address of the applicant's head office or its registered office;
   (c) the identity of the members of the applicant's management or administrative organ and the persons who hold qualifying holdings within the meaning of Article 4(1), point (36), of Regulation (EU) No 575/2013;
   (d) evidence that the applicant fulfils the conditions laid down in Article 5(1), points (b) and (c);
   (e) evidence that the persons who hold qualifying holdings within the meaning of Article 4(1), point (36), of Regulation (EU) No 575/2013 fulfil the conditions laid down in Article 5(1), point (d), of this Directive;
   (f) evidence of the governance arrangements and internal control mechanisms referred to in Article 5(1), point (e);
   (g) evidence of the policy referred to in Article 5(1), point (f);
   (h) evidence of the internal procedures referred to in Article 5(1), point (g);
   (i) evidence of the procedures referred to in Article 5(1), point (h);
   (j) where relevant, evidence of the existence of a separate account in a credit institution as provided for in Article 6(2), point (a);
   (k) any outsourcing agreement as referred to in Article 12(1).
3. Member States shall ensure that the competent authorities of a home Member State assess, within 45 days of receipt of the application for authorisation, whether that application is complete.
4. Member States shall ensure that, within 90 days of receipt of a complete application or, if the application is considered incomplete, of receipt of the required information, the competent authorities of the home Member State

**notify the applicant whether the authorisation is granted or refused and provide reasons for refusal.**

5. **Member States shall ensure that an applicant has the right of appeal before a tribunal in cases where the competent authorities of the home Member State decide to refuse an application for authorisation pursuant to Article 5(3) and also in cases where, within the time limit provided for in paragraph 4 of this Article, no decision is taken by the competent authorities in respect of the application.**



## A. INTRODUCTION

**7.01** The article regulates procedural matters for the authorisation of credit servicers. A list of conditions is required for an applicant to satisfy the requirements set in the directive for the competent authority of the home Member State. The authorisation process includes detailed governance, transparency, and consumer protection standards: credit servicers must obtain authorisation from their home Member State before providing services. In terms of consumer protection, credit servicers have the obligation to provide certain information prior to the amendment of the terms and conditions of a credit agreement and the exercise, where appropriate, of reasonable forbearance before enforcement proceedings are initiated. The directive aims to harmonise the authorisation framework that allows credit servicers of NPL portfolios, acting on behalf of purchasers of NPLs, to scale up their activities in different EU Member States for the first time by using a passport.[1] The directive requires that credit servicers first obtain a licence for their activities and sets out the requirements for their authorisation. The host and home Member States are required to cooperate and share relevant information to ensure compliance with the directive and national implementation. They may also impose administrative sanctions, penalties, or remedial measures in the case of non-compliance. In addition, any transfer of NPLs triggers a notification to the borrower, to be done by the credit purchaser or the credit servicer, and the directive details the content of such notification. Banks must also inform competent authorities about the details of the loans they transferred. National competent authorities (NCAs)

1 European Parliament, 'Credit Servicers Directive' (October 2021), https://www.europarl.europa.eu/RegData/etudes/ATAG/2021/698749/EPRS_ATA(2021)698749_EN.pdf.

must introduce an authorisation procedure for credit servicers requiring them to prove they meet all the conditions; decide within 90 days whether to grant or refuse authorisation; have supervisory, investigatory, and sanctioning powers; and may, in certain circumstances, withdraw an authorisation; maintain a publicly accessible online register of all credit servicers; allow, subject to certain conditions, credit servicers authorised in one Member State to practise elsewhere in the EU.[2] Member States are responsible for establishing appropriate administrative penalties and remedial measures for breaches of the directive. Member States regulate credit servicing activities that do not fall within the scope of the directive, such as services offered for credit agreements issued by non-credit institutions or credit servicing activities performed by natural persons.

**7.02** Credit servicers authorised in one Member State can provide credit servicing activities in other EU countries provided they notify the original authorising Member State. They notify borrowers of an NPL sale and ahead of the first debt collection, providing specific information, including the date of transfer, identification, contact details, and authorisation of the new credit servicer or credit service provider. The credit servicer must also avoid misleading borrowers. Keeping records for a period of 10 years of all correspondence with the credit purchaser and the borrower, all instructions received from the credit purchaser, and all instructions provided to credit service providers. Credit servicers are required to provide the borrower with the following information after the transfer of a creditor's rights and before the first debt collection, or whenever a borrower so requests: the date of the transfer and identity and contact details of the credit purchaser; the amounts the borrower owes, broken down into capital, interest, fees, and other charges; a statement certifying that all relevant EU and national laws continue to apply; the name, address and contact details of the relevant national authorities.[3] The credit servicer shall have in place adequate and specific internal procedures that ensure the recording and handling of complaints from borrowers. Credit servicers are

2 To avoid lengthy procedures and uncertainty, it is necessary to establish requirements regarding the information that applicants for authorisation as a credit servicer are required to submit, as well as reasonable deadlines for the issue of an authorisation and the circumstances for its withdrawal. Where competent authorities withdraw an authorisation of a credit servicer that provides credit servicing activities in other Member States, competent authorities of the host Member State and also of the Member State where the credit was granted, when different from the host and the home Member States, should be informed. Equally, an up-to-date public register or list should be established in the home and the host Member States and made publicly available on the website of the competent authorities to ensure transparency as regards the number and identity of authorised credit servicers.

3 See 'Framework for Credit Servicers and Credit Purchasers' (27 April 2022), https://eur-lex.europa.eu/legal-content/EN/TXT/?uri=LEGISSUM:4572717.

responsible for making sure that the outsourcing of their credit servicing activities to credit service providers does not result in undue operational risk, nor in non-compliance by the credit service provider with any requirements of Union or national law, nor restrict the capacity of a regulatory supervisor to perform its duty and safeguard borrower rights.

## B. THE APPLICATION PROCESS

Before transmitting the application to the NCA, the applicant may contact the authority to request information on the need for an authorisation as credit servicer, the application documentation for the authorisation file or any other important question relating to the applicant's project. The applicant submits a completed application form with supporting documentation and the NCA acknowledges receipt of the application submission. The authority assesses whether the application submission contains the key information and documentation required; where all key information and documentation have been provided, the NCA completes an assessment of the application submission and may issue detailed comments and seek additional information. The applicant is provided with the opportunity to address the comments and requests issued by the authority in a revised application submission. The NCA assesses the subsequent application submission and notifies the applicant of its assessment and next steps. The applicant is provided with a further opportunity to address any concerns arising at this stage in the process and the NCA notifies the applicant of its decision in respect of the application submission. Where a credit servicer does not intend to receive and hold funds from borrowers as part of its business model, the credit servicer must convey that intention in its application for authorisation. The NCA assesses within 45 days of receipt of the application for authorisation whether that application is complete. The decision of the authority with respect to an application for authorisation must be duly substantiated and notified to the applicant within 90 days of receipt of a complete application or, if the application is considered incomplete, of receipt of the required information. Such a decision must in any event be adopted within twelve months of receipt of the application, failing which the absence of a decision shall be deemed to constitute notification of a refusal. The authorisation can be refused if the conditions for the grant thereof are not fulfilled. **7.03**

In the assessment stage, the application material submitted is reviewed against the relevant authorisation requirements to determine whether sufficient information has been provided to enable the NCA to proceed with the notification of assessment. The NCA generally issues initial comments to the applicant **7.04** based on its review of the application material submitted and any subsequent comments based on its review of responses submitted by the applicant. The NCA can issue guidelines regarding the processing of applications for authorisation and in the context of meeting those guidelines, the timeframe to which the authority has committed for the assessment phase of the application process is 90 working days. However, it should be noted that in the event of further and subsequent information being sought, this 90-day threshold is paused until such information is received by the NCA from the applicant. The guidelines do not apply to applications where another regulatory authority has to be contacted; which are subject to interview; where significant legal issues arise; where significant fitness and probity issues arise; where the business model of an applicant is complex or novel in nature; where significant changes to the business model, the applicant's shareholder structure or other key aspects of an application arise during the review process, or where the application becomes dormant; and where the NCA is going to refuse an application. Applications that remain dormant with no positive engagement from an applicant are returned; assessment and specific interviews are also conducted in respect of applications where specific fitness and probity-related concerns arise.

## C. NOTIFICATION AND REFUSAL OF THE AUTHORISATION

**7.05** The NCA notifies the applicant of the outcome of the assessment stage of the application process as follows: where the assessment is favourable, the NCA communicates to the applicant by letter that it proposes to authorise the applicant on the basis of the information provided in its application submission, provided any specified final steps are taken and specified final items of information and evidence are received. This letter also specifies any specific conditions the NCA proposes to impose on the authorisation itself once granted. This letter explains the reasons for these proposed conditions and the applicant is afforded the opportunity to make representations in respect of the proposed conditions before the NCA makes any decision on the application. In the event that the NCA is not satisfied on foot of the assessment stage such that it can issue a notification of assessment, the authority advises the applicant of this by letter. The letter sets out the areas to be addressed and affords the applicant the opportunity to do so and to make any submissions it wishes to the NCA in respect of these matters.

**7.06** Once the NCA has assessed any further information, evidence, representations submitted by the applicant, it notifies the applicant, via letter, of its decision on the application. The principal outcomes are as follows: (a) authorisation

– the NCA has decided to grant an authorisation; (b) authorisation with specific conditions – the NCA has decided to grant an authorisation with specific conditions attached to the authorisation. The specific conditions to be attached to the authorisation are outlined in the letter; (c) proposed refusal of authorisation – the NCA is inclined to refuse the application for authorisation. In this case, the NCA notifies the applicant of the grounds for the proposed refusal of the authorisation. The applicant then has an opportunity to make submissions in response to the proposed refusal. The submissions are considered by the NCA, following which a decision is taken by the authority to grant or refuse the authorisation applied for, as appropriate. The NCA offers the facility of an optional pre-application meeting to firms to answer specific questions about any aspect of the application process and completing the application form. The NCA recommends that firms which avail of this facility have reviewed the application material in full before requesting such a meeting and have their specific questions prepared in advance in order to make the meeting as productive as possible.

# ARTICLE 8

# WITHDRAWAL OF AUTHORISATION

**Georgios Psaroudakis**

**1. Member States shall ensure that the competent authorities of the home Member State have the necessary supervisory and investigatory powers, and sanctioning powers, in accordance with Article 22 in order to withdraw the authorisation granted to a credit servicer, where any of the following applies to such a credit servicer:**

**(a) does not make use of the authorisation within 12 months of its grant;**

**(b) expressly renounces the authorisation;**

**(c) has ceased to engage in the activities of a credit servicer for more than 12 months;**

**(d) has acquired an authorisation through false statements or other irregular means;**

**(e) no longer fulfils the requirements for the granting of an authorisation as a credit servicer set out in Article 5(1) and, where relevant, in Article 6(2) point (a);**

**(f) commits a serious infringement of the applicable rules, including the national provisions transposing this Directive, or of other consumer protection rules, including applicable rules of the host Member State and of the Member State where the credit was granted.**

**2. Where an authorisation is withdrawn in accordance with paragraph 1 of this Article, Member States shall ensure that the competent authorities of the home Member State immediately inform the competent authorities of the host Member State in cases where the credit servicer provides services under Article 13, and also the competent authorities of the Member State where the credit was granted, when different from the host and the home Member States.**

## A. NATURE AND APPLICATION OF WITHDRAWAL

### 1. Competence to withdraw authorisation

Article 8 first serves to clarify that the competent authority, designated in each Member State according to Article 21(3) of the Directive, is also competent to withdraw authorisation. This is only reasonable, as withdrawal is the *actus contrarius* of the granting of authorisation by the same authority, and it is mostly based on findings that the competent authority comes across while exercising its ongoing supervisory function. Notably, the same conclusion, i.e. that the competent authority also has the power to withdraw authorisation, can be derived from Article 22(1)(b) of the Directive as well. **8.01**

### 2. Withdrawal as a part of supervisory powers

The connection between ongoing supervision and its findings on the one hand, and the withdrawal of authorisation on the other, is also expressed in the requirement that the same competent authority has all other (supervisory, investigative, sanctioning) powers necessary, in order to ultimately reach and implement a decision on the withdrawal of authorisation. It should be noted here that the withdrawal of authorisation is mentioned together with other measures in the list of administrative penalties and remedial measures in Article 23(2) of the Directive, without a clarification on whether it is a penalty or a remedial measure. On the one hand, it may be (but is not necessarily) the consequence of a serious infringement, and it is certainly unfavourable to the credit servicer (except when it is decided upon request of the servicer itself). On the other hand, the remedial nature, which might be thought to prevail in an overall analysis, is connected with the fact that withdrawal, most importantly, removes the servicer from the market and thus fosters the proper functioning of the latter. **8.02**

**8.03** In any case, even if it is not, or is not primarily, a penalty, withdrawal is still a measure that typically affects the servicer adversely. Therefore, the servicer has the right to be heard before the competent authority withdraws authorisation. Indeed, this right, beyond its position in national legal traditions, is guaranteed at the EU level as well, namely in Article 41(2)(a) of the Charter of Fundamental Rights. In this context, the servicer may try to suggest that the circumstances invoked by the competent authority to justify withdrawal are not as described by it, or that the servicer itself is able to remedy these circumstances in a timely manner. The argument, in the latter case, would be that it is disproportionate to withdraw authorisation if a solution is imminent; of course, this argument could only be successful if established in a solid and reliable manner. In particular, it should be noted that alternative measures can be considered in the analysis of the necessity of withdrawal only if they are equally effective.[1] Moreover, the assessment on proportionality must be compatible with the discretion available to the competent authority.[2]

### 3. Cross-border aspects of withdrawal

**8.04** The withdrawal of authorisation must be made known to the competent authorities in other Member States in two cases, as stipulated in Article 8(2). First, if the credit servicer has been providing services on a cross-border basis as well, using the "passport" under Article 13 of the Directive, then the competent authority of the home Member State must communicate the withdrawal to the competent authority of the host Member State. Just like withdrawal is the *actus contrarius* of authorisation, this communication of withdrawal to the authority of the host Member State is the *actus contrarius* of the communication, under Article 13(3), that the authorised credit servicer intends to provide services in that host Member State. Second, if the credit institution or credit purchaser, as the case may be, had itself provided credit in a different Member State (other than the home and any host Member State), it is possible that the credit servicer is providing services (to the credit institution or credit purchaser) with regard to such credit granted in a third Member State. In this case, the withdrawal must be communicated to the competent authority of the third Member State as well.

1 GCEU, Case T-351, 584/18 *Versobank* at [320], dealing with the withdrawal of authorisation of a credit institution, but with an analysis that is of relevance here as well.

2 CJEU, Case C-450/17 P *Landeskreditbank Baden-Württemberg* at [53]; GCEU, Case T-351,584/18 *Versobank* at [308].

## B. GROUNDS FOR WITHDRAWAL

### 1. General remarks

#### (a) Minimum harmonisation

The present provision contains a list of grounds for withdrawal that the Directive requires Member States to introduce in their national laws. More precisely, the Directive requires these grounds to be available to competent authorities, without excluding the possibility that other grounds are introduced at the initiative of the national legislator. Therefore, this should be read as a case of minimum harmonisation. 8.05

Thus, while the present provision lacks a formulation such as in Article 18(3) CRD IV on credit institutions, which explicitly refers to "other cases where national law provides for withdrawal of authorisation", the result is not different. Lastly, it should be noted that, even without an additional ground for withdrawal in national law beyond those mentioned in Article 8(1) of the Directive, the last among them, i.e. the infringement of rules applicable to the credit servicer, which go beyond rules implementing the Directive and include other national rules in the area of consumer protection, allows for some flexibility on the basis of national law. 8.06

#### (b) Categorisation

If a categorisation of the grounds for withdrawal is to be drawn, one comes up with two broad categories. On the one hand, there are grounds that are based on objective circumstances regarding the activity of the credit servicer, or rather the lack of such activities (though it will be explained that even the application of these grounds for withdrawal may involve a degree of assessment). These grounds are examined below. On the other hand, there are grounds for withdrawal that require, always and even more clearly, a material assessment of that activity, and they are examined below. 8.07

### 2. Individual grounds for withdrawal

#### (a) Grounds not involving an assessment (or involving only a limited assessment) of the credit servicer's behaviour: Article 8(1)(a)–(c)

Regarding the three grounds in Article 8(1)(a)–(c), it is noteworthy that the grounds for withdrawal corresponding to them in Article 18(a) CRD IV on credit institutions may be used, if national law so chooses, as a basis for authorisation to lapse. The difference between withdrawal and lapsing of authorisation is that the former requires an administrative act of the competent 8.08

authority, while the latter occurs by operation of law, when its condition is fulfilled. Given that the present provision does not refer to the lapsing of authorisation as an alternative, it follows that this is not available in the case of credit servicer and that an administrative act is always required. This is indeed preferable for the sake of legal certainty, while it also allows for a (comparatively limited) degree of discretion to be exercised by the competent authority. Regarding each individual ground, authorisation may be withdrawn under Article 8(1)(a) if no use has been made of it within 12 months of its granting. This suggests that the credit servicer is not willing or able to attract clients for its activity; the servicer does not engage, or does not engage successfully, with the market. Moreover, even if the servicer's internal governance has been deemed to be adequate at the time that authorisation was granted, its inactivity for 12 months casts heavy doubts on the suitability of its (unused) internal procedures to perform well, if needed. This ground for withdrawal is also found in Article 18(a) CRD IV on credit institutions. Preparatory acts on the part of the servicer (in particular relating to the infrastructure for its activity, such as hiring staff or developing the IT system) are not a "use" of the authorisation in the sense of this provision, which would require the occurrence of credit servicing as such.[3] Thus, such preparatory acts do not prevent the withdrawal in principle. However, it is not impossible, in the context of proportionality, that the competent authority, taking into account, in its reasonable discretion, the extent of such preparatory acts, any concrete potential for a use of the authorisation in the near future and the market circumstances, allows the servicer a somewhat longer time without withdrawing the authorisation. Moreover, authorisation may be withdrawn under Article 8(1)(b) if the servicer renounces it. Obviously, the servicer may not be required to keep operating if it lacks the will to do so any more. Still, an administrative act must be issued, practically upon application of the servicer, in this case as well. This ground for withdrawal is also found in Article 18(a) CRD IV on credit institutions. Lastly, authorisation may be withdrawn under Article 8(1)(c) if the servicer has ceased engaging in its activities for more than 12 months. This ground for withdrawal complements the one in Article 8(1)(a). The overarching idea is that the servicer that remains inactive, initially or later, for more than 12 months, should not retain its authorisation. This ground for withdrawal is also found in Article 18(a) CRD IV on credit institutions, though with the remarkable difference that the authorisation of the credit institution is withdrawn after 6, rather than 12, months of inactivity. In other words, in the case of credit institutions

3 Reinfrid Fischer/Kaspar Krolop, in: Fischer/Schulte-Mattler (eds.), *KWG, CRR-VO* (6th edn. 2023), § 35 KWG para. 5, on the relevant provision in the case of banks.

the law is stricter with subsequent inactivity than with the initial one, directly following the granting of authorisation.[4] This is not repeated in the present provision, which deals with both initial and subsequent inactivity in the same manner, setting 12 months as the limit, by which activity must be taken up or resumed.

(b) Grounds involving an assessment of the credit servicer's behaviour

The following grounds for withdrawal require a material assessment of the servicer's behaviour, as this behaviour occurred either at the time of applying for authorisation or during its functioning. In other words, these are the grounds connected with the ongoing supervision of the servicer, out of which the competent authority becomes aware of relevant circumstances. Therefore, there is a close link between the requirements for authorisation and ongoing supervision, given that in the context of the latter it must be continuously examined whether the servicer fulfils the said requirements. In this sense, the requirements for authorisation are guiding ongoing supervision as well. Moreover, these grounds for withdrawal often involve a complex and fact-specific analysis on the part of the competent authority, to be made in light of proportionality but also on the basis of a significant margin of appreciation for this authority, which needs to protect the integrity of the credit servicing market. **8.09**

Authorisation may be withdrawn under Article 8(1)(d) if it was acquired on the basis of false statements or other irregular means. For example, it may be that the governance arrangements and internal control mechanisms, or the knowledge and experience of the management or administrative organ were misrepresented at the time of the application. This ground for withdrawal may (but does not necessarily) concur with the next one in Article 8(1)(e), if the credit servicer not only misrepresented compliance with the requirements for authorisation at the stage of application but also does not fulfil such requirements at the time that withdrawal is examined either. Article 8(1)(e) refers to the case that these requirements are "no longer" fulfilled, but there can be an additional ground for withdrawal on the present basis if the said requirements have never been fulfilled from the beginning (e.g. there have never been robust governance arrangements, as required by Article 5(e)). Then, the application of Article 8(1)(d) is based on the initial misrepresentation and the application of Article 8(1)(e) is based on the condition discerned at a later **8.10**

4 The reason behind this is that it is thought to be harder to establish a running business, immediately after authorisation, than to re-establish a business that has operated in the past, so that the former case is treated more leniently: Fischer/Krolop, in: Fischer/Schulte-Mattler (eds.), KWG, CRR-VO, § 35 KWG para. 16, on the relevant provision in the case of banks.

stage. However, Article 8(1)(d) may also function as a ground for withdrawal independently. This is the case, when there has been a misrepresentation at the time of application, but the affected issue has been corrected in the meantime; for example, robust governance arrangements have actually been developed in the meantime. In this case, Article 8(1)(e) is not applicable, but Article 8(1)(d) remains applicable. Indeed, this is its independent significance of the latter provision, as it is related to the unreliable conduct of the credit servicer as such. Authorisation may be withdrawn under Article 8(1)(e) if the servicer does not comply with the requirements for authorisation any more. Therefore, these requirements are not only to be met at the time that authorisation is granted, but they form the basis of the ongoing supervision of the servicer too. Given that there are numerous requirements for authorisation under Article 5(1) and Article 6(2)(a), this ground for authorisation can in effect be analysed as a number of particular grounds. Therefore, generally corresponding to the requirements in Article 5(1), authorisation may be withdrawn if:

- it is established that the members of the management or administrative organ are not of sufficiently good repute, in particular on the basis of developments that are subsequent to the granting of authorisation (e.g. new criminal proceedings);
- it emerges that the management or administrative organ does not have adequate knowledge and experience, perhaps due to changes in its composition;
- the persons having qualifying holdings in the servicer are established not to be in good repute, in particular due to new developments (which may refer to initial shareholders or to persons that have acquired holdings subsequently);[5]
- governance arrangements or internal control mechanisms are proven in practice to be inadequate;
- the compliance policy is inadequate, at least as applied;
- AML procedures are not adequate, at least as applied;
- the servicer does not comply in practice with the requirement to keep a separate account in a credit institution in order to protect the funds received from borrowers and held by the servicer until channelled to the credit purchaser.

**8.11** Not every case of such breach of requirements leads to the withdrawal of authorisation. The latter is subject to an examination of proportionality, in which potential milder measures (sanctions or remedial measures) are considered, and which depends on the extent of the breaches. Authorisation may be withdrawn under Article 8(1)(f) if the servicer commits a serious infringement of the "applicable rules". There is more than one category of such applicable rules: the provision itself refers to rules implementing the Directive itself in

5 Fischer/Krolop, in: Fischer/Schulte-Mattler (eds.), KWG, CRR-VO, § 35 KWG para. 34, on the relevant provision in the case of banks.

the law of the home Member State, and to consumer protection rules of the home Member State and, as the case may be, the host Member State and the third Member State where credit was granted. Since this reference is indicative, one may add other national rules applicable to the servicers. For example, national law may introduce capital requirements (which the Directive itself does not introduce), the breach of which may lead to withdrawal, in particular if the servicer is unable to remedy it. Again, withdrawal must be a proportional reaction to the particular infringement, which is expressed, in the wording of the provision, in the reference to a "serious" infringement.

# ARTICLE 9

# LIST OR REGISTER OF AUTHORISED CREDIT SERVICERS

**Georgios Psaroudakis**

**1. Member States shall ensure that the competent authorities establish and maintain at least a list or, where considered more appropriate, a national register, of all credit servicers authorised to provide services within their territory, including credit servicers providing services under Article 13 of this Directive.**

**The EBA shall develop guidelines in accordance with Article 16 of Regulation (EU) No 1093/2010 for establishing and maintaining such lists or registers and specifying the types of information included in them in order to guarantee a level playing field across the Union and transparency for credit purchasers and for borrowers.**

**2. The list or register referred to in paragraph 1 shall be made publicly accessible online on the website of the competent authorities and shall be updated on a regular basis.**

**3. Where an authorisation has been withdrawn pursuant to Article 8, the competent authorities shall update the list or register referred to in paragraph 1 of this Article without delay.**



## A. INTRODUCTION

**9.01** The aim of this provision is to provide transparency (as explained in recital 30 to the Directive) as to the credit servicers that are authorised to provide services within the territory of each Member State. This includes servicers that have been authorised in the Member State itself, as well as those who have been authorised in a different (home) Member State, but the competent authority of the host Member State has received a communication from the competent authority of the home Member State to the effect that the servicer intends to provide services at the host.[1] The reference to Article 13 establishes this latter point. Therefore, all interested parties, i.e. credit institutions, credit purchasers and (perhaps more importantly, given that their access to information is harder) borrowers must, according to the present provision, be able to easily establish whether a credit servicer lawfully provides services in the relevant territory. This facilitates procedurally the overall objective of the Directive, which is to foster the secondary market for NPLs, as explained in recital 9 to it.[2]

## B. EBA GUIDELINES 2024/02: CONTENT OF THE LIST OF REGISTER

EBA has published Guidelines 2024/02 on the establishment and maintenance of such national lists or registers. The Guidelines specify the content to be included in the lists or registers: mainly, name, address, authorisation status of the servicer, its home Member State, list of host Member States for which a notification to the competent authority of the home Member State has been made and contact details (including in connection with consumer complaints; in this respect, the list or register supports, as a publicity tool, the procedures for the handling of complaints provided for in Article 24). 9.02

In particular, the authorisation status of the servicer consists of two aspects. First, this status may be "valid" or "withdrawn", according to para. 9(i) of the Guidelines, as to whether the entity mentioned may provide credit servicing activities. This is to say that servicers, the authorisation of which has been withdrawn, are still displayed in the list or register (with reference to withdrawal), which serves transparency regarding their status. The question arises, whether the display of the "withdrawn" status is required to be indefinite or can be limited in time in national law. While it is a valid consideration that the informational value of the display (which needs to be balanced against the reputational cost to the former servicer) reduces with time, this balancing 9.03

1 An alternative idea would be to establish a "pan-EU" register, which would be kept by the national competent authorities collectively: see for such a proposal Cătălin-Gabriel Stanescu, 'The Impact of the Debt Servicing Directive on Regulating Abusive Debt Collection in the European Union: A Step Forward or a Missed Opportunity?' (2023) 12(1) *Journal of European Consumer and Market Law* 4. This proposal certainly has a significant appeal, as it seems to fit well with the move towards an integrated secondary market for NPLs. The main difficulty seems to be the lack of a competent authority at the European level, which would be keeping the register by itself. On the other hand, there is the example of payment institutions, in the case of which there are both national registers and a central EBA register according to Articles 14–15 of Directive 2015/2366/EU (the "PSD II" Directive).

2 Andrea Miglionico, 'The NPLs Services Directive. The Restructuring Toolkit for Asset Quality' in Georgios Psaroudakis (ed.), *Risk Sharing in the Euro Area. Legal Aspects* (Springer 2023) 5.

has been performed by the EBA, which has come to the explicit conclusion that the interest of consumers in transparency remains more important, also given that loan agreements may be long-lasting (para. 17 of the Background and rationale to the Guidelines). Therefore, compliance with the Guidelines requires that this display is indefinite (para. 10 of the Guidelines).

**9.04** Second, the authorisation status is connected to whether the servicer may receive or hold funds from borrowers as per Article. 6, or not. According to para. 9(j) of the Guidelines, there are three options as to the display of this aspect of the authorisation status: "approved", "prohibited for this credit servicer" and "generally prohibited for credit servicers based in [name of Member State]". Therefore, a differentiation is made, in the display as well, between a "horizontal" prohibition (either in the law of the host Member State, which then applies to all servicers in its list or register, or in the law of the home Member State of the servicer, which the host Member State takes note of in its list of register) and a prohibition deriving from the non-authorisation of a particular servicer. Lastly, if the authorisation status of the servicer, as per para. 9(i) of the Guidelines, is "withdrawn", then the servicer is obviously unable to receive or hold funds from borrowers, so that the determination of status regarding funds from borrowers is non-applicable.

## C. EBA GUIDELINES 2024/02: PROCEDURAL ASPECTS

**9.05** Care is taken that the list of register is updated appropriately, as required by paras. 2–3 of the provision examined here and by the underlying idea of transparency. In general, it must be updated at least once a week (para. 16 of the Guidelines), while in case of withdrawal of authorisation (either a general withdrawal or a withdrawal as to receiving and holding funds from borrowers) an update is required within two working days (para. 17 of the Guidelines).

**9.06** The list or register must be accessible with no prior registration or other precondition and free of charge (para. 12–13 of the Guidelines), and it must also be available for download (para. 14 of the Guidelines), which the Guidelines should be deemed to also require to be free of charge. An interesting provision is found in para. 15, according to which the list or register should be made available in the national language(s) "and at least in an official EU language customary in the field of finance". Given the circumstances in the field of finance (as well as more broadly), the latter part of the provision implies in effect (without spelling it out) that the list or register must be available in English as well.

# ARTICLE 10

# RELATIONSHIP WITH THE BORROWER, COMMUNICATION OF THE TRANSFER AND SUBSEQUENT COMMUNICATIONS

**Georgios Psaroudakis**

**1. Member States shall require that credit purchasers and credit servicers, in their relationships with borrowers:**
**(a) act in good faith, fairly and professionally;**
**(b) provide information to borrowers that is not misleading, unclear or false;**
**(c) respect and protect the personal information and privacy of borrowers;**
**(d) communicate with borrowers in a way that does not constitute harassment, coercion or undue influence.**

**2. Member States shall ensure that, after any transfer of a creditor's rights under a non-performing credit agreement, or of the non-performing credit agreement itself, to a credit purchaser, and always in advance of the first debt collection, but also whenever requested by the borrower, the credit purchaser or, when appointed to perform credit servicing activities, the entity referred to in Article 2(5), point (a)(i) or (iii), or the credit servicer, sends to the borrower a communication, on paper or on another durable medium, that includes at least the following:**
**(a) information on the transfer that took place, including the date of transfer;**
**(b) the identification and contact details of the credit purchaser;**
**(c) when appointed, the identification and contact details of the credit servicer or of the entity referred to in Article 2(5), point (a)(i) or (iii);**
**(d) when appointed, evidence regarding the authorisation of a credit servicer granted pursuant to Article 7;**
**(e) where relevant, the identification and contact details of the credit service provider;**
**(f) presented in a prominent way, a contact reference point at the credit purchaser or, when appointed to perform credit servicing activities, at the entity referred to in Article 2(5), point (a)(i) or (iii), or at the credit servicer and, where relevant, at the credit service provider, from which to receive information when needed;**

**(g) information on the amounts due by the borrower at the time of the communication, detailing what is due as capital, interests, fees and other permitted charges;**

**(h) a statement to the effect that all relevant Union and national law concerning in particular the enforcement of contracts, consumer protection, borrower's rights and criminal law continues to apply;**

**(i) the name, address and contact details of the competent authorities of the Member State in which the borrower is domiciled, or its registered office is situated or, if under its national law it has no registered office, the Member State in which its head office is situated and to which the borrower can submit a complaint.**

**The communication provided for in the first subparagraph shall be written in language which is clear and understandable for the general public.**

**3. Member States shall ensure that, in all subsequent communications with the borrower, the credit purchaser or, when appointed to perform credit servicing activities, the entity referred to in Article 2(5), point (a)(i) or (iii), or the credit servicer, includes the information set out in paragraph 2, point (f) of this Article, except where it is the first communication after the appointment of a new credit servicer, in which case the information set out in paragraph 2, points (c) and (d) of this Article, shall also be included.**

**4. Paragraphs 2 and 3 shall be without prejudice to any additional requirements regarding communications provided for in other applicable Union or national law.**



## A. INTRODUCTION

**10.01** The present provision refers to the relationship between the credit servicer and purchaser on the one hand and the borrower on the other. The Directive cannot actually regulate this relationship comprehensively, because this is a matter of non-harmonised, national civil law. It does however introduce some principles on the functioning of the said relationship, while also introducing a duty of information. In other words, the present provision is more concrete in the area of transparency, while it does not proceed beyond the establishment of relatively abstract principles in the area of material duties between the parties of the credit contract.

The context, in which this provision applies, is derived from the definition of credit servicing in Article 3(9). While this is not the proper place to go into detail in this respect, it is recalled here that the main activities included in credit servicing are collection and renegotiation, both of which the servicer performs on behalf of the purchaser. 10.02

## B. MATERIAL DUTIES

Article 10(1) contains the material duties of both the servicer and purchaser vis-à-vis the borrower. The provision does not attempt to delineate the duties of the servicer and the purchaser separately from each other, but rather establishes principles that both of them must follow. This allows national law some discretion as to the functioning of the relationship between servicer, purchaser and borrower. It also makes clear that the level of protection that is afforded to the borrower must remain steady, whatever modalities exist as to the credit servicing agreement and the division of duties between servicer and purchaser. Four duties are mentioned. 10.03

*First*, there is a duty of good faith, fair and professional behaviour. Obviously, these are open-ended terms, which are dealt with differently in different Member States. One way to analyse this duty is to regard it as a programmatic introduction to the material duties of the servicer and the purchaser under this paragraph, which are then concretised in the following passages of the paragraph. Under this view, the reference to good faith etc. is basically a tool of interpretation for the other duties below, without having much independent content itself. An alternative analysis is to regard the same duty as a check to the material choices of the servicer (in particular), when it collects from, or renegotiates with the borrower (as opposed to collection practices, which are caught by para. 1(d)). 10.04

Under the second view, strategies on the management of the relationships with borrowers, and corresponding choices at the individual level, that might be regarded as too aggressive (e.g. seizing assets of the borrower to a degree that is indeed consistent with the rights arising from the credit contract but may be thought to cause significant personal hardship to the borrower) would be contrary to this duty. The same would apply to the refusal of the servicer to engage constructively in renegotiation. Clearly, this could not be turned into a broad second-guessing of business decisions made by the servicer (and perhaps the purchaser as well): the latter should be allowed to pursue its business strategy, while this good faith duty would be applicable in somewhat marginal 10.05

cases. But even so, this is a significant matter relating to the functioning of the contract, which has already been explained to be an issue for national law. Moreover, the precise consequences of a breach of duty in this case would again depend on national law, which ultimately means that the practical significance of the duty would depend thereupon.

**10.06** Ultimately, and given that the reference to a duty of good faith should have some (even if limited) independent normative function, going beyond the other duties mentioned in the present provision, this reference of the Directive cannot be immaterial. Therefore, Member States should provide for some material control of the behaviour of the servicer/purchaser. This comes closer to the second view presented above on the meaning of the good faith duty, and it is also supported by recital 32 to the Directive, which explains that servicers "should act fairly and with due consideration for the financial situation of borrowers". Such control might, however, be based on general clauses, and not necessarily on particular rules relating to servicing, and might thus depend on the manner that such clauses are implemented in national law. Beyond this rather basic observation, it should not be thought that the Directive imposes on Member States a very specific level or method of control on the behaviour of servicers and purchasers; if that was the purpose of the Directive, one would expect a more elaborate provision.

**10.07** *Second*, there is a duty to provide information to borrowers that is not misleading, unclear or false. This should not be taken to refer to the information mentioned in para. 2, as this is separately regulated and refers to the aspects mentioned there, but is a rather a broader principle, relating to transparency in the relationship between the servicer and purchaser on the one hand and the borrower on the other. It is also remarkable that the Directive does not introduce here a positive duty to offer adequate information (such as in para. 2 on the items of information that it covers), but rather a duty to avoid misinforming the borrower. In other words, beyond the rather procedural information required by para. 2, the information that the servicer/purchaser must provide is found in (the contract and) national law, to the extent that such duties can be derived from the latter. What the Directive requires is transparency in the information that the servicer or purchaser provides, either because it is compulsory to be provided or voluntarily.

**10.08** *Third*, there is a duty to respect and protect the personal information and privacy of the borrowers. While this is not formulated with reference to personal data in the sense of the GDPR, and may therefore be broader, the main field of application of this duty should be expected to refer to such personal data, so that the behaviour imposed on the servicer/purchaser is mostly covered by the GDPR anyway.

*Fourth*, there is a duty not to harass, coerce or exercise undue influence on debtors while communicating with them. The rationale behind this duty is to avoid aggressive collecting practices.[1] The duty refers to the manner of communication, which is indeed important in itself, and not to the strategy of the credit servicer/purchaser (which may fall under the general duty of good faith, to the extent explained above). For example, the latter is not prevented by the present provision from rejecting a restructuring proposal made by the debtor. It is also important that this duty overlaps with the prohibition of aggressive commercial practices in Directive 2005/29/EU; indeed, harassment, coercion and undue influence are the main forms of such practices according to Articles 8–9 of the said Directive. The novelty brought by the present provision is that it applies to all borrowers, unlike Directive 2005/29/EU, which only applies to business-to-consumer ("B2C") practices according to Article 3(1) thereof, and does not therefore cover all borrowers.[2] **10.09**

## C. DUTY TO PROVIDE INFORMATION

Para. 2 contains a duty of the credit purchaser/servicer to provide the information listed in the said provision to the borrower. The information is significant, but of rather procedural character. For example, there is no duty to provide information on the strategy followed by the purchaser/servicer in general, under which the treatment of the particular credit contract falls as well. The information is provided at least once, after the credit transfer and prior to the first debt collection, and may then be provided again at the request of the borrower. The consequences of the breach of this duty to provide information are not spelled out in the present provision and need to be determined in national law,[3] provided that the EU law requirements of effectiveness and equivalence are complied with. It is possible that a collection action is void under national law, or that any damages caused to the borrower must be compensated, or **10.10**

1 On the broader issue of dealing with abusive debt collection practices in EU law see Catalin-Gabriel Stanescu, 'A Critical Assessment of the Need for Harmonization of the Legal Framework Concerning Abusive Informal Debt Collection Practices in the European Union' (2021) 44(4) *Journal of Consumer Policy* 531.

2 Catalin-Gabriel Stanescu, 'The Impact of the Debt Servicing Directive on Regulating Abusive Debt Collection in the European Union: A Step Forward or a Missed Opportunity?' (2023) 12(1) *Journal of European Consumer and Market Law* 4.

3 Ibid., 10.

on the other hand that the only consequence is that the purchaser/servicer is subject to administrative sanctions. It is reasonable to conclude that further requests to provide information, after it has been provided once, refer to any updated data that may have come up in the meantime.[4] This is particularly relevant with regard to para. 2(g) on the amounts due, which change constantly, though it might apply to other pieces of information as well, such as contact details. Abusive requests, which are repeated often with no valid reasons, serve no purpose under the Directive and should be able to be rejected by the credit purchaser/servicer.

**10.11** The information to be provided covers, succinctly put, the transfer itself, the identification and contact details of the credit purchaser/servicer; moreover, it includes a reference to the (continuing after the transfer) applicability of relevant law, as well as to the contact details of the relevant competent authority, so that it becomes easier for the borrower to file complaints. A significant part of the information to be provided refers to the amount due at the time of communication (and not at the time of transfer, so that the information is up-to-date at the time it is granted). Indeed, a breakdown of this amount in capital, interest, fees and other permitted charges must be included. This is important for the borrower to be made aware of the exact condition of the loan, as well as to be able to check the accuracy of the calculations made by the credit servicer/purchaser.

4 Ibid., 10–11.

# ARTICLE 11

# CONTRACTUAL RELATIONSHIP BETWEEN A CREDIT SERVICER AND A CREDIT PURCHASER

**Georgios Psaroudakis**

**1. When a credit purchaser does not itself perform credit servicing activities, Member States shall ensure that the appointed credit servicer provides its services in respect of the management and enforcement of a creditor's rights under a non-performing credit agreement, or of the non-performing credit agreement itself, on the basis of a credit servicing agreement with the credit purchaser.**

**2. The credit servicing agreement referred to in paragraph 1 shall provide for the following:**

**(a) a detailed description of credit servicing activities to be carried out by the credit servicer;**

**(b) the level of remuneration of the credit servicer or how the remuneration is to be calculated;**

**(c) the extent to which the credit servicer can represent the credit purchaser in relation to the borrower;**

**(d) an undertaking by the parties to comply with the Union and national law applicable to a creditor's rights under a credit agreement, or to the credit agreement itself, including in respect of consumer and data protection;**

**(e) a clause requiring the fair and diligent treatment of the borrowers.**

**3. Member States shall ensure that the credit servicing agreement referred to in paragraph 1 contains a requirement pursuant to which the credit servicer notifies the credit purchaser prior to outsourcing any of its credit servicing activities.**

**4. Member States shall ensure that the credit servicer keeps and maintains the following records for at least 5 years from the date on which the credit servicing agreement referred to in paragraph 1 is terminated, or for the duration of the statutory limitation period applicable in the home Member State, but in either case for a period of no longer than 10 years:**

**(a) relevant correspondence with both the credit purchaser and the borrower, under the conditions provided for under applicable national law;**

**(b) relevant instructions received from the credit purchaser in respect of a creditor's rights under each non-performing credit agreement, or the**

**non-performing credit agreement itself, that it manages and enforces on behalf of that credit purchaser, under the conditions provided for under applicable national law;**

**(c) the credit servicing agreement.**

**5. Member States shall ensure that the credit servicer makes the records referred to in paragraph 4 available to competent authorities upon request.**



## A. THE CREDIT SERVICING AGREEMENT

### 1. Form and content of the agreement

**11.01** In case the credit purchaser does not perform credit servicing activities itself, it must appoint a credit servicer for this purpose. Then, a credit servicing agreement must be made between these two parties. This agreement is regulated by the present provision. Unlike in Article 12 on outsourcing agreements, there is no explicit requirement in the present provision that the agreement must be in writing. However, given that a record of the agreement must be kept by the credit servicer under para. 4, it follows indirectly that the agreement must be in writing; otherwise there could be no such record. The requirement of a written agreement, derived from the text of the Directive in this indirect manner, is furthermore corroborated by recital 32 to the Directive; it obviously corresponds to practical needs too, not least the need of "competent authorities to verify how such a relationship is determined" (as explained, again, in recital 32 to the Directive).

**11.02** Regarding the content of the agreement, para. 2 stipulates that the basic obligations of the parties as well as some more particular issues must be covered. As to the former, the agreement must refer to the activities assigned to the servicer and to the remuneration payable to it (or the method for its calculation). These are matters to be determined, as regards their substance, by the parties themselves. The Directive only requires clarity, or in other words, their inclusion in the agreement, which also contributes to the stability of the contractual relationship between the parties.

Moreover, an issue that typically arises in the context of credit servicing is the extent to which the servicer represents the purchaser in relation to the borrower, and in particular the representation of the purchaser by the servicer in judicial proceedings on debt collection (as well as in negotiations); this must be clarified in the agreement. While representation in negotiations is certainly a matter governed by private autonomy, representation in judicial proceedings is possible subject to national procedural law and its rules on the modalities of such representation by a different party. In this case, the agreement is formulated within the framework defined by such rules. **11.03**

According to para. 2(d) and 2(e), the agreement must state that the parties will comply with applicable law (including on consumer protection and data protection), and that they will treat borrowers in a fair and diligent manner; the latter can also be said to be a case of the duty of compliance with applicable law, given that this treatment of borrowers is required by Article 10. Obviously, the parties must comply with these statutory rules anyway, even without such contractual clause. The independent consequence of the clause is that it becomes a breach of contract as well for one party to fail to comply with the said rules. **11.04**

In particular regarding para. 2(e), the reference of the present provision to a fair and diligent treatment of borrowers does not introduce an additional duty towards the latter, but rather incorporates the duties in Article 10(1) into the contract between purchaser and servicer as well. Article 10(1) remains the basis of these duties, given that that provision regulates the "vertical" relationship with borrowers, while the present provision refers to the "horizontal" relationship between purchaser and servicer. The agreement may concretise, or enhance, the requirements in Article 10(1), though without putting at risk compliance with the latter provision (for example, by concretising duties in a rather narrow manner). **11.05**

Lastly, para. 3 introduces a requirement for the agreement to contain a clause, according to which the servicer must notify the purchaser prior to any outsourcing. Recital 32 to the Directive is somewhat unclear in this context, as it mentions that "Member States should be able to provide" that such a notification prior to outsourcing is necessary; however, para. 3 of the present provision makes it clear that this is not a discretion for national law, but rather that national law must make it obligatory that outsourcing is made known to the purchaser in advance. This notification requirement does not extend to a **11.06** need for the purchaser to consent to such outsourcing,[1] though the parties are certainly free to include such a term in the credit servicing agreement if they so wish.

**11.07** The list of items that must be included in the agreement according to the present provision may be expanded in national law, given that this is a case of minimum harmonisation. For example, and with no prejudice to national particularities, it is probably useful to require the servicing agreement to contain a list of the credit agreements that this servicing applies to. While this might be thought to fall under para. 2(a) of the present provision, this is not at all clear; the description of the activities to be carried out, as required by para. 2(a), probably refers to the nature of the work assigned to the servicer and not to the credit agreements affected. A list of these agreements is useful in particular for the scope of the servicer's authority to represent the purchaser to be declared and made clear.

**11.08** It might be questioned why the Directive stipulates in a binding manner items of the content of an agreement between private parties, indeed sophisticated ones, as the purchaser and the servicer are. The rationale seems to be twofold: First, to contribute to clarity, and thus to a smooth functioning of the secondary market involved. Second, to further protect third parties, and in particular borrowers, given that some of these items make a contractual obligation out of rules relating to their protection.

### 2. Consequences of the incompleteness of the agreement

**11.09** One matter that the Directive leaves open is the consequences of the incompleteness of the agreement, or in other words, the failure of the parties to include in it one or more of the binding elements of its content under para. 2. It is rather unlikely that sophisticated parties, such as the purchaser and the servicer, make such an error, in particular regarding terms that are integral parts of the agreement anyway. However, it is not inconceivable, for example, that the "fair and diligent treatment" clause is not included.

**11.10** In this case, the legal effect of the failure to comply with para. 2 is not necessarily that the agreement becomes void. In other words, para. 2 does not turn the items listed therein into *essentialia negotii* of the agreement on the basis of the Directive. Rather, this remains a matter for national law, as evidenced in the lack of a provision in the Directive on this legal effect. This is

1 Catalin-Gabriel Stanescu, 'The Impact of the Debt Servicing Directive on Regulating Abusive Debt Collection in the European Union: A Step Forward or a Missed Opportunity?' (2023) 12(1) *Journal of European Consumer and Market Law* 4, 13–14.

consistent with the connection of this matter with general private law, which is not harmonised.

It may be that national law considers the agreement with such an omission to be void. This may be the case on the basis either of the legislation on credit servicing or of general rules of private law; the latter probably applies in particular with regard to para. 2(a),(b), as the servicing activities to be carried out and the remuneration owed are indeed by their nature *essentialia negotii* of the contract. On the other hand, at least in cases in which general law does not lead to such a result, it is also possible that the agreement remains valid and only administrative sanctions apply. Overall, the effectiveness of the provision and the equivalence of the legal effect of breaches with the treatment of similar breaches in case of rules of national origin must be safeguarded. **11.11**

## B. PROCEDURAL MATTERS

### 1. Records to be kept

Beyond the content of the credit servicing agreement, the present provision requires certain records to be kept. These include the agreement itself, as already mentioned, as well as correspondence of the servicer with both the purchaser and the borrower and instructions that the servicer receives from the purchaser. Such records must be made available to the competent authority upon request. They may be voluminous, which is why para. 4 contains the qualification that national law determines the conditions under which such records must be kept. While the effectiveness of the Directive's provision must certainly be safeguarded, this allows (though it does not impose on) national law to differentiate among such records to an extent and refrain from requiring servicers to keep the entirety of their correspondence available for the specified period of time. **11.12**

Regarding the instructions that the servicer receives from the purchaser and that are mentioned in para. 4, this reference should not be overestimated. It is of procedural nature, in that records of these instructions must be kept by the servicer. It does not introduce a requirement for instructions to be issued by the purchaser to the servicer, and it certainly does not impose a level of specificity or a particular content of such instructions. Such a material requirement should have been found, if at all, in para. 2, which is not the case. Indeed, whether and to what extent the purchaser issues instructions to the servicer, which then assumes a rather ancillary function, or on the other hand expects from the servicer to exercise its own judgement and initiative, is for the parties to decide. **11.13**

# ARTICLE 12

## OUTSOURCING BY A CREDIT SERVICER

**Georgios Psaroudakis**

**1. Member States shall ensure that where a credit servicer uses a credit service provider to perform any of the credit servicing activities, the credit servicer remains fully responsible for complying with all obligations under national provisions transposing this Directive. The outsourcing of those credit servicing activities shall be subject to the following conditions:**

**(a) the conclusion of a written outsourcing agreement between the credit servicer and the credit service provider under which the credit service provider is required to comply with the applicable legal provisions, including national provisions transposing this Directive, and the relevant Union or national law applicable to a creditor's rights under a credit agreement, or to the credit agreement itself;**

**(b) the outsourcing to a credit service provider of all credit servicing activities at the same time is forbidden;**

**(c) the contractual relationship between the credit servicer and the credit purchaser and the obligations of the credit servicer towards the credit purchaser or towards borrowers is not altered by the outsourcing agreement with the credit service provider;**

**(d) the compliance of a credit servicer with the requirements of its authorisation as set out in Article 5(1) is not affected by the outsourcing of some of its credit servicing activities;**

**(e) the outsourcing to the credit service provider does not prevent the supervision by competent authorities of a credit servicer in accordance with Articles 14 and 21;**

**(f) the credit servicer has direct access to all relevant information concerning the credit servicing activities outsourced to the credit service provider;**

**(g) after the outsourcing agreement is terminated, the credit servicer has the expertise and resources to be able to provide the outsourced credit servicing activities.**

**The outsourcing of credit servicing activities shall not be undertaken in such a way as to impair the quality of the credit servicer's internal control, or the soundness or continuity of its credit servicing activities.**

**2. Member States shall ensure that the credit servicer informs the competent authorities of the home Member State and, where applicable, of the host Member State, prior to outsourcing its credit servicing activities in accordance with paragraph 1.**

**3. Member States shall ensure that the credit servicer keeps and maintains records of relevant instructions provided to the credit service provider, in accordance with the conditions provided for under applicable national law, and of the outsourcing agreement referred to in paragraph 1 for a period of at least 5 years from the date on which the outsourcing agreement is terminated, or for the duration of the statutory limitation period applicable in the Member State, but in either case up to a maximum period of 10 years.**

**4. Member States shall ensure that the credit servicer and the credit service provider make the information referred to in paragraph 3 available to competent authorities upon request.**

**5. Member States shall ensure that credit service providers are not permitted to receive and hold funds from borrowers.**



## A. MATERIAL ASPECTS OF OUTSOURCING

### 1. Permissibility and limits of outsourcing

The present provision accepts, as it is indeed reasonable and well-known in the whole financial system,[1] that credit services may outsource part of their activities (i.e. the credit servicing activities as defined in Article 3(9)) to external providers. This is a business choice that, depending on circumstances, may enhance efficiency and reduce costs, in particular if the provider is achieving economies of scale or has specialised knowledge or may apply scalability of services. The last point refers to the possibility that a certain activity may need to be applied to a higher or lower extent from time to time, so that it is much more efficient for the credit servicer to outsource it than to engage in it by itself, with staff that would become redundant, or developing capacities that are then superfluous when there is less need for such activity. In particular, it has been remarked that "IT has become one of the most commonly outsourced activities".[2] **12.01**

1 Cf. in particular EBA Guidelines 2019/02 on outsourcing arrangements.
2 EBA Guidelines on outsourcing arrangements, para. 2.

12.02 On the other hand, outsourcing carries an inherent risk, given that it is not the licensed institution that is performing directly the activities outsourced, but rather a service provider as defined in Article 3(7).[3] Therefore, it is reasonable that certain safeguards are put in place to promote the integrity of the activities performed by the external provider, as well as the overall proper functioning of the credit servicer.

12.03 A significant exception from the permissibility of outsourcing is found in para. 5. The service provider may not undertake to receive and hold funds from borrowers. This is regarded as a sensitive and sophisticated part of the credit servicer's activity (given "the risks that could arise in cases of insolvency … as well as in cases of the discharge of the borrower", as explained in recital 29 to the Directive), which cannot be assigned to the service provider. Indeed, the latter's credibility and organisation has not been similarly assessed by the competent authority. Indeed, it is recalled here that it is uncertain (and depends on national law) whether the credit servicer itself may receive and hold funds, according to Article 6(1). If the permissibility of receiving and holding funds is uncertain in the case of the credit servicer, it is only reasonable that the non-licensed service provider is not able to engage in such activity.

12.04 Para. 1 of the present provision introduces a number of conditions for outsourcing, in the area to which it may apply (i.e. except for receiving and holding funds). To structure their analysis, it is possible to regard these conditions as falling under three categories (which are of course interconnected with each other): those relating to the protection of the legal and contractual status quo (para. 1(a) and 1(c)), those preserving the overall proper functioning of the credit servicer (para. 1(b), 1(f), and 1(g)), and those relating to proper prudential supervision (para. 1(d) and 1(e)).

### 2. The legal and contractual status quo

12.05 In order to preserve the legal status quo of the time at which an activity is outsourced, para. 1(a) stipulates that a written agreement must be made between the credit servicer and the service provider, under which the latter is obliged to comply with all legal provisions applicable to the credit agreement and the

3 Catalin-Gabriel Stanescu, 'The Impact of the Debt Servicing Directive on Regulating Abusive Debt Collection in the European Union: A Step Forward or a Missed Opportunity?' (2023) 12(1) Journal of *European Consumer and Market Law* 8, criticises the distinction between the servicer and the service provider, regarding it as difficult to understand. However, it is in the context of outsourcing in particular that the distinction becomes clear. The servicer is authorised and may outsource activities to the service provider, subject to the conditions of the present provision.

creditor's rights under it. Of course, such legal provisions remain applicable anyway vis-à-vis the borrower and may not be influenced by the content of the outsourcing agreement. Thus, a contractual clause to this effect in the outsourcing agreement is useful in that it creates a contractual duty of the service provider to not disrupt the legal and contractual status quo between the credit servicer and the borrower.

The consequence of a breach of para. 1(a), which may consist in not making a written agreement or not including a clause under which the service provider is required to comply with the credit agreement and with the law applicable to it, is not determined in the Directive itself and is rather a matter for national law. The latter should abide by the well-known requirements arising from EU law, i.e. the effectiveness of the sanction and its equivalence with sanctions for similar breaches of rules of national origin. In any case, national law retains some margin of discretion as to the sanction. It is possible, but not necessary, that the outsourcing contract is void in this case, but alternative sanctions are conceivable as well, such as that compliance with the credit agreement and the law applicable to it is obligatory for the service provider *ex lege*, and any clauses of the outsourcing agreement to the contrary are void, while the agreement itself remains otherwise valid. **12.06**

Lastly, para. 1(c) clarifies that the credit purchaser may not be made worse off due to outsourcing by the credit servicer. The contractual position of the purchaser vis-à-vis the credit servicer remains unaffected by this outsourcing. This is really an application of the broader principle that the contract (in this case, between the credit servicer and the service provider) may not develop any adverse effects on a third party (in this case, the credit purchaser). **12.07**

### 3. The overall proper functioning of the credit servicer

It is the credit servicer, and not the service provider, that has been licensed to perform the activity regulated by the Directive. Therefore, some conditions are introduced to ensure that outsourcing does not undermine compliance with the Directive. **12.08**

Para. 1(b) clarifies that the credit servicer may not outsource its entire operation to a service provider. Such a "global" outsourcing would, in effect, turn the credit servicer into a shell and substitute this particular service provider for the credit servicer, while the former has not been licensed. This would be the extreme case of what recital 31 to the Directive calls "undue operational risk" connected with outsourcing. **12.09**

12.10 It should be noted though that it is the outsourcing of all service activities to one service provider at the same time that is prohibited. The case of more than one outsourcing agreement to different service providers, which covers, if added up, all service activities of the credit servicer, is not prohibited by para. 1(b). This is not at all to say that this case is unproblematic. It is just not submitted to this particular prohibition, apparently because there is not a single service provider which would in effect operate as if a licence had been granted to the provider itself. Still, the supervisory authority should be able to assess this case, and potentially reject such an arrangement, in particular under para. 1(d) and (g).

12.11 Para. 1(f) should be understood in a similar vein to para. 1(b). Given that the credit servicer, and not the service provider, is the business authorised to perform the respective activity, as well as the party that has made a contract with the credit purchaser, the servicer must be able to directly access all information available to the service provider and relating to the outsourced activities. This allows the credit servicer to comply with its regulatory duties as well as with its contractual duties to the credit purchaser. Therefore, the service provider is not able to withhold information (e.g. by invoking a business secret) from the credit servicer, to the extent that such information refers to the activities falling under the latter's authorisation. Moreover, although this provision only refers to access to information and does not explicitly introduce audit rights for the credit servicer, this access to information is a sufficiently broad term to also include such audit rights. This is in particular the case, if merely receiving information from the service provider is not adequately effective.[4]

12.12 Para. 1(g) is remarkable, in that it aims to preserve the fitness of the credit servicer for the business it is involved in, as well as, more specifically in the same context, an exit strategy from outsourcing itself.[5] Thus, the credit servicer must remain able to perform the outsourced activities on its own. This is closely related to the requirement, examined above, that outsourcing is not used as a stratagem, under which one party is the holder of the authorisation and a different party (the service provider) is effectively performing the activities covered by the authorisation. It also allows the credit servicer to retain an adequately strong position in its contractual relationship with the service provider;

---

4 See also EBA Guidelines on outsourcing arrangements, para. 87, referring to "full access to all relevant business premises" and to "unrestricted rights of inspection and auditing relating to the outsourcing arrangement".

5 On the importance of an exit strategy in case of outsourcing see EBA Guidelines on outsourcing arrangements, paras. 106–108.

otherwise, the risk would arise that the servicer becomes too dependent on the provider. Lastly, under this provision, it is still possible that the servicer scales down its own business structure; otherwise, outsourcing would be pointless. However, the servicer must retain enough expertise and access to resources to be able to assume the outsourced activities again in a prompt and efficient manner.

### 4. Proper prudential supervision

Outsourcing may not harm the compliance of the servicer with the require- **12.13**
ments for authorisation under Article 5(1), with which the servicer must indeed comply continuously, or the ability of the supervisory authority to exercise its competence regarding the servicer. As to the first point, covered by para. 1(d) of the present provision, it is for example important that the government arrangements and internal control mechanisms of the servicer are not affected by outsourcing; they should rather be formulated in a manner that covers the relationship with the service provider too. As to the second point, covered by para. 1(e), supervision may not be affected operationally; therefore, it is important that the supervisor has full access to information regarding the activities outsourced and can effectively exercise inspections which may not be hindered or delayed by the service provider. To this effect, it is significant that the outsourcing agreement contains a term on the obligation of the provider to not hinder such inspections.

## B. PROCEDURAL ASPECTS OF OUTSOURCING

### 1. Notification and records

Two procedural rules regarding outsourcing are introduced in paras. 2–4 of **12.14**
the present provision. According to para. 2, the credit servicer must notify outsourcing to the competent authority in advance. It is recalled that the credit purchaser must be informed as well according to Article 11 (3). One might wonder whether this is to say that the competent authority must be informed before the agreement is made or before the agreement is implemented, in other words outsourcing starts operating in practice. The former answer should be preferred, as it contributes to the effectiveness of the provision by imposing notification before the credit servicer assumes contractual duties with regard to outsourcing.

On the basis of this notification, the competent authority has the opportunity **12.15**
to assess the compatibility of outsourcing with the conditions set out in the

present provision. If it finds it to be incompatible with these conditions, it may direct the credit servicer to terminate or modify the agreement, or take other measures to correct the problem. However, para. 2 does not require prior approval from the competent authority for outsourcing. Certainly, the competent authority includes outsourcing in its ongoing assessment of the credit servicer and may take related measures at a later stage too. National law may be stricter, or in other words, may introduce a requirement of prior approval.

**12.16** Paras. 3–4 contain a procedural duty of the credit servicer to keep records of the outsourcing agreement and of the instructions given to the service provider for the period of time prescribed in para. 3. Servicer and provider must make such information available to the competent authority upon request according to para. 4, which is really a procedural tool that supports the conditions set out in para. 1(d),(e), according to which compliance with prudential requirements, as well as the exercise of prudential supervision, may not be harmed by outsourcing.

# CHAPTER 2

# CROSS-BORDER CREDIT SERVICING ACTIVITIES

# ARTICLE 13

# FREEDOM TO PROVIDE CREDIT SERVICING ACTIVITIES IN A HOST MEMBER STATE

Andrea Miglionico

**1. Member States shall ensure that a credit servicer having obtained an authorisation in accordance with Article 4(1) in a home Member State has the right to provide in the Union those services that are covered by that authorisation, without prejudice to any restrictions or requirements established in the national law of the host Member State in accordance with this Directive, including, where applicable, a prohibition on receiving and holding funds from borrowers, that are not related to other authorisation requirements of credit servicers, or to those established for the renegotiation of the terms and conditions related to a creditor's rights under a credit agreement or of the credit agreement itself.**

**2. Member States shall ensure that where a credit servicer having obtained an authorisation in accordance with Article 4(1) in a home Member State intends to provide services in a host Member State, the credit servicer submits to the competent authority of the home Member State the following information:**

**(a) the host Member State in which the credit servicer intends to provide services and, where that information is already known to the credit servicer, the Member State where the credit was granted, when different from the host and the home Member States;**

**(b) where applicable, the address of the credit servicer's branch established in the host Member State;**

**(c) where applicable, the identity and address of the credit service provider in the host Member State;**

**(d) the identity of the persons responsible for managing the provision of credit servicing activities in the host Member State;**

**(e) where applicable, details of the measures taken to adapt the internal procedures, governance arrangements and internal control mechanisms of the credit servicer in order to ensure compliance with the laws applicable to a creditor's rights under a credit agreement or to the credit agreement itself;**

(f) a description of the procedure established in order to comply with the anti-money laundering and counter terrorist financing rules, whereby the national law of the host Member State transposing Directive (EU) 2015/849 designates credit servicers as obliged entities for the purpose of preventing and combating money laundering and terrorist financing;
(g) that the credit servicer has appropriate means to communicate in the language of the host Member State or in the language of the credit agreement;
(h) whether or not the credit servicer is authorised in its home Member State to receive and hold funds from borrowers.

3. The competent authorities of the home Member State shall, within 45 days of receipt of all information referred to in paragraph 2, communicate that information to the competent authorities of the host Member State, which shall acknowledge receipt thereof without delay. The competent authorities of the home Member State shall thereafter inform the credit servicer of the date on which the information was communicated to the competent authorities of the host Member State and the date on which those competent authorities acknowledge receipt of the information. The competent authorities of the home Member State shall also communicate all information referred to in paragraph 2 to the competent authorities of the Member State where the credit was granted, when different from the host and the home Member States.
4. Member States shall ensure that a credit servicer has the right of appeal before a tribunal where the competent authorities of the home Member State fail to communicate the information referred to in paragraph 2.
5. Member States shall ensure that the credit servicer is able to start providing services in the host Member State from the earlier of the following:
   (a) receipt of the communication from the competent authorities of the host Member State acknowledging receipt of the communication referred to in paragraph 3;
   (b) in the absence of any receipt of the communication referred to in point (a) of this paragraph, after the expiry of 2 months from the date of submission of all information referred to in paragraph 2 to the competent authorities of the host Member State.
6. Member States shall ensure that a credit servicer informs the competent authorities of the home Member State of any subsequent change to the information that is required to be communicated in accordance with paragraph 2. In such cases, Member States shall ensure compliance with the procedure set out in paragraphs 3, 4 and 5.
7. Member States shall ensure that the competent authorities of the host Member State record in the list or register referred to in Article 9 the credit servicers which are authorised to provide credit servicing activities in their territory and the details of the home Member State.

## A. INTRODUCTION

**13.01** The article regulates cross-border activities of credit servicers in the Member States. The directive introduces a comprehensive and complex system of regulatory requirements while setting up a procedure for the exercise of the right of an authorised credit servicer to operate cross-border in the EU. The passporting regime allows authorised credit servicers to provide cross-border services and access the EU loan markets. The article confers passporting rights to credit servicers authorised in one Member State in order to provide services covered in its authorisation in other Member States, if it has made the appropriate notification to its competent authority. This is a mechanism similar to the passporting frameworks set out in other EU financial services directives.[1] Credit servicers that intend to engage in cross-border activities are required to complete and submit an application for authorisation to the competent authority and will not be able to engage in such activities until the competent authority has granted authorisation to the person. The competent authority may also refuse to grant authorisation: it is an offence for such persons to commence engaging in credit servicing until authorisation as a credit servicing firm has been obtained. The directive specifies the procedures that home and host state competent authorities should follow in these circumstances. In this context, communication between national competent authorities (NCAs) of the home and the host Member States and credit servicers should take place within reasonable deadlines. The competent authorities of the Member State where the credit was granted should also receive information on cross-border activities from the competent authorities of the home Member State. A credit servicer carrying out activities in a host Member State is subject to the restrictions and requirements established in the national law of that host Member State according to the directive, including, where applicable, the prohibition on receiving and holding funds from borrowers, that are not related to other authorisation requirements of credit servicers. If, under the national provisions of a host Member State transposing the directive, additional requirements for authorisation as a credit servicer are imposed, such additional requirements should not apply to credit servicers performing cross-border credit servicing

1 Danny Busch, 'The Future of EU Financial Law' (2022) 17(1) *Capital Markets Law Journal* 84–85.

activities in that host Member State. The provision covers a set of harmonised requirements for passporting rights of cross-border credit servicers activities, establishing conditions on the disclosure of information about the servicing activities provided in the Member States. Further, it also requires a list of host Member States for which the credit servicer has notified the competent authority of the home Member State that it intends to provide credit servicing activities and for which that competent authority has sent a notification to the competent authority of the host Member State (only to be completed by the competent authority of the home Member State); as well as the date when the credit servicer is able to start providing services in the host Member State and where applicable the date on which the competent authority of the host Member State received the notification from the competent authority of the home Member State that the credit servicer no longer intends to provide services in the host Member State (only to be completed by the competent authority of the host Member State). Where the authorisation of a credit servicer has been withdrawn, the competent authority should include in the list or register, on an indefinite basis, the information that was updated and relevant at the time of the withdrawal of the authorisation.

## B. COOPERATION BETWEEN AUTHORITIES

The regulatory framework of passporting rights refers to credit service providers authorised in one Member State where the loans concerned are located in another (host) Member State, while the credit purchaser may even be in a third Member State, or indeed based in a non-EU location. Credit servicers complying with these standards in one Member State have a right to provide services elsewhere in the EU. Member States are required to introduce harmonised standards on authorisation, notification, and supervision. The authorisation process involves comprehensive assessments of financial stability, business conduct, and consumer protection law adherence.[2] To ensure effective and efficient supervision of cross-border credit servicers, a regulatory framework is placed for cooperation between the competent authorities of the home and of the host Member States and, where appropriate, the competent authorities of the Member State where the credit was granted. The framework allows the exchange of information, while preserving its confidentiality, professional secrecy, protection of individual and business rights, inspections, the provision 13.02

2 Jean-Baptiste Poulle, Arut Kannan, Nicolas Spitz, Sandra Kahn and Anastasia Sotiropoulou (eds), *EU Banking and Financial Regulation* (Edward Elgar 2024) ch.14.

of assistance, and the notification of results of checks and inspections and of any measures taken. Authorised or passported credit service providers can access the credit servicing passport to enter other EU markets. However, the credit servicing market remains fragmented as it often requires local expertise, e.g., language skills, and larger independent credit servicers may take advantage of the passport regime to consolidate their corporate structures and operations in lenient Member States.[3]

## C. LISTS OF REGISTERS

**13.03** Competent authorities should make their list or register accessible 24 hours a day and 7 days a week. The list or register should be accessible on the competent authorities' websites or on other electronic tools accessible to the public unless under maintenance. Competent authorities should ensure that public access to the list or register does not require prior registration or any other precondition for access and should provide access to the list or register free of charge. Competent authorities should make the list or register available for download and should include the date of the last update of the list or register.

**13.04** Competent authorities should process information relevant to the list or register and update the list or register at least once per week. In the specific case where the competent authority in the home Member State has taken the decision to withdraw the authorisation of a credit servicer to provide credit service activities or to receive and hold funds from borrowers, the competent authority from the home Member State should update the information. Once the competent authority in the host Member State has received the information from the competent authority in the home Member State, it should update its list or register no later than by the end of the following two working days. The competent authority in the home Member State should inform the competent authority in the host Member State of any changes that are of relevance to their list or register, no later than when the competent authority in the home Member State updates its list or register. The competent authority in the home Member State should send the information to the competent authority in the host Member State.

3 See 'Irish Credit Servicing – Transposition of the EU Credit Servicing Directive' https://maples.com/knowledge/irish-credit-servicing---transposition-of-the-eu-credit-servicing-directive.

## D. ACCESSIBILITY REQUIREMENTS

The article states that a credit servicer authorised by a competent authority in an EU Member State may provide its credit servicing activities that are covered by the authorisation in another EU Member State on a passporting basis. This is subject to the credit servicer complying with the relevant national laws giving effect to the directive in the host Member State to which the credit servicer intends to passport its credit servicing activities. The article sets out the information the notifying credit servicer must provide to the competent authority when advising of its intention to passport its credit servicing activities to a host Member State. A credit servicer authorised in one EU Member State is permitted to exercise passport rights and provide those services on a cross-border basis into another EU Member State. Credit servicers seeking authorisation are required to demonstrate to the competent authority that they are in a position to meet each of the authorisation requirements and standards prior to an authorisation being granted. The requirements and standards are imposed on all credit servicing firms as a condition of authorisation and must be complied with on an on-going basis. **13.05**

Member States, through their competent authority, must ensure that authorised credit servicers may carry out servicing activities in any other host Member State by ensuring scope for adherence to relevant national law provisions on authorisation. Authorised credit servicers that intend to carry out activities in a host Member State must submit detailed branch and address information to their home Member State, as well as compliance with anti-money-laundering provisions. The home Member State must furnish this information to the host Member State within 45 days of receiving it, and the host Member State must provide an acknowledgement of receipt without delay. The credit servicer may begin providing activities in the host Member State upon confirmation of receipt from the host Member State or, if no receipt arises, within 2 months of submitting the information above. The credit servicer must also notify home Member States of any changes to the above information.[4] **13.06**

4 Padraic Kenna, 'Public Consultation on Credit Servicers Directive' (7 March 2023), University of Galway, p. 17, https://www.universityofgalway.ie/media/housinglawrightsandpolicy/Submission-Credit-Servicers-Directive-Public-Consultation-PK-UoG[21].pdf.

# ARTICLE 14

# SUPERVISION OF CREDIT SERVICERS THAT PROVIDE CROSS-BORDER SERVICES

**Andrea Miglionico**

1. **Member States shall ensure that the competent authorities of the home Member State review and evaluate the ongoing compliance, by a credit servicer which performs credit servicing activities in a host Member State, with the requirements of this Directive.**
2. **Member States shall ensure that the competent authorities of the home Member State are empowered to supervise, investigate and impose administrative penalties and remedial measures on credit servicers in respect of the requirements of this Directive when performing their credit servicing activities in a host Member State.**
3. **Member States shall ensure that the competent authorities of the home Member State communicate the measures taken in respect of the credit servicer to the competent authorities of the host Member State and, where appropriate, of the Member State where the credit was granted, when different from the host and the home Member States.**
4. **Member States shall ensure that where a credit servicer performs credit servicing activities in a host Member State, the competent authorities of the home Member State and the competent authorities of the host Member State and, where appropriate, of the Member State where the credit was granted, when different from the host and the home Member States, shall cooperate closely in the performance of their functions and duties, in particular when carrying out checks, investigations and on-site inspections.**
5. **Member States shall ensure that the competent authorities of the home Member State, in the exercise of their functions and duties provided for in this Directive, ask the competent authorities of the host Member State for their assistance in carrying out an on-site inspection of a branch set up, or of a credit service provider appointed, in a host Member State. The on-site inspection of a branch or of a credit service provider shall be conducted in accordance with the law of the Member State where the inspection is carried out.**
6. **Member States shall further ensure that the competent authorities of the host Member State are entitled to decide on the most appropriate measures**

**to be taken in each individual case in order to meet the request of assistance by the competent authorities of the home Member State.**

7. **Where the competent authorities of the host Member State decide to conduct on-site inspections on behalf of the competent authorities of the home Member State, they shall inform the competent authorities of the home Member State of the results thereof without delay.**
8. **On their own initiative, the competent authorities of the host Member State may conduct checks, inspections and investigations in respect of credit servicing activities provided within their territory by a credit servicer authorised in a home Member State. The competent authorities of the host Member State shall provide the results of those checks, inspections and investigations to the competent authorities of the home Member State without delay.**
9. **Member States shall ensure that where the competent authorities of the host Member State have evidence that a credit servicer performing credit servicing activities within its territory, as provided for in Article 13, infringes the applicable rules, including obligations arising from the national provisions transposing this Directive, they transmit that evidence to the competent authorities of the home Member State and request that they take appropriate measures, without prejudice to the supervisory, investigatory and sanctioning powers of the competent authorities of the host Member State regarding the credit servicer under national law, namely those applicable to the credit or the credit agreement.**
10. **Member States shall ensure that where the competent authorities of the Member State where the credit was granted, when different from the host and the home Member States, have evidence that a credit servicer infringes the obligations provided for in this Directive, or in the national rules applicable to the credit or the credit agreement, they transmit that evidence to the competent authorities of the home Member State and request that they take appropriate measures, without prejudice to the supervisory, investigatory and sanctioning powers of the competent authorities of the Member State where the credit was granted, when different from the host and the home Member States.**
11. **Member States shall ensure that the competent authorities of the home Member State communicate details of any administrative or other procedure initiated in respect of the evidence provided by the host Member State, or of any administrative penalties and remedial measures taken against the credit servicer, or of a reasoned decision why no measures were taken, to the competent authorities of the host Member State that referred the evidence no later than 2 months from the date of the request referred to in paragraph 9. Where a procedure has been initiated, the competent authorities of the home Member State shall regularly inform the competent authorities of the host Member State about its status.**
12. **Where a credit servicer continues to infringe the applicable rules, including its obligations under this Directive, and after the competent authorities of the host Member State have informed the home Member State thereof, Member States shall ensure that the competent authorities of the host**

**Member State are entitled to impose appropriate administrative penalties and remedial measures in order to ensure compliance with this Directive when either of the following apply:**

**(a) no adequate and effective steps were taken by the credit servicer to rectify the infringement in a reasonable time; or**

**(b) in an urgent case, where immediate action is necessary in order to address a serious threat to the collective interests of the borrowers.**

**The competent authorities of the host Member State may impose the administrative penalties and remedial measures referred to in the first subparagraph notwithstanding any administrative penalties and remedial measures already imposed by the competent authorities of the home Member State.**

**In addition, the competent authorities of the host Member State may prohibit further activities of a credit servicer that infringes the applicable rules, including its obligations under this Directive, until such time as an adequate decision is taken by the competent authority of the home Member State or the credit servicer takes steps to remedy the infringement.**



## A. INTRODUCTION

14.01 The article regulates the procedures that home and host state competent authorities should follow in the passporting regime for credit servicers. It specifies the procedures to follow for home and host state competent authorities in the supervision of credit servicers providing cross-border services. The directive provides that national competent authorities (NCAs) arrange inspections and impose injunctions or administrative sanctions with respect to credit servicers and credit purchasers. In each European Economic Area (EEA) country, a national authority is responsible for the protection of the rights of consumers when they interact with credit servicers. The provision empowers the NCAs of the home Member State to review and evaluate the ongoing compliance by a credit servicer that performs credit servicing activities in a host Member State. The NCAs of the home Member State carry out the supervision and enforcement procedures on credit servicers: administrative penalties and remedial measures can be issued in case of a lack of compliance with the reporting duties of service providers. This stringent regime of monitoring between Member States and NCAs responds to the need for transparency in the credit servicers' cross-border activities, which are subject to periodic reports. The NCAs have powers to supervise not only the credit servicers, but also the third-party service providers to which the credit services have outsourced their services, as well as credit purchasers (even if they are unregulated, and even if they are based outside the EU). However, it has been noted that the directive does not set minimum financial sanctions contrary to other European directives.[1]

The passporting system for credit servicers represents a step toward harmonisation, allowing firms authorised in one Member State to operate in others. Despite the promising scope, its objective is limited to NPLs issued by EU credit institutions, meaning national restrictions still apply in many cases. This has left several inefficiencies unresolved, slowing the pace of standardisation across the EU's fragmented secondary NPL market.[2] The complex system of national regulations governing fees, debt collection, and forbearance further complicates cross-border NPL transactions. These costs and procedures remain highly variable across EU Member States, shaped by national laws, consumer protection frameworks, and judicial processes. While the directive has introduced harmonisation efforts, it applies only to bank-originated credit, excluding non-bank debts such as utility bills, telecom arrears, and e-commerce financing. This concern creates an uneven regulatory landscape, where different categories of debt – and debtors – are subject to divergent legal and financial consequences depending on jurisdiction.[3] For servicers operating across multiple Member States, these inconsistencies increase the complexity of structuring deals, assessing enforcement costs, and managing borrower interactions. However, the shift toward secondary NPL sales has helped lower costs in some segments, as investors can acquire restructured portfolios with reduced legal complexities. In the long term, regulatory misalignment may distort pricing in secondary NPL markets, limiting investor appetite, and creating inefficiencies in debt resolution. **14.02**

1 See 'Initial Feedback Following the Transposition of the Non-performing Loans Directive' (11 March 2024), https://www.gide.com/en/news-insights/initial-feedback-following-the-transposition-of-the-non-performing-loans-directive-1/.

2 Johannes Kasinger et al., 'Non-performing Loans – New Risks and Policies? NPL Resolution after COVID-19: Main Differences to Previous Crises' (2021) SAFE White Paper No. 84, Leibniz Institute for Financial Research SAFE, https://www.econstor.eu/bitstream/10419/232027/1/1751693937.pdf.

3 Timur Peters, 'Review of the Market Report from the NPL Advisory Panel at the European Commission' (19 February 2025), https://www.debitos.com/news/europes-npl-sector-braces-for-new-distress-as-secondary-market-expands/.

## B. CREDIT INFORMATION DISCLOSURE

**14.03** Credit servicers which obtained authorisation to provide their activities in one Member State may offer their services in another Member State. Accordingly, the credit servicer informs the competent authorities of the home Member State, which, in turn, communicates to the competent authorities of the host Member State. The supervision of the credit servicer is carried out by the competent authority of the home Member State (with the assistance of the host Member State and, where appropriate, of the Member State where the credit was granted). The directive establishes a number of reporting obligations for credit institutions selling NPLs vis-à-vis purchasers and the competent authority.[4] Credit institutions and purchasers selling purchased NPLs shall report the sales they make to the competent authority on a biannual basis, identifying the purchaser, the aggregate outstanding balance, the number of NPLs transferred, details of the NPLs transferred that correspond to consumer agreements and the guarantees, if any, securing these NPLs. It has been noted that 'credit information sharing, which attenuates the opportunistic tendencies of borrowers, represents one of the potent responses to NPLs in credit markets. It refers to lenders sharing proprietary information about their loan clients either through private credit bureaus or public credit registries'.[5] Transparency around NPLs is therefore key in enabling banks, regulators and interested external parties to understand where risk might be building up on balance sheets, and when either higher provisioning or capitalisation is required. This in turn might lower the probability of bank crises, or at least dampen their impact. Where crises do occur, a method to ensure swift identification of problem loans enables swifter policy responses. Banks may, particularly in times of crisis, be incentivised not to draw attention to NPLs in order to avoid scrutiny as to the level of loan loss provisions raised against them. Given the potential systemic consequences that can result from NPLs, higher levels of loan loss provisioning and their early recognition would seem desirable.[6] However, both early identification of NPLs and proper consideration

---

4 EBA, 'Peer Review Follow-Up Report on Supervision of Non-performing Exposure Management by Credit Institutions' (7 November 2024), EBA/REP/2024/23, https://eba.europa.eu/publications-and-media/press-releases/eba-observes-improvement-competent-authorities-practices-supervision-non-performing-loans.

5 Michael Adusei and Ngozi Adeleye, 'Credit Information Sharing and Non-performing Loans: The Moderating Role of Creditor Rights Protection' (2022) 27(4) *International Journal of Finance & Economics* 4756.

6 Carla Stamegna, 'Minimum Loss Coverage for Non-performing Loans' (May 2019), European Parliamentary Research Service, https://www.europarl.europa.eu/RegData/etudes/BRIE/2019/635553/EPRS_BRI(2019)635553_EN.pdf.

of them for provisioning purposes require factoring in the complex strategic choices banks face when making provisioning decisions. However, the timely recognition of problem loans and credit loss by banks, and proper transparency such that asset positions are well understood by the market, regulators, and the general public, is critical to averting and mitigating crises.

Banks can be incentivised by accounting, regulatory and tax considerations in various ways when considering how to identify, and provide against, problem loans. This in turn can result in under-provisioning, particularly when the economic environment is relatively benign. But the early recognition of expected losses in good times is generally agreed by policymakers to contribute to greater bank resilience and mitigate the impact of crises on banks' balance sheets. This in turn lowers the probability of downturns resulting in debt crises that last several years or even decades.[7] Even before provisioning, problem loans need to be identified according to criteria that are transparent, understandable and economically meaningful. There is currently no universal consensus as to what these criteria should be. The introduction of expected loss provisioning methodologies that require loans to be classified into different categories amplifies the need for more understandable methods of asset quality classification.[8] Understanding the nature and quality of bank assets remains vital to assessing the health of the banking system as a whole, and so the transparency of NPLs is critical for financial stability. **14.04**

## C. THE ENFORCEMENT MECHANISMS

The article regulates procedural matters of enforcement measures to credit servicers that do not comply with the requirements set in the directive. The cooperation between the competent authorities of the home Member State and the competent authorities of the host Member State about remedial actions and administrative penalties is substantiated by the sharing of information on the most appropriate measures to be taken in each individual case. This is an articulated and complex system of controls and monitoring against credit servicers that infringe the applicable rules: cross-border credit servicing activities are subject to scrutiny and thorough investigations by the NCAs. In case the credit servicer does not take steps to remedy the infringement, the competent **14.05**

7 David Bholat et al., 'Non-performing Loans at the Dawn of IFRS 9: Regulatory and Accounting Treatment of Asset Quality' (2018) 19 *Journal of Banking Regulation* 46.

8 Benjamin H. Cohen and Gerald Edwards, 'The New Era of Expected Credit Loss Provisioning' (March 2017), *BIS Quarterly Review*, https://www.bis.org/publ/qtrpdf/r_qt1703f.pdf.

authorities of the host Member State may impose additional administrative penalties and remedial measures although it is not clear if the directive prohibits certain activities until the violation has been solved. The enforcement regime on cross-border activities of credit servicers seems more intrusive with respect to the authorisation regime: NCAs have the sanctioning power to investigate and carry out inspections in order to address a serious threat to the collective interests of the borrowers. Concerns have been voiced that retail debtors are often confronted with a different creditor than the bank with which they have initially established a relationship.[9] The consumer protection as well as the interest to protect loan markets align with the supervision over credit servicers that are assessed as part of the supervisory activities that Member States and competent authorities conduct to check compliance with the accessibility requirements.

**14.06** The supervision of credit servicers responds to the aim of the directive to develop secondary markets for NPLs by tackling undue obstacles to credit servicing and to the transfer of bank loans to credit purchasing. Legal safeguards and transparency rules are set out to ensure that the transfer of a loan does not affect the rights and interests of consumers. Common standards are established for authorisation and supervision to regulate conduct rules across the EU. Purchasers of bank loans are required to notify authorities when acquiring a loan, and third-country purchasers of consumer loans are required to utilise authorised EU credit servicers. The ability, by competent authorities, to impose administrative sanctions and other corrective measures to hold credit servicers liable for breaches of their obligations is one of the cornerstones of an effective supervisory regime. To be effective, administrative sanctions or measures should be proportionate to the breach and the nature and size of the firm, and dissuasive to change the firm's behaviour and that of its peers. Credit servicers' compliance with accessibility requirements is fundamental to ensuring their safety and soundness and the stability of the NPLs markets. It is crucial that the competent authorities have the powers to take timely and appropriate action as soon as they have reason to suspect that a supervised entity is not complying with these requirements. Further, it is essential to ensure compliance not only with substantive authorisation requirements but also with the related reporting obligations. These enable the competent authorities to make an overall assessment of the risks to which the supervised entities are exposed

9 Rebecca Segall, Cristina Dias, Kristina Grigaitė and Marcel Magnus, 'The EU's Regulatory and Supervisory Response to Addressing Non-performing Loans' (February 2021) European Parliament, Economic Governance Support Unit (EGOV), https://www.europarl.europa.eu/RegData/etudes/IDAN/2021/659634/IPOL_IDA(2021)659634_EN.pdf.

and exercise their powers accordingly. By taking specific measures when such infringements are detected, the NCAs aim to ensure that all supervised entities fully comply with their obligations. However, competent authorities may on occasion face serious difficulties in identifying breaches, especially when deliberate actions are taken to conceal them. These led to follow-up actions such as requesting documents and explanations from the entity concerned, organising on-site inspections, or initiating sanctioning proceedings.

When forecasting future losses and loan performance, judgement inevitably **14.07** plays a role. The implication of this observation is that, in addition to initiatives to harmonise NPL definition and asset classification for purposes of loan loss provisioning, considerable vigilance is required of the competent authorities and Member States to enhance the quality of the data for the purpose of assessing asset quality to aid that judgement. Although credit servicers are required to disclose how they determine whether a significant increase in credit risk has occurred, the criteria used in internal classifications more generally are often opaque so users of financial statements may not be able to understand the full context in which a loan is reclassified, or to what extent loans have not been determined to have undergone a significant increase in credit risk even where some deterioration has occurred. A more comprehensive classification of asset quality, showing how credit quality changes from one period to the next, arguably provides further colour in understanding how the bank goes about applying the three-stage classification in practice. The global financial crisis of 2008–9 is a stark reminder of the dangers posed to economic and financial stability by over-indebtedness, under-provisioning, and NPLs. The focus of authorities should be on getting banks, prudential regulators, investors, and other stakeholders the right data to monitor asset quality in a more timely and transparent way. Bad lending is the root of many banking crises, which in turn are often the source of economic downturns and depressions. In these situations, uncertainty with respect to the quality, and therefore ultimately the value, of banks' assets can prove to be a major stumbling block to bank recapitalisation and economic recovery. Co-ordination to better collect and disclose asset quality data increasingly available in the era of 'big data' together with cooperative oversight is paramount in the regulatory standards adopted to supervise and enforce cross-border credit servicers in the EU.[10] This responds to the need for NCAs to enhance their approach in the authorisation, ongoing supervision and enforcement work, relating to firms'

10 George Kladakis, Lei Chen and Sotirios K Bellos, 'Bank Asset and Informational Quality' (2020) 69 *Journal of International Financial Markets, Institutions and Money* 101256.

cross-border activities. NCAs have established adequate processes in relation to the passport notifications and in the context of cooperation. This includes calibrating their supervisory work to the nature, scale, and complexity of those firms' cross-border activities and the risks they pose.

# TITLE III

# CREDIT PURCHASERS

# ARTICLE 15

# RIGHT TO INFORMATION REGARDING A CREDITOR'S RIGHTS UNDER A NON-PERFORMING CREDIT AGREEMENT OR THE NON-PERFORMING CREDIT AGREEMENT ITSELF

**Kyriaki Vasileiou**[1]

1. **Member States shall ensure that a credit institution provides a prospective credit purchaser with necessary information regarding a creditor's rights under a non-performing credit agreement, or the non-performing credit agreement itself, and, if applicable, the collateral, so as to enable the prospective credit purchaser to conduct its own assessment of the value of the creditor's rights under the non-performing credit agreement, or of the non-performing credit agreement itself, and the likelihood of recovery of the value of that agreement prior to entering into a contract for the transfer of that creditor's rights under the non-performing credit agreement, or of the non-performing credit agreement itself, while ensuring the protection of information made available by the credit institution and of the confidentiality of business data.**
2. **On a biannual basis, Member States shall require credit institutions that transfer to a credit purchaser a creditor's rights under a non-performing credit agreement, or the non-performing credit agreement itself, to inform the competent authorities of the host Member State designated in accordance with Article 21(3) of this Directive, and the competent authorities referred to in Article 4(5) of Directive 2013/36/EU of the European Parliament and of the Council, of at least the following:**
   (a) **the legal entity identifier (LEI) of the credit purchaser or, where applicable, of its representative designated in accordance with Article 19, or where such identifier does not exist, of:**
      (i) **the identity of the credit purchaser or of the members of the credit purchaser's management or administrative organ and the persons**

---

1 The author is grateful to Professor Vincenzo Bavoso for his comments on an earlier draft. Any errors are, of course, entirely my own.

**who hold qualifying holdings in the credit purchaser within the meaning of Article 4(1), point (36), of Regulation (EU) No 575/2013; and**

**(ii) the address of the credit purchaser or, where applicable, its representative designated in accordance with Article 19;**

**(b) the aggregate outstanding balance of the creditor's rights under the non-performing credit agreements or of the non-performing credit agreements transferred;**

**(c) the number and size of the creditor's rights under the non-performing credit agreements or of the non-performing credit agreements transferred;**

**(d) whether the transfer includes the creditor's rights under the non-performing credit agreements, or the non-performing credit agreements themselves, concluded with consumers and the types of assets securing the non-performing credit agreements, when applicable.**

**3. The competent authorities referred to in paragraph 2 may require credit institutions to provide the information referred to in that paragraph on a quarterly basis whenever they deem necessary, including in order to better monitor a high number of transfers that might occur during a crisis period.**

**4. Member States shall ensure that the competent authorities of the host Member State communicate without delay the information referred to in paragraphs 2 and 3, and any other information that they might consider to be necessary for carrying out their functions and duties in accordance with this Directive, to the competent authorities of the home Member State of the credit purchaser.**

**5. Paragraphs 1 to 4 shall be applied in accordance with Regulations (EU) 2016/679 and (EU) 2018/1725.**



## A. INTRODUCTION

This EU Directive is aimed at facilitating the creation of a secondary market for non-performing loans (NPL) across the Union, and in particular, it seeks to provide a harmonised framework for the sale of distressed assets from credit institutions to credit purchasers, and to assign their management to credit servicers, without compromising in the process the rights of borrowers. This in itself is ambitious from a supervisory angle of analysis, given the diverging legal regimes that exist in terms of the borrowers' rights at the Member State 15.01

level.[2] Creating a secondary market for NPL entails eliminating barriers created by individual national regimes, and the compliance costs may create on credit purchasers and servicers that are likely to be incorporated in a jurisdiction different from that of the credit institutions or the borrowers'.[3]

**15.02** The regulatory strategy at the heart of this Directive follows the well-known principle of 'Passporting'. This is premised on a single authorisation granted by the home Member State to a financial institution. This authorisation is then valid across the EU, and the authorised financial institution can provide services and operate throughout the Single Market, eventually through the establishment of a branch in a host Member State.[4]

**15.03** While the above is not new, it fits within the idea of fostering a system of cross-border risk-sharing capable of absorbing the risks of distressed assets, before the volume of NPLs reaches excessive build-ups with ensuing risks of spillover and financial stability concerns.[5] This is the macroprudential rationale behind this Directive, namely, private risk-sharing that is designed to prevent instances of public risk-sharing, where the risks of NPLs would translate into social costs.[6] It is important to stress that the success of this policy design hinges on the development of a more competitive EU-wide banking sector, which in turn rests on the hard tasks of completing the banking union and implementing the capital markets union.[7]

**15.04** Title III of the Directive sets out a common framework for the transfer of NPLs from credit institutions to credit purchasers. In essence, these provisions lay down the operational rules for the transfer of NPLs. It covers the ex ante and ex post obligations of the parties to the credit agreement, including the rights of credit purchasers in the enforcement, or transfer, of the non-performing credit agreement itself. At the core of these provisions, there lies

2 See for an overview Andrea Miglionico, 'Restructuring Non-Performing Loans for Bank Recovery: Private Workouts and Securitisation Mechanisms' (2019) 16(6) *European Company and Financial Law Review* 746–770.

3 See Directive (EU) 2021/2167, Preamble, paras 8–11.

4 See European Banking Authority, 'Passporting and Supervision of Branches', available at https://www.eba.europa.eu/regulation-and-policy/passporting-and-supervision-branches.

5 See Javier Suarez and Antonio Sánchez Serrano, 'Approaching Non-Performing Loans from a Macroprudential Angle', Reports of the Advisory Scientific Committee, European Systemic Risk Board, N.7, September 2018, pp. 13–16.

6 Ibid., p. 11.

7 See Johannes Kasinger, Jan Pieter Krahnen, Steven Ongena, Loriana Pelizzon, Maik Schmeling and Mark Wahrenburg, 'Non-performing Loans, New Risks and Policies? – NPL Resolution after COVID-19 – Main Differences to Previous Crises' European Parliament (March 2021) https://data.europa.eu/doi/10.2861/454107 > (accessed 2 May 2025).

an assumption that credit purchasers, and their servicers, are to act in good faith by respecting the rights of borrowers.[8] These provisions, taken together, seek to promote transparency, ensure the protection of debtors' rights, and enable the effective oversight by competent authorities across the EU.[9]

## B. PRE-SALE DISCLOSURES

Article 15 of the Directive imposes extensive disclosure obligations and other reporting requirements for credit institutions selling NPLs. Article 15(1) starts by setting out the duty upon Member States to ensure that credit institutions provide prospective credit purchasers with all relevant information regarding the NPL. Credit institutions should disclose that information any time prior to the completion of a contract of transfer, though the exact timing remains unclear. Emphasis should be put on the type of information that is to be shared. This is limited to what is deemed 'necessary' to enable prospective credit purchasers to make an informed decision. The content and method by which information is to be communicated to prospective credit purchasers is qualified in Article 16 of this Directive. This entails the use of a standardised set of data templates provided for by the EBA. Member States should ensure that the provision of such information, and its subsequent use, complies with the applicable Union data protection framework provided in Article 15(5) of this Directive.[10] **15.05**

The rationale behind this disclosure obligation is, simply stated, to equip potential credit purchasers with such information so as to enable a better assessment of both the value of the creditor's rights under the non-performing credit agreement, and where possible, taking into account information regarding the collateral, the extent of recovery. Under current banking practices, NPLs have been traded on a *caveat emptor* basis – the purchaser being responsible for ensuring they are not disadvantaged in financial transactions. **15.06**

From the perspective of the credit purchaser, Article 15(1) of the Directive is welcomed as it partially reverses this position and assists credit purchasers **15.07**

8 See Directive (EU) 2021/2167, Preamble, para 20, and Article 10.

9 Note, European Commission DG Competition *Case M.8888 – Apollo Management/Cyprus Cooperative Bank/Altamira Cyprus*. The case involves public interest concerns in respect of large-scale transfers of NPLs from banks to asset management firms/funds. Although decided on competition grounds, it helps unpack some of the wider issues or challenges in debt management that the Directive seeks to address. To put it pithily, it highlights the need for regulation in the area.

10 That said, insufficient guidance is provided on how the duty to disclose said information is to be balanced against the protection of personal data.

in their due diligence.[11] This is also likely to help bridge the gap between the credit institutions' expectations and prospective purchasers' pricing of the NPL during the auction/bidding stage. From the perspective of the credit institution, the disclosure obligation is likely to come into conflict with their pre-existing duties in regard to confidentiality or secrecy rules which prevent banking institutions from disclosing certain information to third parties, especially those regarding data protection laws or those pertaining to insolvency.[12] To that end, the obligation may appear to be onerous on their part.

## C. POST-SALE REPORTING

**15.08** Article 15(2) of this Directive requires credit institutions to report details of said transfer to the competent authorities of its own home Member State, and to the competent authorities of the host Member State of the credit purchaser.[13] In terms of frequency of reporting, this should be done on a biannual basis, but the relevant competent authorities have the power, under Article 15(3), to require that credit institutions provide these on a quarterly basis instead.

**15.09** The information to be reported is as follows. First, the legal entity identifier (LEI) of the credit purchaser, or if a third-country credit purchaser, the representative in accordance with Article 19 of this Directive. In case the LEI does not exist, then, under Article 15(2)(a), the credit institution shall provide the identity of the credit purchaser, or if a body, the members of its managing/administrative body and the individuals who hold qualifying holdings, and their addresses. Second, under Article 15(2)(b), the credit institution should report upon the aggregate outstanding balance of the creditor's rights under the non-performing agreement. Third, under Article 15(2)(c), the credit

11 For the sake of clarity, it needs to be noted that the information, or lack thereof, does not of itself constitute a barrier to a sale of an NPL where credit purchasers are willing to price the resulting uncertainty into their offer.

12 Confidentiality is underpinned by Regulation (EU) 2016/679 of the European Parliament and of the Council of 27 April 2016 on the protection of natural persons with regard to the processing of personal data and on the free movement of such data, and repealing Directive 95/46/EC (General Data Protection Regulation); and Directive (EU) 2016/680 of the European Parliament and of the Council of 27 April 2016 on the protection of natural persons with regard to the processing of personal data by competent authorities for the purposes of the prevention, investigation, detection or prosecution of criminal offences or the execution of criminal penalties, and on the free movement of such data, and repealing Council Framework Decision 2008/977/JHA. For an interesting discussion, see *Promontoria (Oak) Ltd v Emanuel* [2021] EWCA Civ 1682.

13 See Directive (EU) 2021/2167, Article 4(5): 'Member States shall require that institutions provide the competent authorities of their home Member States with all the information necessary for the assessment of their compliance with the rules adopted in accordance with this Directive and Regulation'.

institution should report on the number and size of the creditor's rights. This is believed to be useful in assessing the book debt value of the NPL. Finally, under Article 15(2)(d), credit institutions shall report on whether the transfer includes credit agreements concluded with consumers, and if this is the case, then the type of collateral that is used to secure the credit agreement.

To allow for the effective monitoring of the transfer of the non-performing credit agreement, Article 15(4) requires the competent authorities of the host Member State to communicate the details under Article 15(2) to the competent authorities of the home Member State of the credit purchaser. This position is reinforced in Article 26(1) of the Directive, which imposes a duty upon Member States to ensure that the competent authorities cooperate with each other whenever necessary for the purpose of carrying out their functions and duties or of exercising their powers under the national provisions transposing this Directive. **15.10**

It is important to note that notification requirements to competent authorities in respect of a credit portfolio, once such portfolio has been transferred to a credit purchaser, remain the responsibility of the credit servicer. **15.11**

# ARTICLE 16

# IMPLEMENTING TECHNICAL STANDARDS FOR DATA TEMPLATES

**Kyriaki Vasileiou**

**1. The EBA shall develop draft implementing technical standards to specify the templates to be used by credit institutions for the provision of information referred to in Article 15(1), in order to provide detailed information on their credit exposures in the banking book to credit purchasers for the analysis, financial due diligence and valuation of a creditor's rights under a non-performing credit agreement, or of the non-performing credit agreement itself.**

**2. The EBA shall specify in the draft implementing technical standards referred to in paragraph 1 of this Article the data fields, including which data fields are mandatory, and the data treatment for confidential information as set out in Article 15(1).**

**3. The draft implementing technical standards shall be proportionate to the nature and size of credits and credit portfolios.**

**4. When preparing the draft implementing technical standards referred to in paragraph 1, the EBA shall take into consideration all of the following:**
- **(a) existing market practices in data sharing between buyers and sellers;**
- **(b) the feedback received from users of their experience of using existing EBA non-performing loans transaction templates;**
- **(c) existing similar requirements at Member State level;**
- **(d) the importance of minimising processing costs for credit institutions and credit purchasers.**

**5. The EBA shall submit the draft implementing technical standards referred to in paragraph 1 to the Commission by 29 September 2022.**

**6. Power is conferred on the Commission to adopt the implementing technical standards referred to in paragraph 1, in accordance with Article 15 of Regulation (EU) No 1093/2010. 8.12.2021 EN Official Journal of the European Union L 438/25.**

**7. The data templates shall be used for transactions relating to credits issued on or after 1 July 2018 that become non-performing after 28 December 2021. For credits that originate between 1 July 2018 and the date of entry into force of the implementing technical standards referred to in paragraph 1, credit institutions shall complete the data template with the information already available to them.**

**8. Member States shall ensure that credit institutions also apply the implementing technical standards referred to in paragraph 6 to the transfer of a creditor's rights under a non-performing credit agreement, or of the non-performing credit agreement itself, to other credit institutions. The data templates shall be used by credit institutions for the provision of information between credit institutions in cases where there is only a transfer of a creditor's rights under a non-performing credit agreement, or of the non-performing credit agreement itself.**



## A. INTRODUCTION

The need to strengthen the data infrastructure with "uniform and standardised" data for NPL has been recognised by the EU Council in its 2017 Action Plan.[1] Notably, the Council underlines the opportunity to set out guidelines that stipulate the minimal detailed information required from credit institutions for the provision of information on their credit exposures in the banking book.[2] **16.01**

In this context, the EBA produced the draft 'Implementing Technical Standards' (ITS) which provides the prescribed data templates to be used for the application of Article 16(1) of this Directive.[3] The ITS specifies granular loan-by-loan information that is to be provided by credit institutions when selling or transferring non-performing credit agreements, with the aim of enabling prospective credit purchasers to conduct their analysis, financial due diligence, and valuation of NPL in the context of a transaction. **16.02**

The main objective of the ITS is to facilitate cross-country comparisons of NPLs by standardising the content and format of disclosures, and to reduce **16.03**

1 Council of the EU, 'Council Conclusions on Action Plan to Tackle Non-performing Loans in Europe', 459/17 (11 July 2017), 2, https://www.consilium.europa.eu/en/press/press-releases/2017/07/11/conclusions-non-performing-loans/pdf (accessed 4 June 2025).

2 ECOFIN Council, 'Report of the FSC Subgroup on Non-Performing Loans', 9854/17 (31 May 2017), 74, https://data.consilium.europa.eu/doc/document/ST-9854-2017-INIT/en/pdf (accessed 4 June 2025).

3 EBA, Final Report on Draft Implementing Technical Standards (16 December 2022) https://www.eba.europa.eu/legacy/regulation-and-policy/regulatory-activities/credit-risk/implementing-technical-standards-npl (accessed 4 June 2025).

information asymmetries between sellers and prospective buyers by safeguarding a minimum standard of disclosure.[4] Such steps are likely to assist potential credit purchasers in their assessment of the transaction, facilitating this way the operation of the secondary market.

**16.04** This position has now been adopted by virtue of the Commission Implementing Regulation (EU) 2023/2083.[5]

**16.05** Article 16 is to be read as the companion to the provision of information obligation found in Article 15(1) of this Directive.

## B. IMPLEMENTING TECHNICAL STANDARDS

**16.06** Article 16(2) of the Directive provides that the EBA shall specify the data fields and identify which of those are "mandatory" for reporting purposes. The ITS templates have 135 data fields, of which 78 of those are mandatory. The distinction between mandatory and non-mandatory fields was decided in light of the proportionality principle provided under Article 16(3) of this Directive. On this basis, mandatory data fields are those that are deemed essential for financial due diligence and for loan valuation purposes. This includes information regarding: the counterparties to the loan; the contractual characteristics of the loan itself, including any forbearance measure and any lease agreement; any collateral and guarantee provided with the associated enforcement procedures; and historical collection of loan repayments.[6] Credit institutions must complete all mandatory fields but are encouraged to complete all fields whenever possible.

**16.07** To facilitate the proportionate application of the templates, as reflected in Article 16(4) of the Directive, the ITS specify the types of transactions where all the data fields should be dealt with on a non-mandatory basis. This includes NPLs under syndicated credit agreement facilities; NPLs to third-country borrowers; NPLs between credit institutions belonging to the same group; NPLs that have been acquired by the credit institutions from entities other than credit institutions, in which case required data fields may not be available

4 Ibid.

5 Commission Implementing Regulation (EU) 2023/2083 of 26 September 2023 laying down implementing technical standards for the application of Article 16(1) of Directive (EU) 2021/2167 of the European Parliament and of the Council with regard to the templates to be used by credit institutions for the provision to buyers of information on their credit exposures in the banking book.

6 EBA, Draft Implementing Technical Standards, 6–8.

to the selling credit institutions; unsecured NPLs to natural persons; a single NPL or several NPLs linked to a single borrower.[7]

## C. TREATMENT OF PERSONAL DATA AND CONFIDENTIAL INFORMATION

In addition to the fields of disclosure, credit institutions must observe the guidance provided as to the treatment of confidential information. Any information deemed confidential by credit institutions shall be shared with the appropriate confidentiality arrangements in place. The ITS notes that credit institutions may use non-disclosure agreements, drafted in compliance with applicable legislation and market practices, or provide the information through secure channels, such as electronic virtual data rooms. Having regard to the detail of such information and related confidentiality concerns, credit institutions should only communicate the information to potential buyers who are seriously interested in purchasing the non-performing credit agreement. **16.08**

That said, it is unclear how the duty to disclose said information is to be balanced against the protection of personal data, independent of the guidance provided herein.[8] Many of the mandatory fields would present significant challenges for credit institutions. Take the collateral template as an example. This requires the credit institution to provide access to internal and external valuations of the collateral. This clearly undermines consumer protection law, and comes with liability concerns for the credit institution itself. There also lies the risk that such information may be abused by potential credit purchasers who do not intend to buy the specific portfolio but eventually use that information to buy the collateral at an extremely low price later down the line. Credit institutions are, in essence, enabling someone to create a complete profile on their loan quality. Similar information has been used in the past to take over distressed credit institutions. **16.09**

---

7 EBA, Draft Implementing Technical Standards, 9–10.

8 In fact, this provision has received much objection, see European Data Protection Supervisor, 'Formal Comments of the EDPS on the Proposal for a Directive of the European Parliament and of the Council on Credit Servicers, Credit Purchasers and the Recovery of Collateral' (24 January 2019) https://www.edps.europa.eu/sites/default/files/publication/19-01-24_comments_proposal_directive_european_parliament_en.pdf (accessed 5 June 2025); European Data Protection Supervisor, 'Formal Comments on the Draft Proposal for a Commission Implementing Regulation Laying Down Implementing Technical Standards for the Application of Article 15(1) of Directive(U) 2021/2167 with Regard to the Templates to be Used by Credit Institutions for the Provision to Buyers of Information on their Credit Exposures in the Banking Book' (25 July 2023), https://www.edps.europa.eu/system/files/2023-07/2023-0712_formal_comments_en.pdf (accessed 5 June 2025).

**16.10** Furthermore, and independent of this, it is unclear as to the extent to which information disclosure can serve as a viable regulatory mechanism for NPLs traded on the secondary market.

## D. EXEMPTIONS

**16.11** The ITS does not apply to sales or transfers of loans not classified as "non-performing" in accordance with Article 47a of the Capital Requirements Regulation (CRR).[9] Article 16(1) also restricts the application of said templates to "credit exposures in the banking book", i.e., loans kept on a hold to maturity basis. Excluded from application are, therefore, loans held in the trading book by means of other arrangements such as credit default swaps, total return swaps, and any other type of derivative contract, insurance contracts, and sub-participation contracts in relation to NPL. The ITS also do not apply to sales or transfers of NPLs through transferable debt securities, derivatives, or other financial instruments that fall within the scope of Directive 2014/65/EU. It also does not cover securities financing transactions, other than margin lending transactions, within the meaning of Regulation (EU) 2015/2365 or financial or other leases of movable or immovable property that are not covered by Directive 2008/48/EC or sales or transfers of rights under such instruments, transactions, or leases. Excluded are also sales of NPLs that are subject to insolvency procedures and proceedings.

**16.12** The list is extensive. It is unclear, though, if transactions that fall outside the scope of the ITS, as outlined here, remain in the scope of the Directive for other obligations, i.e., the general obligation of credit institutions to disclose "necessary information" to prospective credit purchasers. If that is the case, the securitisation exemption is likely to have significant implications in terms of the effectiveness of the Directive, as in essence highly risky NPLs will continue to be traded on a *caveat emptor* basis.

## E. SCOPE OF APPLICATION

**16.13** In terms of the relevant period, guidance here is provided by Article 16(7) of the Directive. Credit institutions must use the ITS data templates for transfers

9 A bank loan is considered non-performing when more than 90 days pass without the borrower paying their dues. See, Articles 47a(3) and 178(1)(b) of the Regulation (EU) No 575/2013 of the European Parliament and of the Council of 26 June 2013 on prudential requirements for credit institutions and amending Regulation (EU) No 648/2012.

of non-performing credit agreements taking place on or after 30 December 2023 where the credits have been issued on or after 1 July 2018 and become non-performing after 28 December 2021. However, for credits that originate between 1 July 2018 and the date of entry into force of the ITS, credit institutions shall complete the data template with the information already available to them.

# ARTICLE 17

# OBLIGATIONS OF CREDIT PURCHASERS

**Kyriaki Vasileiou**

**1. Member States shall ensure that:**

**(a) a credit purchaser domiciled in the Union, or that has its registered office or, if under its national law it has no registered office, its head office in the Union appoints an entity referred to in Article 2(5), point (a)(i) or (iii), or a credit servicer, to perform credit servicing activities in respect of a creditor's rights under a non-performing credit agreement, or of the non-performing credit agreement itself, concluded with consumers;**

**(b) where a credit purchaser is not domiciled in the Union, or does not have its registered office or, if under its national law it has no registered office, its head office in the Union, its representative designated in accordance with Article 19(1) appoints an entity referred to in Article 2(5), point (a)(i) or (iii), or a credit servicer, except in cases where the representative is itself an entity referred to in Article 2(5), point (a)(i) or (iii), or a credit servicer, to perform credit servicing activities in respect of a creditor's rights under a non-performing credit agreement, or of the non-performing credit agreement itself, concluded with:**

**(i) natural persons, including consumers and independent workers;**

**(ii) micro, small and medium-sized enterprises (SMEs), as defined in Article 2 of the Annex to Commission Recommendation 2003/361/EC.**

**Host Member States may extend the requirement provided for in the first subparagraph to other credit agreements.**

**2. Member States shall ensure that a credit purchaser is not subject to any additional requirements for the purchase of a creditor's rights under a non-performing credit agreement, or of the non-performing credit agreement itself, other than as provided for by the national provisions transposing this Directive, or by provisions of applicable consumer protection law, contract law, civil law or criminal law. Member States shall ensure that relevant Union and national law concerning in particular the enforcement of contracts, consumer protection, borrowers' rights, credit origination, bank secrecy rules and criminal law continues to apply to the credit purchaser upon the transfer**

**of the creditor's rights under the credit agreement, or of the credit agreement itself, to the credit purchaser. The level of protection provided under Union and national law to consumers and other borrowers, as well as insolvency rules, shall not be affected by the transfer of the creditor's rights under the credit agreement, or of the credit agreement itself, to the credit purchaser, without prejudice to national and international rules on promissory notes and bills of exchange.**

**3. This Directive is without prejudice to national powers regarding credit registers, including the power to require information from credit purchasers regarding a creditor's rights under a credit agreement, or the credit agreement itself, and its performance.**

**4. Member States may allow credit purchasers to engage natural persons to service the credit agreements that they have acquired. Those natural persons shall be subject to a national regulation and supervision regime and shall not benefit from the freedom provided for in this Directive to perform credit servicing activities in another Member State.**

**5. Member States shall ensure that the appointed credit servicer, or entity referred to in Article 2(5), point (a)(i) or (iii), complies, on behalf of the credit purchaser, with the obligations imposed on the credit purchaser pursuant to paragraph 2 of this Article and Articles 18 and 20. In cases where no credit servicer or entity referred to in Article 2(5), point (a)(i) or (iii), is appointed, the credit purchaser or its representative shall remain subject to those obligations.**

**Member States may require that the appointed credit servicer, or entity referred to in Article 2(5), point (a)(i) or (iii), complies, on behalf of the credit purchaser, with the obligations imposed on the credit purchaser in accordance with national law including in relation to paragraph 3 of this Article.**



## A. INTRODUCTION

Article 17 sets out the obligations of credit purchasers. This provision facilitates the transfer of NPLs by removing authorisation requirements as to credit purchasers. 17.01

## B. APPOINTMENT OF CREDIT SERVICERS

Article 17(1)(a) of the Directive sets out the duty upon Member States to ensure that credit purchasers domiciled in the Union, or third-country credit 17.02

purchasers that have their registered or head office in the Union, appoint a "credit servicer", or on an "entity" referred to in Article 2(5), point (a)(i) and (iii) of the Directive, to perform servicing activities in respect of non-performing credit agreements concluded with consumers. Although the provision applies only in respect of consumer NPLs, the obligation can be extended to other credit agreements by stipulation.

**17.03** A credit servicer is defined in Article 3(8) of the Directive as an entity that acts on behalf of a credit purchaser in the management and enforcement of creditors' rights and obligations under the non-performing credit agreement, or the agreement itself, and carries out servicing activities of the NPL. The credit servicer can be a credit institution, a non-credit institution supervised by a competent authority of a Member State,[1] or an authorised credit servicer that performs credit servicing functions. As to entities mentioned under Article 2(5) point (a)(i) or (iii), these include credit institutions established in the EU and non-credit institutions supervised by competent authorities of a Member State when carrying out activities in that Member State.[2] Although these entities ordinarily fall outside the scope of the Directive when servicing creditors' rights, the present provision allows for their appointment in respect of non-performing agreements concluded with consumers. This is a major point of concern, as to put it succinctly, it allows credit purchasers to bypass the protection it provides to borrowers.[3]

**17.04** Under Article 17(1)(b), third-country credit purchasers are required to appoint an EU representative responsible for the performance of their obligations under this Directive. The rationale here is fairly simple. This is to ensure that third-country credit purchasers do not take advantage of the diverging legal regimes, making it harder for borrowers to rely on their rights under Union law. Rather, by assigning a representative, the national authorities will be able to closely supervise and monitor the enforcement of the non-performing credit agreements. Under the present provision, the representative would be responsible for the obligations imposed on credit purchasers, and is therefore tasked with the appointment of a credit servicer in respect of NPLs to natural persons,

---

1 Directive 2008/48/EC or with Directive 2014/17/EU.

2 See Directive 2008/48/EC of the European Parliament and of the Council of 23 April 2008 on credit agreements for consumers and repealing Council Directive 87/102/EEC, Article 20; Directive 2014/17/EU of the European Parliament and of the Council of 4 February 2014 on credit agreements for consumers relating to residential immovable property and amending Directives 2008/48/EC and 2013/36/EU and Regulation (EU) No 1093/2010, Article 35.

3 See Article 10(1) of this Directive. It is unclear if this provision applies to the other entities referred to in Article 2(5)(i) and (iii).

including consumers and workers, or NPLs to micro, small, or medium-sized enterprises. Again, this can be extended to other credit agreements by stipulation of the host Member State.

The aim here is to ensure that borrowers do not interact with unregulated or opaque entities after their loans have been sold. Credit servicers are subject to licensing, regulatory oversight, and conduct standards that protect borrowers from abusive practices. By mandating the involvement of a regulated intermediary, the Directive maintains a layer of accountability that would otherwise risk being lost in the secondary market for NPLs. This is further reinforced in Article 17(5), which states that the appointed credit servicer must comply with obligations set out in the Directive, particularly those concerning borrower protections (i.e., Articles 17(2), 18, and 20 of the Directive). If no servicer is appointed, the credit purchaser or its representative remains directly responsible to perform these functions. This ensures there is no regulatory vacuum or loophole that could harm borrowers' rights in the secondary market. **17.05**

## C. BORROWER PROTECTION

According to Article 17(2) of the Directive, credit purchasers are exempted from authorisation requirements in respect of credit agreements that fall within the scope of the Directive. This provision prohibits Member States from imposing additional requirements on credit purchasers beyond those stipulated by the Directive or applicable consumer, contract, civil, or criminal law. The logic behind this is that the purchase of credit agreements does not amount to the creation of new credit, but merely a relocation of an existing one. On this basis, credit purchasers' contribution to systemic risk is negligible and their exemption from the authorisation requirement does not threaten the stability of the financial system. It is important, however, for the transfer of the non-performing credit agreement to be conducted in accordance with Union and national consumer protection rules, and to ensure that the borrowers' rights continue to be those arising from the initial credit agreement – the same standards of consumers' rights are preserved. **17.06**

This provision strikes a balance between creating a harmonised market for NPLs while at the same time respecting the national law of the relevant Member State. Importantly, this provision affirms that all relevant Union and national law continues to apply post-transfer, and that the rules on the enforcement of contracts, consumer protection, borrower rights, credit origination standards, banking secrecy, and criminal liability are to be followed. **17.07**

For example, if a borrower had the right to contest a contract clause under national consumer protection law while the loan was held by a bank, that right remains intact even after the loan is sold to a private investment firm. This provision also confirms that insolvency protections remain unaffected by the operation of the Directive.

## D. CREDIT REGISTERS

**17.08** Article 17(3) preserves the power of Member States to regulate access to, and the use of credit registers, which are national databases used to track credit agreements, borrower performance, and creditor activity. It explicitly affirms that this Directive does not prejudice national powers in this area, including the ability to require credit purchasers to submit data on the performance of the acquired non-performing credit agreements. This provision ensures that competent authorities retain oversight over credit market developments, assess systemic risk, monitor borrower treatment, and intervene in cases of misconduct. For Member States, this is a key element in retaining financial stability and consumer trust. Given the cross-border nature of many NPL transactions, continued national control over credit registers also serves to anchor supervisory coordination between Member States and the ECB.

## E. NATURAL PERSONS

**17.09** Article 17(4) of the Directive introduces a degree of flexibility by allowing Member States to permit natural persons – individuals – to act as credit servicers, provided they are regulated and supervised under national law. It should be noted, however, that these individual servicers can only operate within the Member State concerned and cannot provide services cross-border. In essence, the passport benefit is not afforded to individual servicers. This restriction ensures that natural persons acting as servicers do so only within a controlled, national context, where their activities can be closely monitored. The risk of inconsistent borrower treatment and lack of standardisation is mitigated by confining such servicing to national frameworks. This can be particularly relevant in smaller Member States or specific niche segments of the credit servicing market, such as local debt recovery.

## F. ROLE OF CREDIT SERVICER

Article 17(5) of the Directive mandates that the appointed credit servicer, or regulated entity under Article 2(5) point (a)(i) or (iii), must comply, on behalf of the credit purchaser, with the obligations set out in Article 17(2) of this Directive and with the provisions provided for under Articles 18 and 20 of the Directive. These include obligations relating to fair borrower treatment, complaint handling, and transparency. This ensures the effective supervision of the credit servicer's operational practices. **17.10**

# ARTICLE 18

## USE OF CREDIT SERVICERS OR OTHER ENTITIES

**Kyriaki Vasileiou**

1. **Where the credit purchaser or, where applicable, its representative designated in accordance with Article 19 appoints an entity referred to in Article 2(5), point (a)(i) or (iii), or a credit servicer, to perform credit servicing activities in relation to the transferred creditor's rights under a non-performing credit agreement, or the non-performing credit agreement itself, Member States shall require that credit purchaser or its representative to inform the competent authorities of its home Member State of the identity and address of the entity referred to in Article 2(5), point (a)(i) or (iii), or of the credit servicer, at the latest on the date on which the credit servicing activities start.**
2. **Where the credit purchaser or, where applicable, its representative designated in accordance with Article 19 appoints an entity other than the one notified under paragraph 1 of this Article, it shall notify the competent authorities of its home Member State thereof at the latest on the date of that change and shall indicate the identity and address of the new entity that it has appointed to perform credit servicing activities in relation to the transferred creditor's rights under a non-performing credit agreement or the non-performing credit agreement itself.**
3. **Member States shall require the competent authorities of the home Member State of the credit purchaser to transmit without undue delay to the competent authorities of the host Member State, to the competent authorities of the Member State in which the credit was granted, and to the competent authorities of the home Member State of the new credit servicer, the information received in accordance with paragraphs 1 and 2.**

## A. INTRODUCTION

Article 18 of the Directive sets out the rules by which credit purchasers should inform the competent authorities of their home Member States, in regards to the appointment of credit servicers or other similar entities. This provision ensures that the details of the credit servicer are communicated to the relevant authorities in a timely manner, allowing for the effective and efficient supervision of credit servicers that fall under the umbrella of this Directive.[1] **18.01**

## B. PURPOSE AND EFFECT OF ARTICLE 18

Article 18(1) starts by setting out the duty upon Member States to ensure that credit purchasers, or in the case of third-country credit purchasers, their representatives, inform the competent authorities of their home Member States of the identity and address of the credit servicer or entity appointed to perform credit servicing activities in respect of the non-performing credit agreement. This information must be submitted no later than the date on which the credit servicing activities commence. **18.02**

The underlying objective here is to ensure that competent authorities of the home Member States are informed of any servicing activities on non-performing credit agreements. This notification of appointment is deemed necessary so as to allow relevant competent authorities to exercise their supervisory powers as regards the conduct of the credit servicer, or of the credit institution, or of the non-credit institution supervised by a competent authority of a Member State in accordance with Directive 2008/48/EC or with Directive 2014/17/EU, vis-à-vis the borrower. **18.03**

Article 18(2) deals with the situation where the originally appointed credit servicer is replaced. If a different entity is subsequently designated to carry out credit servicing activities, then the credit purchaser or, where applicable, its representative must inform the competent authorities of its home Member State on or before the date the change takes effect, providing again the identity and address of the new credit servicer or entity. This ensures that the authorities are continuously aware of who is responsible for servicing the loans in question and helps prevent regulatory gaps that could arise from unexpected or unreported transitions between servicers. **18.04**

---

1 See Directive (EU) 2021/2167, Preamble, para 45.

**18.05** Article 18(3) introduces an obligation for regulatory cooperation and communication across Member States. Once the competent authority of the credit purchaser's home Member State receives the relevant information, whether regarding the initial appointment or a change in servicer, it is required to transmit this information without undue delay to three sets of authorities: the competent authority of the host Member State (where the credit servicing is carried out), the authority in the Member State where the original credit was granted, and the home authority of the newly appointed credit servicer. This multi-jurisdictional reporting obligation reflects the cross-border nature of the secondary market for NPLs in the EU and ensures that all relevant competent authorities are kept informed in real time. It is an essential safeguard for regulatory coordination and borrower protection.

# ARTICLE 19

# REPRESENTATIVE OF A THIRD-COUNTRY CREDIT PURCHASER

**Kyriaki Vasileiou**

1. **Member States shall provide that where a transfer of a creditor's rights under a non-performing credit agreement, or of the non-performing credit agreement itself, is concluded, a credit purchaser that is not domiciled in the Union, or that does not have its registered office or, if under its national law it has no registered office, its head office in the Union designates in writing a representative that is domiciled in the Union or that does have its registered office or, if under its national law it has no registered office, its head office in the Union.**
2. **The representative referred to in paragraph 1 shall be addressed in addition to, or instead of, the credit purchaser by competent authorities on all issues related to the ongoing compliance with this Directive and be fully responsible for compliance with the obligations imposed on the credit purchaser under the national provisions transposing this Directive.**



## A. INTRODUCTION

Article 19 of the Directive provides the criteria for permitting third-country credit purchasers to participate in the secondary market for NPLs. **19.01**

## B. PURPOSE AND EFFECT OF ARTICLE 19

Although access to the secondary market is to a great extent liberalised, in the sense that there are no authorisation requirements for credit purchasers, this provision imposes some restrictions for third-country credit purchasers seeking to enter the market. The rationale behind this is fairly simple. Due to the **19.02** diverging legal regimes, a third-country credit purchaser would make it more difficult for the borrower to rely on their rights under national law for protection, and for the national authorities to supervise and monitor the enforcement of the non-performing credit agreement. The issue of conflicts of law would be presented here. For these reasons, the Directive allows third-country credit purchasers to access the market with the requirement that they will assign someone within the EU to act as their representative on all matters that fall within the ambit of this Directive.

**19.03** Article 19 starts by setting out the duty upon Member States to transpose into national law that where a sale or a transfer of a credit agreement is concluded with a third-country credit purchaser – that is, a credit purchaser that is not domiciled in the Union, or that does not have its registered or head office in the Union – the third-country credit purchaser should designate, in writing, a representative to act on its behalf. That representative must be domiciled in the EU or have their registered or head office in the EU. No guidance is provided by the Directive as to the legal status of the representative – natural person, credit institution, or non-credit institution.

## C. ASSUMPTION OF LIABILITY

**19.04** Under Article 19(2) of the Directive, representatives of third-country credit purchasers are to be addressed by competent authorities on all matters of compliance with the Directive and are to be fully responsible for compliance with the obligations imposed on the credit purchaser under the national provisions transposing this Directive. This means that they are to assume all responsibilities and obligations of the third-country credit purchaser.

**19.05** This is reinforced in Article 21(2) of the Directive, which requires the competent authorities of the home Member State of the representative to supervise compliance in respect of obligations set out in Articles 10, 17–20 of this Directive. The representative is answerable for non-compliance with any of these provisions.

**19.06** Therefore, generally corresponding to the above, the Directive imposes sanctions on the representative for:

- failure to communicate mandatory information (Articles 18 and 20);
- failure to appoint an entity or credit servicer to perform credit servicing activities (Articles (5)(a)(i)–(ii) and Article 17, respectively); and
- failure to act in good faith towards the borrower (Article 10).

The representative will be held accountable by virtue of Article 23(1)(e) if it fails to communicate the information provided for by national provisions transposing Articles 18, or by virtue of Article 23(1)(f) if it fails to comply with the requirement of the national provisions transposing Article 17. **19.07**

# ARTICLE 20

# TRANSFER OF A CREDITOR'S RIGHTS UNDER A NON-PERFORMING CREDIT AGREEMENT, OR OF THE NON-PERFORMING CREDIT AGREEMENT ITSELF, BY A CREDIT PURCHASER AND COMMUNICATION TO THE COMPETENT AUTHORITIES

**Kyriaki Vasileiou**

1. **Member States shall require a credit purchaser or, where applicable, its representative designated in accordance with Article 19, that transfers a creditor's rights under a non-performing credit agreement, or the non-performing credit agreement itself, to inform the competent authorities of its home Member State on a biannual basis of the legal entity identifier (LEI) of the new credit purchaser and, where applicable, of its representative designated in accordance with Article 19 or, where such identifier does not exist, of:**
   (a) **the identity of the new credit purchaser or, where applicable, its representative designated in accordance with Article 19, or of the members of the new credit purchaser's or its representative's management or administrative organ and the persons who hold qualifying holdings in the new credit purchaser or its representative within the meaning of Article 4(1), point (36), of Regulation (EU) No 575/2013; and**
   (b) **the address of the new credit purchaser or, where applicable, of its representative designated in accordance with Article 19.**

   **Additionally, the credit purchaser or its representative shall inform the competent authorities of its home Member State of at least the following:**
   (a) **the aggregate outstanding balance of the creditor's rights under the non-performing credit agreements, or of the non-performing credit agreements transferred;**
   (b) **the number and size of the creditor's rights under the non-performing credit agreements or of the non-performing credit agreements transferred;**

(c) **whether the transfer includes a creditor's rights under a non-performing credit agreement, or a non-performing credit agreement itself, concluded with consumers and the types of assets securing the non-performing credit agreement, when applicable.**

2. **The competent authorities referred to in paragraph 1 may require credit purchasers or, where applicable, their representatives designated in accordance with Article 19, to provide the information referred to in that paragraph on a quarterly basis whenever those competent authorities deem necessary, including in order to better monitor a high number of transfers that might occur during a crisis period.**

3. **Member States shall ensure that the competent authorities referred to in paragraphs 1 and 2 transmit without undue delay the information received in accordance with those paragraphs to the competent authorities of the host Member State and to the competent authorities of the home Member State of the new credit purchaser.**



## A. INTRODUCTION

Article 20 introduces reporting obligations on credit purchasers transferring non-performing credit agreements to 'new' credit purchasers. This provision reflects, to a great extent, the reporting obligations imposed upon credit institutions under Article 15 of this Directive. Several key differences can be noted in terms of requirements. First, under Article 20 there is no correlative duty upon credit purchasers, transferring non-performing credit agreements, to disclose necessary information to prospective new credit purchasers. This is understandable as we are now entering the realm of shadow banking. The parties to the transferred non-performing credit agreement are likely to be non-credit institutions. Second, these obligations are related to the monitoring interests of Member States and non-compliance does not imply any potential sanctions under this Directive. **20.01**

Reporting obligations are, under Article 20, not mandatory. **20.02**

## B. REPORTING OBLIGATIONS

Article 20(1) of this Directive imposes the duty upon Member States to require that credit purchasers transferring a creditor's rights under non-performing **20.03** credit agreements shall inform the competent authorities of their home Member State, on a biannual basis, of the LEI of the new credit purchaser, or where applicable, its representative. In cases where such an identifier does not exist, under Article 20(1)(b), credit purchasers are required to provide the identity of the new credit purchaser or the members of the new credit purchaser's management or administrative organ, and the persons with qualifying control in the latest credit purchaser, as well as the address of the new credit purchaser.

**20.04** In addition to these, credit purchasers are required to inform the competent authorities of their home Member State of the aggregate outstanding balance of the creditor's rights under the transferred non-performing credit agreement, the number and size of the creditor's rights under the transferred non-performing credit agreement, whether the transfer includes a creditor's rights arising from credit agreements with consumers, and the types of assets securing the non-performing credit agreement.

**20.05** Pursuant to Article 20(2) of the Directive, competent authorities should be able to require that the information be provided on a quarterly basis instead, whenever they consider it necessary, including due to the high number of transactions during a crisis period. The information should be communicated to the competent authorities of the host Member State and to the competent authorities of the home Member State of the new credit purchaser in a timely manner (Article 20(3)).

**20.06** It appears that the intention of Article 20 is to monitor the activities of the shadow banking system. It is unclear whether this provision will be of any value in monitoring the EU market for NPLs.

# TITLE IV

# SUPERVISION

# ARTICLE 21

# SUPERVISION BY COMPETENT AUTHORITIES

**Andreas Kokkinis and Shunqi Yang**

**1. Member States shall ensure that credit servicers and, where applicable, credit service providers to whom credit servicing activities have been outsourced in accordance with Article 12, comply with the national provisions transposing this Directive on an ongoing basis and shall ensure that those activities are subject to adequate supervision by the competent authorities of the home Member State in order to assess such compliance.**

**2. The home Member State of a credit purchaser or, where applicable, its representative designated in accordance with Article 19, shall ensure that the competent authorities referred to in paragraph 1 of this Article are responsible for the supervision of the obligations set out in Article 10 and in Articles 17 to 20 in respect of the credit purchaser or, where applicable its representative designated in accordance to Article 19.**

**3. Member States shall designate the competent authorities responsible for carrying out the functions and duties under the national provisions transposing this Directive.**

**4. Where Member States designate more than one competent authority pursuant to paragraph 3, they shall determine their respective tasks and designate one of them to be a single point of entry for all necessary exchanges and interactions with competent authorities of home or host Member States.**

**5. Member States shall ensure that appropriate measures are in place to enable the competent authorities designated pursuant to paragraph 3 of this Article to obtain from credit purchasers or their representatives designated in accordance with Article 19, credit servicers, credit service providers to whom a credit servicer outsources credit servicing activities under Article 12, borrowers and any other persons or public authority, the information necessary to carry out the following:**

**(a) assess ongoing compliance with the requirements laid down in the national provisions transposing this Directive;**

**(b) investigate possible infringements of those requirements;**

**(c) impose administrative penalties and remedial measures in accordance with the national provisions transposing Article 23.**

**6. Member States shall ensure that the competent authorities designated pursuant to paragraph 3 have the expertise, resources, operational capacity and powers necessary for the exercise of their functions and duties laid down in this Directive.**



## A. INTRODUCTION

The article defines the roles and responsibilities of competent authorities, including monitoring, enforcement, and cross-border cooperation. The provision contains six paragraphs. Paragraph 1 highlights the importance of continuous adherence to the Directive, requiring Member States to ensure that credit servicers and credit service providers consistently comply with national laws derived from the Directive. Compliance is supervised by the competent authorities of the home Member State. Paragraph 2 extends the supervisory responsibility of the home Member State to credit purchasers or their representatives, as referenced in Article 19 of the Directive. It mandates oversight of compliance with obligations outlined in Article 10 and Articles 17–20. These obligations consist of matters such as borrower relations, notification of NPL transfers, credit purchasers' rights, the use of credit servicers, the role of third-country credit purchasers, and the transfer of creditor rights under NPL agreements. Paragraph 3 assigns Member States the responsibility of appointing competent authorities to ensure effective implementation and oversight of the Directive. Paragraph 4 requires Member States with multiple authorities involved in supervision to clearly define their roles and responsibilities. It also mandates the designation of one authority as the primary communication hub for interactions with other Member States. Paragraph 5 stresses the necessity for competent authorities to have access to essential information from all entities involved in credit servicing and borrowers. Paragraph 6 concludes by clarifying that Member States must ensure that their competent authorities are equipped with the requisite expertise, resources, operational capacity, and powers to fulfil their duties effectively. This requirement is also stated in Preamble (28), which emphasises the need for credit servicers to possess adequate knowledge and experience. **21.01**

**21.02** This article requires the establishment of a robust supervisory framework to ensure compliance with the Directive. NPLs need regulatory intervention as a high stock of NPLs can undermine the stability of the banking and financial system, thereby hindering economic growth.[1] However, monitoring NPLs can be rather difficult due to the opacity of the value of distressed loans, conflicts of interest, and information asymmetries. For example, senior management often has incentives to conceal or delay the recognition of NPLs to avoid sending negative signals about the bank's financial health, and risk a reduction in their variable remuneration. [2] A high level of NPLs is perceived as a sign of weakness, and by obscuring these exposures, managers exacerbate information asymmetries regarding asset quality for both internal and external stakeholders.[3] Cyclical economic movements lead to an accumulation of NPLs during downturns, challenging banks' balance sheets.[4] Furthermore, the lack of harmonisation in definitions, accounting practices, and provisioning methods creates obstacles for assessing and comparing NPLs across the EU, complicating regulatory oversight.[5] Even the effectiveness of corporate governance mechanisms (audit committee, CEO duality, and independent commissioners) on reducing NPLs is limited and not mediated significantly by financial performance.[6] Thus, unsurprisingly, early recognition and provisioning for NPLs are emphasised as essential to mitigating systemic risks.[7]

**21.03** Financial regulation aims to enhance the functioning of the financial system,[8] and the aim of regulating NPLs is to address financial stability issues while prioritising market efficiency and consumer protection. A key component of this regulatory framework is prudential regulation, which focuses on mitigating

1 Preamble (2).

2 Andreas Kokkinis and Andrea Miglionico, 'The Role of Bank Management in the EU Resolution Regime for NPLs' (2020) 6(2) *Journal of Financial Regulation* 204, 206.

3 Ibid.

4 Charles AE Goodhart, 'The Historical Pattern of Economic Cycles and Their Interaction with Asset Prices and Financial Regulation' in William C Hunter, George G Kaufman and Michael Pomerleano (eds), *Asset Price Bubbles: The Implications for Monetary, Regulatory, and International Policies* (Massachusetts Institute of Technology Press 2003) ch.33.

5 David Bholat and others, 'Non-performing Loans: Regulatory and Accounting Treatments of Assets' (2016) Bank of England Staff Working Paper No 594, 23, https://www.bankofengland.co.uk/-/media/boe/files/working-paper/2016/non-performing-loans-regulatory-and-accounting-treatments-of-assets.pdf.

6 Indri Kartika, 'Corporate Governance and Non-performing Loans: The Mediating Role of Financial Performance' (2022) 9(1) *Cogent Business & Management*, https://www.tandfonline.com/journals/oabm20?src=pdf.

7 Ibid., 42.

8 John Armour et al., *Principles of Financial Regulation* (Oxford: Oxford University Press 2016) 52. Major goals of financial regulation include investor protection, consumer protection, financial stability, market efficiency, competition, the prevention of financial crime, and fairness.

systemic risks by ensuring the safety and soundness of financial institutions such as banks, insurance companies, and mutual funds.[9] Designed to promote cautious and responsible behaviour within regulated firms, prudential regulation ultimately safeguards the interests of stakeholders who depend on these institutions.[10] The dual focus of financial regulation encompasses prudential supervision and conduct regulation.[11] Prudential supervision prioritises systemic stability and market soundness by ensuring the operational efficiency of financial institutions. In contrast, conduct regulation emphasises consumer protection and the fairness of market operations. However, these goals can sometimes be in tension.[12] For example, while consumer protection centres on providing access to information and ensuring fairness, financial stability requires systemic supervision to address broader risks.[13] An overemphasis on investor protection could inadvertently undermine financial stability by reducing market discipline and introducing inefficiencies, but equally ignoring consistent negative outcomes for customers can ultimately weaken the financial system too.

The 2007 financial crisis exposed the limitations of relying solely on traditional prudential regulation to address systemic risks and prevent financial contagion. Before the crisis, it was widely assumed that protecting investors and maintaining market confidence would naturally ensure financial stability.[14] However, the crisis revealed that these measures were inadequate in scenarios involving systemic risk.[15] Consequently, broader macro-prudential measures have become essential to mitigate systemic vulnerabilities and maintain stability. NPLs exemplify the challenges of financial stability. They highlight inefficiencies and failures in risk assessment and regulatory supervision, often stemming from inadequate capital controls and an inability to anticipate market corrections.[16] Addressing the risks associated with NPLs is crucial not only for safeguarding financial stability but also for improving overall market **21.04**

9 Erik Gerding, *Law, Bubbles, and Financial Regulation* (Routledge 2013) 15.

10 Ibid., 64.

11 Dirk Schoenmaker and Nicolas Véron, 'A "Twin Peaks" Vision for Europe' in Andrew Godwin and Andrew Schmulow (eds), *The Cambridge Handbook of Twin Peaks Financial Regulation* (Cambridge: Cambridge University Press 2021) 283.

12 Armour et al. (n 8), 72.

13 Frank Partnoy, 'Financial Systems, Crises, and Regulation' in Niamh Moloney, Eils Ferran and Jennifer Payne (eds), *The Oxford Handbook of Financial Regulation* (Oxford: Oxford University Press 2015) 99.

14 Armour et al. (n 8), 65 and 66.

15 Franklin Allen and Elena Carletti, 'Systemic Risk from Real Estate and Macro-prudential Regulation' (2011) at Regulation of Systemic Risk Conference, https://www.federalreserve.gov/events/conferences/2011/rsr/papers/paper7/index.html.

16 Armour et al. (n 8), 72.

efficiency. As financial stability is considered a public good, regulatory oversight must be robust to ensure its provision, balancing this objective with the need for effective consumer protection.

## B. PRUDENTIAL SUPERVISION AND REGULATORY MODELS

**21.05** Article 21 does not dictate the regulatory structure of national competent authorities but instead it allows broad discretion to Member States to make these decisions in line with national policy priorities and path dependence. Generally, if two separate supervisory authorities are responsible for prudential supervision and conduct regulation respectively, this is known as the twin peak model; while if a single authority oversees both supervisory objectives, it then adopts the integrated model.[17] The United Kingdom, for example, adopts a type of twin peaks model. Under this framework, the Prudential Regulation Authority (PRA), a division of the Bank of England, is primarily responsible for prudential supervision. This includes the management of NPLs, ensuring the stability of the financial system, and safeguarding the soundness of financial institutions such as banks and insurance companies.[18] Meanwhile, the Financial Conduct Authority (FCA), an independent market regulator, focuses more on consumer protection and conduct regulation. The PRA enforces Basel requirements, developed by the Basel Committee on Banking Supervision (BCBS), and adapts them to the domestic financial rules established post-Brexit, particularly in the regulation of NPLs securitisations.[19] The twin peaks model thus represents a separation between prudential supervision and conduct regulation, with the former often – but not necessarily – embedded within the central bank.[20] There are various supervision models across the EU, including the twin peaks model. For instance, both the Netherlands and France implement this approach. In the Netherlands, De Nederlandsche Bank (DNB) oversees prudential matters,[21] while the Autoriteit Financiële Markten

17 Ibid., 284.

18 Bank of England, 'What is the Prudential Regulation Authority (PRA)?' https://www.bankofengland.co.uk/explainers/what-is-the-prudential-regulation-authority-pra.

19 PRA, *Implementation of Basel Standards: Non-performing Loan Securitisations* (Policy Statement, PS24/21 October 2021).

20 ECB, Recent Developments in Supervisory Structure (October 2010), https://www.ecb.europa.eu/pub/pdf/other/report_on_supervisory_structures2010en.pdf, 4.

21 DNB, 'Prudential Supervision', https://www.dnb.nl/en/sector-information/open-book-supervision/open-book-supervision-themes/prudential-supervision/. Its main focuses are the soundness of financial enterprises and the stability of the financial system.

(AFM) is responsible for market conduct.[22] Similarly, in France, the Autorité de Contrôle Prudentiel et de Résolution (ACPR) supervises NPLs management and ensures that institutions comply with EU and national prudential standards.[23] The Autorité des Marchés Financiers (AMF), on the other hand, serves as the market regulator.[24]

Depending on the relationship between the prudential supervisory body and the central bank, different regulatory models exist within the integrated model. In some cases, the central bank acts as the integrated supervisor, combining prudential and macroprudential oversight under one institution, as seen in Spain, where the Banco de España (Bank of Spain) oversees prudential regulation while collaborating with sector-specific agencies like the Comisión Nacional del Mercado de Valores (National Securities Market Commission) for securities markets. The Bank of Spain manages NPLs supervision and other prudential responsibilities in collaboration with the European Central Bank (ECB) under the Single Supervisory Mechanism (SSM).[25] This partnership aims to reduce NPLs levels, ensure compliance with EU prudential standards, and implement directives related to NPLs management. The ECB directly supervises significant institutions (large banks) in Spain under the SSM framework. Evidently, the same applies to the vast majority of EU Member States as they are parts of the Banking Union and SSM. **21.06**

## C. THE ROLE OF SUPERVISORY AUTHORITIES

Hybrid models exist where responsibilities are shared between the central bank and specialised regulators. For example, in Italy, the central bank, Banca d'Italia (Bank of Italy) leads prudential supervision, including NPLs management, and is involved in market infrastructure and financial stability.[26] The Commissione Nazionale per le Società e la Borsa (Consob) handles securities markets and consumer protection.[27] These two entities coordinate closely to minimise regulatory overlap while ensuring comprehensive oversight. In 2018, the Bank of Italy and Consob jointly issued regulations on central counterparties and securities depositories, aligning with EU frameworks like the Central **21.07**

22 AFM, 'About the AFM', https://www.afm.nl/en/over-de-afm. AFM is an independent market regulator and aims to promote fair and transparent financial markets.

23 ACPR, 'About the ACPR – Tasks', https://acpr.banque-france.fr/en/acpr/about-acpr/tasks.

24 AMF, 'Our Missions', https://www.amf-france.org/en/amf/our-missions.

25 Bank of Spain, 'About Us', https://www.bde.es/wbe/en/sobre-banco/.

26 Bank of Italy, 'Our Role', https://www.bancaditalia.it/compiti/index.html.

27 Consob, 'Consob and its Activities', https://www.consob.it/web/consob-and-its-activities/contents.

Securities Depositories Regulation (CSDR).[28] The Bank of Italy has long played a central role in Italy's financial system. Germany represents another variation with a decentralised approach, which reflects the shared supervisory model. In Germany, Bundesanstalt für Finanzdienstleistungsaufsicht (BaFin) is such an authority, working with the Deutsche Bundesbank to oversee prudential matters and ensure compliance with EU standards.[29] BaFin is responsible for regulatory compliance, capital adequacy, and risk management, including NPLs, while the Bundesbank provides operational support and monitors systemic risk. These variations reflect the flexibility within the integrated model, but the presence of different regulatory models within the EU is likely to pose challenges in the achievement of the harmonisation and cross-border coordination objectives of the NPL Directive, points to which we will return in the commentary of subsequent articles.

28 Bank of Italy, 'Rules Governing Central Counterparties, Central Securities Depositories and Central Depository Services: New Joint Regulation' (August 2018), https://www.bancaditalia.it/media/notizia/rules-governing-central-counterparties-central-securities-depositories-and-central-depository-services-new-joint-regulation/?com.dotmarketing.htmlpage.language=1&dotcache=refresh.

29 BaFin, 'Function & History', https://www.bafin.de/EN/DieBaFin/AufgabenGeschichte/aufgabengeschichte_node_en.html;jsessionid=DEEB4D12C141BF9F21CF3348385CF24A.internet011.

# ARTICLE 22

# SUPERVISORY ROLE AND POWERS OF COMPETENT AUTHORITIES

**Andreas Kokkinis and Shunqi Yang**

**1. Member States shall ensure that the competent authorities of the home Member State designated pursuant to Article 21(3) are given all supervisory, investigatory and sanctioning powers, necessary for the exercise of their functions and duties laid down in this Directive, including at least the following:**

**(a) the power to grant or refuse an authorisation pursuant to Articles 5 and 6;**

**(b) the power to withdraw an authorisation pursuant to Article 8;**

**(c) the power to prohibit any of the credit servicing activities;**

**(d) the power to conduct on-site and off-site inspections;**

**(e) the power to impose administrative penalties and remedial measures in accordance with the national provisions transposing Article 23;**

**(f) the power to review outsourcing agreements concluded between credit servicers and credit service providers in accordance with Article 12(1);**

**(g) the power to require credit servicers to remove members of their management or administrative organ when they fail to comply with the requirements set out in Article 5(1), point (b);**

**(h) the power to require credit servicers to modify or update their internal governance arrangements and internal control mechanisms in order to effectively ensure respect for borrowers' rights in accordance with the laws governing the credit agreement;**

**(i) the power to require credit servicers to modify or update their policies adopted to ensure the fair and diligent treatment of borrowers, and the recording and handling of complaints from borrowers;**

**(j) the power to request further information pertaining to the transfer of a creditor's rights under the non-performing credit agreement, or of the non-performing credit agreement itself.**

**2. Member States shall ensure that the competent authorities of the host Member State designated pursuant to Article 21(3) and of the Member State where the credit was granted, when different from the host and the home Member States, are given all necessary powers for the exercise of their functions and duties laid down in this Directive.**

**3. Member States shall ensure that the competent authorities of the home Member State evaluate, by applying a risk-based approach, the**

**implementation by a credit servicer of the requirements set out in Article 5(1), points (e) to (h).**

4. **Member States shall determine the extent of the evaluation referred to in paragraph 3, having regard to the size, nature, scale and complexity of the activities of the credit servicer concerned.**
5. **The competent authorities of the home Member State shall inform the competent authorities of the host Member State, or of the Member State where the credit was granted, when different from the host and the home Member States, of the results of the evaluation referred to in paragraph 3 upon request of one of those competent authorities, or where the competent authorities of the home Member State consider it appropriate. The details of any administrative penalties or remedial measures imposed shall be transmitted by the competent authorities of the home Member State to the competent authorities of the host Member State and, where appropriate, of the Member State where the credit was granted, when different from the host and the home Member States.**
6. **Member States shall ensure that when carrying out the evaluation referred to in paragraph 3, the competent authorities of the home and of the host Member States, and of the Member State where the credit was granted, when different from the host and the home Member States, exchange all information necessary to enable them to carry out their respective functions and duties laid down in this Directive.**
7. **Member States shall ensure that the competent authorities of the home Member State are able to require a credit servicer, credit service provider or credit purchaser or its representative designated in accordance with Article 19 that does not meet the requirements of the national provisions transposing this Directive to take, at an early stage, all necessary actions or steps in order to comply with those provisions.**



## A. INTRODUCTION

**22.01** This article sets out requirements for cross-border cooperation, transparency, and the application of risk-based approaches, ensuring that regulated entities can be held accountable at an early stage to protect borrowers and maintain regulatory standards. Paragraph 1 outlines the powers that national laws must grant to the competent authorities, ensuring that they have sufficient powers to enforce compliance. These powers include granting, denying, and revoking authorisations, prohibiting specific credit servicing activities, conducting inspections, imposing penalties, and ensuring adherence to good governance and the protection of borrower rights. Paragraph 2 requires Member States to ensure that competent authorities—whether home or host—have adequate legal authority to fulfil their roles under the Directive. In Article 22(3), a risk-based approach is explicitly mandated for competent authorities in home Member States. This approach guides the evaluation of whether a credit servicer complies with requirements, particularly those concerning the ethical treatment of borrowers, robust internal governance, and operational safeguards. Paragraph 4 tasks Member States with tailoring supervisory efforts to the risk profile and operational complexity of each credit servicer, avoiding a 'one-size-fits-all' regulatory approach. Paragraph 5–6 highlight the importance of access to information, transparency, and cross-border cooperation. This includes sharing evaluation results, details of sanctions imposed, and other necessary information to enable competent authorities to perform their duties effectively. Finally, Paragraph 7 focuses on preventive measures to address non-compliance before it escalates. These measures apply to all legal entities that fall within the scope of the Directive, including credit servicers, service providers, and purchasers.

The overall purpose of Article 22 is to define the powers and responsibilities **22.02** of competent authorities in supervising, investigating, and enforcing compliance with the Directive. As stated in Article 22(1)–(2) and (5)–(7), Member States are instructed to grant competent authorities sufficient powers to oversee NPLs management. Different supervision models can indeed impact the efficiency of regulatory objectives, such as financial stability.[1] Referring to the regulatory models outlined in the commentary on Article 21, impartiality is enhanced in the twin peaks model as prudential supervision is separated from conduct supervision.[2] In the meantime, this separation can present challenges in sharing information between prudential and conduct supervisors, particularly when NPLs data must be communicated across borders. In the integrated model, the coordination in prudential and market conduct financial supervision is prioritised. It offers advantages in policy coordination, information sharing, and financial stability without evident downsides in macroeconomic outcomes.[3] Among the variations of the integrated model, centralised integration as in Spain emphasises efficiency and streamlined decision-making

1 Miguel Ampudia and others, 'The Architecture of Supervision' (European Central Bank Discussion Paper No 2287, May 2019), 5.

2 Andrew Godwin, Timothy Howse and Ian Ramsay, 'A Jurisdictional Comparison of the Twin Peaks Model of Financial Regulation' (2016) 18(2) *Journal of Banking Regulation* 103, 105.

3 Ampudia (n 1), 50.

but may risk overlooking the need for specialised focus. This streamlines operations, ensures seamless access to regulatory data, and reduces duplications of effort. This centralised model shares similarities with the integration of banking and insurance regulation under the China Banking and Insurance Regulatory Commission, which enhances the supervisory independence by centralising appointment and integrating oversight functions, leading to the reduction of the ratio of NPLs in Chinese banks.[4] However, it may lead to risks of reduced specialisation or prioritisation conflicts, as the integrated authority must balance multiple responsibilities.[5] The hybrid integration in Italy highlights flexibility and task-specific expertise but may face challenges in ensuring seamless communication and coordination between supervisory authorities. Meanwhile, the decentralised German pattern, or a shared supervisory governance model, stresses institutional independence and balanced responsibilities. As both the central bank and a separate agency oversee banking, it mitigates the risk of supervisory capture and may succeed in reducing the amount of NPLs, particularly in environments with higher corruption risks.[6] It may, however, encounter difficulties in maintaining cohesive oversight and avoiding fragmentation, which can hinder information flows between sectoral supervisors, particularly as EU directives often require cross-sector harmonisation.

## B. THE PRINCIPLES OF RISK-BASED REGULATION AND PROPORTIONALITY

**22.03** Articles 22(3) and (4) embody the principles of risk-based regulation and proportionality. In EU financial law, risk-based regulation is a fundamental concept and it is also embedded in Basel III.[7] A 'risk' refers to an adverse event that may occur in the future.[8] Risk-based regulation involves allocating resources based on the level of risk posed by regulated entities, focusing on identifying, assessing, and addressing risks most likely to cause harm. In short, regulators should prioritise mitigating the most significant risks that could impede the

4 Xianhang Qian and Xue Yang, 'Supervisory Independence and Banks' Non-Performing Loans: Quasi-Experimental Evidence from China' (2022) 54(60) *Applied Economics* 6938.

5 Ampudia (n 1), 50.

6 Nicolò Fraccaroli, 'Supervisory Governance, Capture, and Non-Performing Loans' (2019) Bank of England Staff Working Paper No 820, 3–4, https://www.bankofengland.co.uk/-/media/boe/files/working-paper/2019/supervisory-governance-capture-and-non-performing-loans.pdf.

7 Basel Committee on Banking Supervision, 'Basel III: A Global Regulatory Framework for More Resilient Banks and Banking Systems' (rev June 2011) 4.

8 Robert Baldwin and Julia Black, 'Driving Priorities in Risk-based Regulation: What's the Problem?' (2016) 43(4) *Journal of Law and Society* 565, 566.

achievement of their objectives.[9] However, as this approach targets uncertainties, rules and individual decisions stemming from a risk-based approach can sometimes be uncertain, complex, or even self-contradictory.[10] As discussed earlier, different regulatory objectives may conflict with one another. In the case of NPLs, the primary concern is to address financial stability—a value that may conflict with the goal of borrower protection. Nevertheless, this does not imply maintaining financial stability at the expense of borrower protection. Instead, the risk-based approach seeks to balance these different regulatory objectives. For instance, while the primary focus of regulating NPLs is to ensure financial stability, Article 24 of the Directive highlights the importance of protecting borrowers. Further, the principle of proportionality is a cornerstone of EU law, enshrined in the Treaty on European Union (TEU) and the Treaty on the Functioning of the European Union (TFEU).[11] It mandates that regulatory measures must be appropriate and suitable for achieving their objectives, necessary to fulfil those objectives, and must not exceed what is required.[12] For instance, under the EU's General Data Protection Regulation (GDPR), small businesses have fewer obligations compared to large corporations processing sensitive data.[13]

Similarly, the Directive avoids a one-size-fits-all supervision model for NPL issues. Instead, competent authorities are encouraged to tailor regulations to the size and complexity of regulated entities. This approach aligns with the principle of subsidiarity, which seeks to avoid unnecessary centralisation and safeguard the legislative autonomy of Member States.[14] Subsidiarity requires that decisions are made at the most appropriate level, with EU intervention occurring only when Member States cannot achieve the desired outcomes effectively. Despite its theoretical appeal, the principle of subsidiarity is not always applied consistently, as its success relies heavily on legislative design and the commitment of EU institutions to uphold it in policymaking and **22.04**

9 Ibid., 565.

10 Julia Black, 'Regulatory Styles and Supervisory Strategies' in Niamh Moloney, Eils Ferran and Jennifer Payne (eds), *The Oxford Handbook of Financial Regulation* (Oxford: Oxford University Press 2015) 223.

11 TEU, Article 5 and TFEU, Article 3 and 296.

12 *R v Minister of Agriculture, Fisheries and Food, ex parte Fedesa* [1990] ECR I-4023; *United Kingdom v Commission (Skimmed Milk Powder)* [1998] ECR I-2265 and *R v Secretary of State for Health, ex parte British American Tobacco and Imperial Tobacco* [2002] ECR I-11453.

13 Christina Tikkinen-Piri, Anna Rohunen and Jouni Markkula, 'EU General Data Protection Regulation: Changes and Implications for Personal Data Collecting Companies' (2018) 34(1) *Computer Law & Security Review* 134.

14 TEU, Article 5.

judicial oversight.[15] In practice, despite these principles, there has been a significant increase in the volume of EU-level legislation and regulation, an example being the NPL Directive itself which contains some detailed and prescriptive rules, suggesting that the EU has not always adhered strictly to subsidiarity and proportionality. The rise in EU regulation is attributed to a broad interpretation of the circumstances under which the EU can act. Rather than limiting its actions to areas where Member States cannot achieve objectives alone, the EU has justified intervention in a wide range of areas. In the case of NPLs, the risk-based approach, the principle of proportionality, and the principle of subsidiarity aim to prevent over-regulation and optimise regulatory efforts. There is potential for NPLs to be addressed at the national level instead of the EU level. Ideally, the first two principles are inherently aligned, as the risk-based approach offers an evidence-based methodology to ensure that regulation is proportionate to the risks posed by specific activities.[16] While the risk-based approach emphasises the efficient allocation of resources within the regulatory system, the principle of proportionality focuses on fairness and necessity, ensuring that regulatory measures are appropriately scaled and impactful without exceeding what is required. The principle of subsidiarity, along with the principle of proportionality, indicates that EU directives should be simple, consistent, and accessible for effective enforcement.[17] Precise and prompt implementation is key to ensuring this efficiency.[18] As such the three principles serve as a general guide for both national authorities and EU authorities in exercising the broad discretion afforded by the Directive.

## C. INFORMATION SHARING AND SUPERVISORY PRACTICES

**22.05** Beyond the three key principles, Article 22(6) emphasises the importance of competent authorities having access to information across the EU. Information sharing in such cases may involve three or more states: the home Member State, the host Member State, and the Member State where the credit was issued. Effective information sharing requires harmonisation of regulatory practices, an understanding of the credit institution's cross-border operations,

15 Paul Craig, 'Subsidiarity: A Political and Legal Analysis' (2012) 50(1) *Journal of Common Market Studies* 72, 84.

16 Julia Black and Robert Baldwin, 'Really Responsive Risk-Based Regulation' (2010) 32(2) *Law & Policy* 181.

17 Paul Craig and Gráinne de Búrca, *EU Law: Text, Cases, and Materials* (7th ed, Oxford: Oxford University Press 2024) 359.

18 European Commission, 'Better Regulation: Why and How', https://commission.europa.eu/law/law-making-process/planning-and-proposing-law/better-regulation_en.

and collaboration in decision-making. In this framework, the home Member State is tasked with monitoring the institution's overall risk management, the host Member State ensures local operations comply with the Directive, and the credit-granting Member State oversees borrower protections, collateral recovery, and debt enforcement in line with local laws. Comprehensive and harmonised information sharing minimises gaps and delays in resolving NPLs caused by fragmented national rules. Challenges may also arise within a single Member State due to the differing roles and structures of competent authorities. NPLs often involve cross-border asset sales, impacting multiple jurisdictions. Where the prudential regulator is linked to the central bank, information accessibility is generally improved. If the prudential regulator also handles conduct regulation, market activity information is more easily acquired. For instance, in a twin peaks model, the separation between prudential and conduct regulators can delay information sharing. Similarly, in an integrated model, where regulatory bodies are highly specialised, coordination challenges may emerge. Consequently, the efficiency of information sharing is critical not only between Member States but also within each Member State, to ensure effective supervision and swift resolution of NPL issues. That being said, information sharing cannot in itself resolve the problem arising out of the different legal treatments of loan agreements in different Member States. Indeed, contract law, personal bankruptcy law, corporate insolvency law and civil procedure rules are not harmonised, and there are significant differences across Member States both in the laws themselves and their practical application.

# ARTICLE 23

# ADMINISTRATIVE PENALTIES AND REMEDIAL MEASURES

**Andreas Kokkinis and Shunqi Yang**

**1. Without prejudice to the right of Member States to lay down criminal penalties, Member States shall lay down rules establishing appropriate administrative penalties and remedial measures applicable in at least the following situations:**

**(a) a credit servicer fails to comply with the requirement set out in the national provisions transposing Article 11 or enters into an outsourcing agreement infringing the national provisions transposing Article 12 or the credit service provider to whom the credit servicing activities were outsourced commits a serious infringement of the applicable legal provisions, including the national provisions transposing this Directive;**

**(b) a credit servicer's governance arrangements and internal control mechanisms as set out in Article 5(1), point (e), fail to ensure respect for borrower rights and compliance with personal data protection rules;**

**(c) a credit servicer's policy is inadequate for the proper treatment of borrowers as set out in Article 5(1), point (f);**

**(d) a credit servicer's internal procedures as set out in Article 5(1), point (g), fail to provide for the recording and handling of complaints from borrowers according to the obligations set out in the national provisions transposing this Directive;**

**(e) a credit purchaser or, where applicable, its representative designated in accordance with Article 19 fails to communicate the information provided for by national provisions transposing Articles 18 and 20;**

**(f) a credit purchaser or, where applicable, its representative designated in accordance with Article 19 fails to comply with the requirement of the national provisions transposing Article 17;**

**(g) a credit purchaser fails to comply with the requirement of the national provisions transposing Article 19;**

**(h) a credit institution fails to communicate the information set out in the national provisions transposing Article 15;**

**(i) a credit servicer allows one or more persons not complying with the requirements set out in Article 5(1), point (b), to become or remain a member of its management or administrative organ;**

(j) a credit servicer fails to comply with the requirements set out in the national provisions transposing Article 24;

(k) a credit purchaser or, where applicable, credit servicers or any entity mentioned under Article 2(5), point (a)(i) or (iii), fails to comply with national provisions transposing Article 10;

(l) a credit servicer receives and holds funds from borrowers when this is not permitted in a Member State in accordance with Article 6(1), point (b);

(m) a credit servicer fails to comply with the requirements set out in the national provisions transposing Article 6(2).

2. The administrative penalties and remedial measures referred to in paragraph 1 shall be effective, proportionate and dissuasive and shall include at least the following:

(a) a withdrawal of an authorisation to carry out activities as a credit servicer;

(b) an order requiring the credit servicer or credit purchaser or, where applicable, its representative designated in accordance with Article 19 to remedy the infringement, and to cease the conduct and to desist from a repetition of that conduct;

(c) administrative pecuniary penalties.

3. Member States shall ensure that administrative penalties and remedial measures are effectively implemented.

4. Member States shall ensure that, when determining the type of administrative penalties or remedial measures and the amount of the administrative pecuniary penalties, the competent authorities take into account relevant circumstances, including the following:

(a) the gravity and the duration of the infringement;

(b) the degree of responsibility of the credit servicer or credit purchaser or, where applicable, its representative designated in accordance with Article 19, responsible for the infringement;

(c) the financial strength of the credit servicer or credit purchaser responsible for the infringement, including by reference to the total turnover of a legal person or the annual income of a natural person;

(d) the importance of profits gained or losses avoided because of the infringement by the credit servicer or credit purchaser or, where applicable, its representative designated in accordance with Article 19, responsible for the infringement, insofar as those profits or losses can be determined;

(e) the losses caused to third parties by the infringement, insofar as those losses can be determined;

(f) the level of cooperation by the credit servicer or credit purchaser responsible for the infringement with the competent authorities;

(g) previous infringements by the credit servicer or credit purchaser or, where applicable, its representative designated in accordance with Article 19, responsible for the infringement;

(h) any actual or potential systemic consequences of the infringement.

5. Member States shall ensure that the competent authorities can apply the administrative penalties and remedial measures set out in paragraph 2 to

**members of the management or administrative organ, and to other individuals who under national law are responsible for the infringement.**

6. **Member States shall ensure that before taking any decision imposing the administrative penalties or remedial measures set out in paragraph 2 of this Article, the competent authorities give the concerned credit servicer, credit purchaser or where applicable, its representative designated in accordance with Article 19, the opportunity to be heard.**
7. **Member States shall ensure that any decision imposing the administrative penalties or remedial measures set out in paragraph 2 is properly reasoned and is subject to the right of appeal.**
8. **Member States may decide not to lay down rules for administrative penalties for infringements that are subject to criminal penalties under their national law. In that case, Member States shall communicate to the Commission the relevant criminal law provisions.**



## A. INTRODUCTION

23.01 This article outlines the enforcement framework, including administrative penalties and remedial measures for non-compliance with the Directive. Paragraph 1 requires Member States to establish rules for administrative penalties and remedial actions in cases of specific violations. These violations cover failures related to compliance, governance, borrower rights, communication requirements, and data protection. Article 23 of the Directive aligns with several rules outlined in its preamble. Preamble (6) references Regulation (EU) 2019/630 and Regulation (EU) No 575/2013, which establish requirements for credit institutions to allocate resources for NPLs, create enforcement mechanisms, and regulate the sale of NPLs in secondary markets. Article 23(1) stipulates that mismanagement or failure in the sale or enforcement of NPLs could attract administrative penalties if borrower rights or transparency are not upheld. Furthermore, Article 23(1)(b) connects with preamble (7), which highlights governance arrangements and internal controls required for the management of NPLs. Non-compliance with these governance standards, particularly where borrower rights are compromised, could trigger penalties under this provision. Articles 23(1)(c) and 23(1)(j) relate to preamble (21), which emphasises consumer protection rules, including those outlined in Directive 2005/29/EC. This means that failure to adhere to consumer protection policies, or breaches of borrower rights such as harassment or coercion during enforcement, would result in administrative penalties. Other instances of non-compliance covered by Article 23 include:

- Governance failures by credit institutions under Article 5(1)(b).
- Credit servicers holding borrower funds without authorisation.
- Credit purchasers failing to fulfil obligations under national provisions.
- Credit servicers mishandling borrower complaints due to inadequate delegation procedures.
- Failure to communicate required information or designate a representative.
- Breaches of obligations related to borrower rights, including the appointment of representatives.
- Breaches of consumer protection obligations during enforcement (e.g., harassment or misinformation).
- Failure to report required information or appoint a representative.
- Failure to provide transaction details, such as aggregated balances and portfolio specifics.

Key types of failure identified in the article itself include: (a) non-compliance with national provisions for outsourcing agreements (Article 11 and Article 12); (b) governance failures that jeopardise borrower rights or personal data protection (Article 5(1)(e)); (c) inadequate policies for fair borrower treatment (Article 5(1)(f)); (d) deficiencies in complaint-handling procedures (Article 5(1)(g)); (e)–(g) failures of credit purchasers or representatives to meet reporting obligations under Articles 17, 18, and 20; (h) credit institutions failing to provide required information (Article 15); (i) allowing unqualified individuals to hold management roles (Article 5(1)(b)); (j) non-compliance with governance and procedural requirements (Article 24); (k) breaches of national provisions related to Article 10 and (l)–(m); and unpermitted handling of borrower funds or non-compliance with Article 6. **23.02**

As emphasised in the preamble (51), the principle of effective, proportionate, and dissuasive enforcement is reflected in Article 23(2), which outlines enforcement measures, including withdrawing authorisation to act as a credit servicer, ordering corrective actions to address the infringement and prevent its recurrence, and imposing financial penalties. This emphasis aligns with a systematic approach to regulatory enforcement, whereby prioritising uniformity and strict penalties enhances compliance.[1] Simultaneously, by requiring infringers to 'remedy the infringement' and desist from repeated misconduct, the Directive mirrors a facilitative approach, which emphasises problem-solving **23.03**

1 Peter May and Raymond Burby, 'Making Sense Out of Regulatory Enforcement' (1998) 20(2) *Law & Policy* 135.

rather than pure punishment. Thus, the Directive reflects an effort to balance strict enforcement with cooperative, problem-solving strategies to ensure compliance and maintain stability.

## B. THE ENFORCEMENT MEASURES

**23.04** The effectiveness of penalty implementation is emphasised in Article 23(3) to ensure entities are sufficiently motivated to prevent infringements. Article 23(4) clarifies the factors considered when determining penalties, including the gravity and duration of the violation, the degree of responsibility, financial strength, profits gained, and losses avoided due to the violation, harm caused to third parties, level of cooperation with authorities, previous violations, and the systemic risks that may result from the infringement. These factors are quite generic and identical to the ones used in other pieces of EU legislation. Article 23(5) extends enforcement measures to individuals responsible for the infringement, such as members of management or administrative bodies, in accordance with national law. This provision is crucial as large banks and other large financial firms often manifest agency problems, especially in the context of NPLs management, to the extent that sanctions imposed on the firm may not be sufficient to dissuade directors and senior managers from infringing the relevant rules.[2] Article 23(6) ensures that affected credit servicers, purchasers, or their representatives have the opportunity to present their case before penalties are imposed by competent authorities. Meanwhile, Article 23(7) stresses that all decisions should be properly reasoned, and affected parties must have the right to appeal. Finally, Article 23(8) provides that if Member States opt not to establish administrative penalties for violations that are subject to criminal law, they must inform the Commission about the relevant criminal provisions.

**23.05** It is therefore evident that article 23 primarily focuses on administrative sanctions rather than criminal penalties. According to Article 83(1) and (2) and Article 84 TFEU, it is possible for criminal sanctions to be included in EU directives.[3] For example, Directive 2008/99/EC (the Environmental Crime

2 For a detailed analysis of the incentives of senior bank managers to conceal NPLs, Andreas Kokkinis and Andrea Miglionico, 'The Role of Bank Management in the EU Resolution Regime for NPLs' (2020) 6(2) *Journal of Financial Regulation* 204.

3 In *Commission v Council* [2005] ECR I-7879, the Court of Justice of the European Union (CJEU) confirmed that the EU can require Member States to adopt criminal sanctions if they are necessary for effective implementation of EU law, and the ruling clarified that criminal law is not entirely excluded from EU competence, particularly in areas of environmental protection and public health.

Directive) mandates criminal sanctions for certain severe environmental offences, while Directive 2014/57/EU (the Market Abuse Directive) requires criminal penalties for insider trading and market manipulation. However, the NPL Directive relies primarily on administrative sanctions and allows Member States to impose criminal sanctions instead provided that they inform the Commission accordingly as outlined in Article 23(8). This approach reflects the nature of NPLs, which are predominantly a financial and regulatory issue, rather than a matter of criminal culpability. The purpose of these sanctions is to restore stability, protect borrowers, and promote market efficiency, rather than to punish individual behaviour. In general, criminal penalties are reserved for the most serious and harmful violations, while administrative enforcement is applied to less severe offences.[4]

Furthermore, administrative sanctions, such as fines, are quicker and easier to implement across diverse national legal systems, avoiding the complexities and sensitivities associated with criminal proceedings and the high standard of proof that they involve. This approach is particularly suited to areas where rapid compliance is critical, such as competition law (e.g., cartel fines imposed by the European Commission) or data protection (e.g., penalties under GDPR). Regarding severity, criminal penalties are considered a last resort within EU law. As stated in Article 23(2), which reflects the principle of proportionality, administrative measures are deemed sufficient to address most NPL-related issues. Additionally, the Directive aims to harmonise national laws rather than impose a uniform legal code. As stipulated at the very beginning of this article, these administrative penalties should not undermine the authority of Member States. In line with the principle of subsidiarity, the Union intervenes only when necessary to achieve objectives that Member States cannot effectively address on their own. Criminal sanctions could easily exceed this threshold. However, this does not mean that the Directive takes an indifferent stance. Instead, it requires Member States to adopt a 'comply or explain' approach, justifying any decision not to apply administrative sanctions. Therefore, rather than imposing a mandatory and uniform set of regulations, the Directive seeks to balance Union-wide guidelines with national autonomy. Given that the current Directive emphasises flexibility and efficiency, administrative sanctions allow Member States to align with their financial and regulatory systems while still meeting EU objectives. **23.06**

4 Ian Ayres and John Braithwaite, *Responsive Regulation: Transcending the Deregulation Debate* (Oxford University Press 1992).

## C. CIVIL SANCTIONS

**23.07** It is worth noting that the Directive does not introduce civil sanctions, as these are typically focused on remedies such as compensation, restitution, or injunctions in disputes between private parties. Civil sanctions would primarily relate to customer protection aspects of the issue, offering borrowers an individual right of action. However, the conduct of business regulation in the EU and globally is far less harmonised compared to prudential regulation, which would make it hard for meaningful harmonised civil sanctions to be designed concerning the distinct economic and social features of each Member State. In addition, the Directive is predominantly aimed at the prudential side of NPLs, and its focus on administrative sanctions reflects this objective. Administrative sanctions, which are imposed by regulators, ensure swift and uniform enforcement across Member States, whereas civil sanctions rely on private parties to pursue legal action in courts. Such reliance could lead to inconsistencies, inadequate enforcement, and lengthy court proceedings due to the significant variations in civil law traditions across Member States. Therefore, civil sanctions have been excluded from the NPLs context to maintain regulatory coherence and effectiveness, but in their place, the Directive introduces a complaints mechanism for borrowers as we will see in Article 24.

# TITLE V

# SAFEGUARDS AND DUTY TO COOPERATE

# ARTICLE 24

# COMPLAINTS

**Andreas Kokkinis and Shunqi Yang**

**1. Member States shall ensure that credit servicers establish and maintain effective and transparent procedures for the handling of complaints from borrowers.**

**2. Member States shall ensure that the treatment by credit servicers of complaints from borrowers is free of charge and that credit servicers record the complaints and the measures taken to address them.**

**3. Member States shall ensure that the competent authorities establish and publish a procedure for the handling of complaints from borrowers concerning credit purchasers, credit servicers and credit service providers, and shall ensure that they are treated promptly when received.**



## A. INTRODUCTION

**24.01** This article focuses on establishing safeguards to ensure that borrowers have accessible, transparent, and effective channels for addressing complaints related to credit servicing activities. It highlights the roles and responsibilities of credit servicers, as well as the oversight functions of competent authorities. Paragraph 1 mandates transparency in the handling of complaints, ensuring that borrowers are kept informed about how their issues are being resolved. Article 24(2) further stipulates that complaints should be handled free of charge and recorded by credit servicers. This provision helps reduce financial barriers and enhances traceability. Article 24(3) introduces state-level intervention to protect borrower interests where private mechanisms fail. One example of aggressive credit servicing on borrowers is in the context of predatory lending, which imposes unfair and misleading loan terms on borrowers,[1]

1 Kathleen C Engel and Patricia A McCoy, 'A Tale of Three Markets: The Law and Economics of Predatory Lending' (2002) 80(6) *Texas Law Review* 1255, 1260.

and tends to lead to financial distress and high default rates.[2] By integrating accountability measures for both credit servicers and competent authorities, a more comprehensive protection and complaint resolution mechanism is created within the NPLs regulatory framework.

Unlike other articles in the Directive that focus on regulatory authority powers over specialised institutions, this section is primarily concerned with safeguarding borrower rights, which makes this article conduct focused rather than prudential focused. This aligns with the analysis under Article 21 that this Directive aims to protect financial stability with emphasis on consumer protection as well. Borrowers in NPLs situations often experience financial stress due to their NPLs status, as well as the potentially complex dynamics of loan transfers and third-party servicing. While borrowers have the right to complain about unfair practices by credit purchasers, access information, and utilise complaint procedures free of charge, they can also seek recourse from competent authorities for unresolved complaints. This creates a strong incentive for effective and transparent procedures in handling complaints, fostering accountability. At first glance, both Article 24(1) and 24(3) aim to ensure borrowers have access to complaint mechanisms. However, Article 24(1) requires credit servicers to establish internal procedures to handle complaints from borrowers, while Article 24(3) ensures that competent authorities address complaints against credit servicers, credit purchasers, and credit service providers, providing oversight where a power imbalance exists. In other words, Article 24(1) requires credit servicers to handle complaints from borrowers regarding their management of loans, whereas Article 24(3) ensures that competent authorities handle complaints concerning credit servicers, credit purchasers, and credit service providers. **24.02**

## B. CREDIT SERVICERS' OBLIGATIONS

Article 24(1) makes credit servicers the first point of contact for complaints. As intermediaries managing loans on behalf of credit purchasers, they directly interact with borrowers. This allows them to address issues swiftly at an operational level before they escalate into regulatory concerns. In this sense, servicers act as gatekeepers. However, Article 24(3) acknowledges the potential conflict of interest between servicers and borrowers, necessitating intervention by the relevant authorities. Servicers owe a duty of care primarily to their **24.03**

2 Sumit Agarwal and others, 'Predatory Lending and the Subprime Crisis' (2014) 113(1) *Journal of Financial Economics* 29.

investors, which may not always align with prioritising borrowers' interests. When servicers fail to handle complaints adequately, borrowers' rights—such as fair treatment and prompt communication—are at risk. Therefore, an independent mechanism is essential to escalate unresolved issues. Consequently, Articles 24(1) and (2) focus on efficiency in complaint handling, while Article 24(3) ensures borrower protection within the regulatory framework for NPLs.

**24.04** Regarding the consistency of consumer protection, the European Banking Authority (EBA) amended its existing guidelines on complaints handling for the banking and financial services sectors to include credit servicers under the NPL Directive, particularly in relation to Article 24.[3] The scope and nature of credit servicers' obligations in the NPLs sector align with those in the banking, insurance, and securities sectors, ensuring effective and transparent complaint-handling procedures.[4] In the context of national registers of credit servicers,[5] competent authorities in the aforementioned Member States include the Klachteninstituut Financiële Dienstverlening (Kifid) in the Netherlands, the Autorité de Contrôle Prudentiel et de Résolution (ACPR) in France, the Bank of Italy in Italy, and BaFin in Germany. Currently, Kifid,[6] ACPR,[7] and BaFin[8] have published their procedures for handling complaints against credit servicers within their respective jurisdictions. According to Kifid, the authority will only accept complaints after borrowers have pursued the internal complaints procedure of their financial services providers. Article 24(1) requires internal complaints procedures to be effective and transparent. Therefore, Kifid will process complaints if the service providers fail to respond within a few weeks or if the response does not provide a resolution. Once Kifid receives a complaint, it assesses whether it falls within its remit. If accepted, Kifid engages in a mediation process with the financial institution, aiming for a swift and amicable resolution. If the issue is not resolved through mediation, the Arbitration Commission will issue a final, binding decision. This process, designed by Kifid, is intended to be straightforward and accessible.

---

3 EBA, Guidelines amending Joint Committee Guidelines on complaints-handling. The existing Joint Committee Guidelines (JC Guidelines) applied to the banking, investment and insurance sectors across the EU from 2014.

4 It includes subject matter, complaints management policy, complaints management function, registration, reporting, internal follow-up, provision of information, and procedures for responding to complaints.

5 EBA, National registers and national authorities responsible for handling complaints related to credit servicers https://www.eba.europa.eu/activities/information-consumers/national-registers-and-national-authorities-responsible-handling-complaints-related-credit-servicers.

6 Kifid, 'Procedure', https://www.kifid.nl/procedure/.

7 ACPR, 'Make a Claim', https://acpr.banque-france.fr/page-sommaire/vous-etes-un-particulier.

8 BaFin, 'Complaints', https://www.bafin.de/ref/19584734.

Similar to Kifid, the ACPR recommends consumers contact their financial services providers before filing a complaint, which requires service providers to adhere to specific response timeframes. If the issue remains unresolved, the consumer may file a complaint with the ACPR. The ACPR evaluates the complaint, ensuring that all regulatory requirements are met, and may facilitate mediation between the consumer and the institution. A decision or recommendation is then issued to resolve the issue. BaFin's procedure focuses on regulatory oversight and ensuring that financial institutions comply with fair complaint-handling practices. Consumers are expected to first seek a resolution directly with the institution involved. If this approach fails, they can lodge a complaint with BaFin. BaFin conducts a thorough investigation to ensure that the institution follows the required complaint-handling processes. Emphasis is placed on regulatory compliance, with corrective measures taken if necessary. All three procedures require consumers to initially attempt to resolve their issues directly with the service provider and are designed to promote transparency and accountability, with a strong emphasis on mediation. Competent authorities primarily act in an appellate role to further ensure consumer protection. These procedures reflect clear channels for complaint handling, as required by Article 24. 24.05

## C. COMPLAINT-HANDLING PROCEDURES

The provision of transparent and free complaint procedures helps prevent financial barriers from hindering access to justice. A good reputation among entities can enhance the performance of secondary credit markets.[9] Effective and prompt complaint-handling procedures contribute to service recovery and foster customer trust, ultimately strengthening market confidence.[10] However, the Directive stops short of granting borrowers an actionable right in private law, leaving them reliant on action by competent authorities if credit servicers do not comply with the requirements of Article 24—a limitation that could invite criticism. While the Directive does not grant a private right of action directly, it leaves Member States with the discretion to implement borrower complaint systems. This is further reflected in preamble (22), which stresses that borrowers who lack sufficient resources are entitled to legal aid according to the conditions set out in national law. However, the national laws of Member States often fall short of effectively protecting all types of borrowers, 24.06

9 Ibid., no 54, 4.

10 See Vaishali Singh, Amit Jain and Sapna Choraria, 'Exploring the Role of Complaint Handling among Complaining Consumers' (2016) 20(4) *Journal of Business Perspective* 331.

particularly in terms of timelines for complaint resolution and mechanisms for follow-up. Additionally, Article 24 does not explicitly address whether the complaints and their resolutions will be monitored for systemic issues or patterns of misconduct by credit servicers or purchasers. This is important because although NPLs primarily fall under the domain of prudential supervision due to their implications for financial stability, it is vital not to sideline the equally critical objective of consumer protection. In an integrated supervisory model, authorities typically prioritise systemic stability over consumer protection, potentially diminishing the effectiveness of borrower protections envisioned by the Directive. The post-COVID-19 environment serves as an example: rising levels of over-indebtedness have led to an increase in NPLs, exposing the need for enhanced collaboration between prudential regulators and conduct authorities.[11] By incorporating debt management insights into policy frameworks and broadening regulatory objectives to encompass financial welfare, a more balanced and proactive approach can be achieved, addressing both financial stability and consumer protection concerns.

**24.07** The balancing of the two aspects of the issues is evident in Preamble (20) which reflects the need for borrowers to be treated fairly and with respect. As discussed above, Article 5(1)(e)(f)(g) outlines the protection of borrowers' rights as a key factor. Article 10 further specifies the expectations for the relationships between credit purchasers, credit servicers, and borrowers. In Article 17(2), measures are outlined to ensure borrowers' rights are upheld, particularly in the context of transferring non-performing credit agreements or creditors' rights to credit purchasers. Even in Article 22, when detailing the powers of competent authorities, the Directive establishes a framework to ensure that borrowers' rights are respected. It requires credit servicers to maintain robust internal governance and control mechanisms. Therefore, while the primary concern of the Directive is financial stability, it also aims to protect consumers and safeguard their legal rights. This demonstrates that the distinction between prudential regulators and conduct regulators is increasingly blurred in modern economic activities, especially in the context of NPLs management.

11 Iris Hse-Yu Chiu, Andreas Kokkinis and Andrea Miglionico, 'Addressing the Challenges of Post-pandemic Debt Management in the Consumer and SME Sectors: A Proposal for the Roles of UK Financial Regulators' (2022) 23 *Journal of Banking Regulation* 439, 443.

# ARTICLE 25

# PERSONAL DATA PROTECTION

**Andreas Kokkinis and Shunqi Yang**

**The processing of personal data for the purposes of this Directive shall be carried out in accordance with Regulations (EU) 2016/679 and (EU) 2018/1725.**



## A. INTRODUCTION

25.01 This article emphasises that personal data related to credit servicing must be processed in accordance with EU data protection standards, ensuring the privacy and security of individuals' personal data. The EU data protection framework grants individuals control over their personal data, fostering trust and accountability within the economy. The article references two key data protection regulations. The GDPR focuses on protecting individuals' rights to privacy, outlining how personal data should be collected, used, and shared. It applies to all Member States and governs both public and private entities processing personal data. According to the GDPR, these core principles include lawfulness, fairness, and transparency, requiring that data be processed in a manner that is both ethical and clear to individuals.[1] Purpose limitation mandates that data be collected for specific, legitimate purposes and not used beyond those objectives. Data minimisation ensures that only the data necessary for a given purpose is collected and processed, while accuracy requires that data be kept up-to-date and correct. Storage limitation restricts the retention of data to the period strictly necessary for its intended use. The principle of integrity and confidentiality emphasises the need for robust security

1 See Article 5 of the GDPR.

measures to protect data against unauthorised access, breaches, or loss. Finally, accountability holds data controllers and processors responsible for demonstrating compliance with these principles, fostering transparency and trust in data handling practices. Regulation (EU) 2018/1725 aligns with the GDPR principles but applies specifically to EU-level entities. Additionally, Directive 2009/136/EC (ePrivacy Directive) complements the GDPR by addressing privacy concerns in electronic communications, such as cookies, marketing, and online tracking.

**25.02** Article 25 highlights the intention to uphold the highest standards of data protection in the handling of information. Motivated by modern digital privacy concerns, the GDPR is rooted in the EU tradition of viewing data protection as a human right.[2] It transformed the landscape of personal data protection by imposing strict governance frameworks, emphasising data privacy as a fundamental right, and introducing stringent compliance mechanisms for businesses globally.[3] The GDPR is widely regarded as a law with global reach, lauded for its ability to balance privacy rights with economic considerations.[4] By imposing fines of up to 20 million euros or 4 per cent of a company's total worldwide revenues, it serves as a powerful regulatory tool.[5] This stringent enforcement framework promotes accountability among corporations, encouraging robust data protection measures. However, the significant compliance costs associated with the GDPR can disproportionately burden smaller organisations and those in less developed EU economies. In practice, its efficacy is challenged by implementation gaps, enforcement inconsistencies, and unintended economic consequences.[6]

---

2 Chris Jay Hoofnagle, Bart van der Sloot and Frederik Zuiderveen Borgesius, 'The European Union General Data Protection Regulation: What it is and What it Means' (2019) 28(1) *Information & Communications Technology Law* 65, 69.

3 Ibid., 67.

4 Paul M. Schwartz, 'Global Data Privacy: The EU Way' (2019) 94 *New York University Law Review* 771, 790.

5 GDPR, 83(5).

6 Wenlong Li, 'Mapping the Empirical Evidence of the GDPR's (In-)Effectiveness: A Systematic Review' (2023), https://ssrn.com/abstract=4615186. Implementation gaps result from ambiguity in legal requirements, such as the vague definitions of 'legitimate interests' and 'data minimisation', which create uncertainty for organisations attempting to comply. Furthermore, inconsistent implementation of rights like data access, erasure, and portability, often due to unclear guidelines, exacerbates these gaps. Enforcement inconsistencies arise from disparities in the resources and priorities of data protection authorities across Member States, with some authorities, such as Ireland's, struggling to manage large-scale cases against tech giants. The variation in fines, ranging from symbolic amounts to 50 million euros, and the preference for cooperative rather than adversarial enforcement approaches further weaken the regulation's uniform application. Unintended economic consequences include significant compliance costs that disproportionately burden small and medium-sized enterprises, which often lack the resources to meet the GDPR's rigorous requirements. Additionally, the regulation has been linked to a decline in the launch of new

## B. COMPLIANCE WITH DATA PROTECTION

Data protection in the context of credit servicing presents unique challenges. The sensitive nature of financial data, particularly regarding NPLs, necessitates careful handling. The information is especially sensitive when concerning borrowers who are unable to repay their loans, and it is crucial for companies involved in loan servicing or those purchasing distressed debt to take this into account. Mishandling such data can lead to severe consequences for borrowers, including financial fraud or identity theft. Data processing in this context is generally justified on the grounds of contractual necessity, as loan agreements often include clauses permitting data sharing with third parties for credit servicing purposes. NPLs are frequently sold to third-party credit purchasers or managed by external credit servicers, necessitating the transfer of borrower data. Ensuring compliance with the GDPR during these transfers is critical, including adherence to conditions for data minimisation, purpose limitation, and lawful data processing. **25.03**

Cross-border transfers of NPLs-related data raise additional concerns, particularly if the credit purchaser operates outside the EU and is hence not bound by the GDPR. Legitimate interests, such as compliance with financial regulations, may also justify processing. However, as the processing of personal data for managing NPLs is often justified under the 'legitimate interest' of the lender or credit purchaser, this can lead to challenges if borrowers perceive the processing as invasive or excessive, especially if it involves debt recovery practices. The management of personal data in the context of NPLs is fraught with challenges, particularly regarding data transfers, borrower transparency, and maintaining GDPR compliance. Credit purchasers and servicers must prioritise data security, respect borrower rights, and adopt transparent practices to navigate the complexities of handling sensitive financial information related to NPLs. **25.04**

digital services, termed the 'lost generation of innovative apps', and challenges in cross-border trade due to the GDPR's stringent adequacy requirements.

# ARTICLE 26

# COOPERATION BETWEEN COMPETENT AUTHORITIES

**Andreas Kokkinis and Shunqi Yang**

**1. Member States shall ensure that the competent authorities referred to in Articles 8, 13, 14, 15, 18, 20 and 22 cooperate with each other whenever necessary for the purpose of carrying out their functions and duties or of exercising their powers under the national provisions transposing this Directive. Those competent authorities shall also coordinate their actions in order to avoid possible duplication and overlap when applying supervisory powers and administrative penalties and remedial measures to cross-border cases.**

**2. Member States shall ensure that competent authorities, on request and without undue delay, provide each other with the information required for the purpose of carrying out their functions and duties under the national provisions transposing this Directive.**

**3. Member States shall ensure that competent authorities receiving confidential information in the exercise of their functions and duties under this Directive use that information only in the course of their functions and duties under the national provisions transposing this Directive. The exchange of information between competent authorities shall be subject to the obligation of professional secrecy referred to in Article 76 of Directive 2014/65/EU of the European Parliament and of the Council.[1]**

**4. Member States shall provide that all persons working, or who have worked, for the competent authorities and auditors or experts acting on behalf of the competent authorities are bound by the obligation of professional secrecy.**

**5. Member States shall take the necessary administrative and organisational measures to facilitate the cooperation provided for in this Article.**

**6. The EBA shall facilitate the exchange of information between competent authorities in the Member States and promote their cooperation.**

---

1 Directive 2014/65/EU of the European Parliament and of the Council of 15 May 2014 on markets in financial instruments and amending Directive 2002/92/EC and Directive 2011/61/EU (OJ L 173, 12.6.2014, p. 349).

## A. INTRODUCTION

This article establishes guidelines for cooperation between competent authorities responsible for supervising credit servicers, particularly in cross-border cases. It outlines how these authorities should coordinate, exchange information, and maintain confidentiality to fulfil their supervisory functions. Efficiency is essential to prevent conflicting actions or ineffective supervision in cases involving multiple jurisdictions. Therefore, a coordinated approach among various authorities is advocated in Article 26(1). One aspect of efficiency is timely access to information, as set out in Article 26(2). However, the emphasis on efficient information exchange should not come at the expense of abusing confidential information. It must instead be conducted in accordance with the obligation of professional secrecy, as outlined in Article 76 of Directive 2014/65/EU, which aims to achieve a more secure and efficient financial market, as specified in Article 26(3). As Article 23(5) extends enforcement measures to responsible individuals, anyone working for the competent authorities is also bound by the obligation of professional secrecy, as required in Article 26(4). This ensures that the confidentiality of sensitive information is maintained at every level of supervision. Member States are expected to create the necessary infrastructure to support cooperation among authorities. Article 26(5) advocates a proactive role for Member States in the NPLs regulatory regime. Finally, the European Banking Authority (EBA) is tasked with facilitating the exchange of information and promoting cooperation between competent authorities across Member States. In this role, the EBA can operate as a centralised, authoritative body that supports national authorities and contributes to the overall effectiveness and cooperation of the Directive. **26.01**

While earlier articles, such as Articles 21 and 22, touch on this topic, Article 26 provides more detailed rules, particularly concerning effective collaboration and information sharing. This article emphasises the need for effective collaboration across borders, which is critical in maintaining the stability of the financial system. This Directive was introduced in 2021 following the COVID-19 pandemic. By stressing the avoidance of duplication in the application of supervisory powers, penalties, or remedial measures, Article 26 seeks to streamline regulatory efforts, reduce administrative burdens, and enhance clarity for stakeholders, including credit purchasers and servicers. Timely information sharing is key, which should be achieved without compromising **26.02** sensitive information. The Directive refers to Directive 2014/65/EU (MiFID II) in terms of confidential information protection, which is crucial for maintaining trust among authorities and protecting sensitive borrower or financial institution data from misuse or unauthorised disclosure. Ensuring confidentiality and trust between competent authorities is always important, as the leak of sensitive data could damage financial stability or undermine enforcement actions. Cross-border cooperation often faces challenges because authorities may be reluctant to share too much, fearing that the information could be misused or inadvertently exposed.

## B. THE ROLE OF EBA

**26.03** Turning to the role of the EBA in Article 26(6), it is evident that its leading role in facilitating information sharing and cooperation in handling NPLs is highlighted. The EBA contributes to the European Single Rulebook, which provides a single set of harmonised prudential rules for financial institutions across the EU, as well as consumer protection, by promoting information transparency and fair treatment.[2] Before the introduction of the EBA, banking supervision in the EU was primarily managed at the national level. The banking failures that occurred after the 2008 financial crisis exposed the need for a coordinated mechanism to handle cross-border banking risks in the EU. The European Supervisory Authorities (ESAs), comprising EBA, European Securities and Markets Authority (ESMA), and European Insurance and Occupational Pensions Authority (EIOPA), established under the European System of Financial Supervision (ESFS), represent a move towards more integrated and harmonised financial supervision in the EU.[3] As part of that process, the EBA was established in 2011 through Regulation (EU) No 1093/2010 and was granted jurisdiction over all EU Member States.[4] It aims to support supervisory convergence and improve the functioning of the internal market.[5] The EBA collaborates with the SSM, which ensures consistency in supervision according to the Single Rulebook,[6] and the Single Resolution Mechanism (SRM), which implements the EBA's resolution guidelines to protect financial stability.[7] The European Commission published an action plan

2 EBA, 'Mission, Values and Tasks', https://www.eba.europa.eu/about-us/mission-values-and-tasks.

3 Niamh Moloney, *EU Securities and Financial Markets Regulation* (4th edn, Oxford University Press 2023) ch.1.

4 Regulation (EU) No 1093/2010.

5 Ibid., preamble (11).

6 Regulation (EU) No 468/2014.

7 Regulation (EU) No 806/2014.

to mitigate further financial deterioration caused by NPLs after the crisis.[8] There was an increased risk of borrowers defaulting on their loans during the financial crisis, and this inability to repay further impacted banks' profitability and their capacity to lend to real economy,[9] thereby slowing economic recovery and development.[10] The overall trend of NPLs in the EU decreased from 2019 to 2022 and remained relatively stable at around 2.3% in 2023 and 2024, before declining to 1.9% in Q4 2024.[11] However, disparities persisted among Member States. Countries with resilient banking sectors, such as Germany and the Netherlands, reported lower NPL ratios, while others, particularly those with historically weaker financial stability, such as Cyprus, continued to struggle with higher levels of distressed debt.[12] The transposition deadline was set for 29 December 2023. By that date, 74% of EU Member States—equivalent to 20 countries, including France, Germany, and Italy—had achieved full transposition of the NPL Directive. However, Spain and the Netherlands had not communicated any transposition measures.[13]

The involvement of the EBA as a coordinating body further underscores the **26.04** EU's commitment to a unified supervisory approach, enhancing trust and consistency across jurisdictions. The EBA has provided guidance on managing existing stocks of NPLs, supporting the development of secondary markets for their resolution by enhancing data availability, and strengthening the resilience of the financial system through loan origination guidelines aimed at improving the quality of future lending.[14] In the context of the COVID-19 pandemic, the EBA is dedicated to building the NPL framework by focusing on NPL data standardisation, enhancing data infrastructure and transparency

8 Directorate-General for Financial Stability and Financial Services and Capital Markets Union of the European Commission, 'Action Plan: Tackling Non-performing Loans (NPLs) in the Aftermath of the COVID-19 Pandemic', https://finance.ec.europa.eu/publications/action-plan-tackling-non-performing-loans-npls-aftermath-covid-19-pandemic_en.

9 EBA, 'NPLs', https://www.eba.europa.eu/legacy/risk-analysis-and-data/npls.

10 European Commission, 'Non-performing Loans (NPLs)', https://finance.ec.europa.eu/banking/non-performing-loans-npls_en.

11 European Central Bank (ECB), 'ECB Publishes Supervisory Banking Statistics on Significant Institutions for the Second Quarter of 2024' (23 September 2024), https://www.bde.es/f/webbe/GAP/Secciones/SalaPrensa/ComunicadosBCE/NotasInformativasBCE/24/presbce2024-96en.pdf, and ECB Data Portal, 'Non-performing Loans Ratio (Excluding Cash Balances at Central Banks and Other Demand Deposits), SIs, EU Countries Participating in the Single Supervisory Mechanism (SSM) (Changing Composition), Quarterly', https://data.ecb.europa.eu/data/datasets/SUP/SUP.Q.B01.W0._Z.I7005._T.SII._Z._Z._Z.PCT.C?chart_props.

12 Eurostat, 'Contingent Liabilities and Non-performing Loans in 2023' (31 January 2025), https://ec.europa.eu/eurostat/web/products-eurostat-news/w/ddn-2025013.

13 European Commission, 'Transposition Status – Credit Servicers and Credit Purchasers Directive', https://finance.ec.europa.eu/credit-servicers-and-credit-purchasers-directive_en.

14 EBA (n 9).

in NPL markets, and promoting the sharing of supervisory practices in monitoring banks' NPL management and resolution. Particular attention is given to balancing prudential objectives with consumer protection obligations, as explicitly reflected in the Directive.[15] However, the role of the EBA is limited, as it lacks direct supervisory powers and primarily provides technical standards and mediates disputes.[16] Furthermore, the EBA's position within the EU's multilevel regulatory governance system hampers its effectiveness as a regulatory authority due to a lack of credibility, legitimacy, and transparency.[17]

**26.05** The Single Rulebook has addressed regulatory fragmentation in the EU banking system by harmonising standards, but its implementation faces challenges, including a complex multi-tiered structure, partially harmonised areas, and national discretions that may undermine the uniformity it aims to achieve.[18] In this context, while Article 26 stresses the importance of cooperation between competent authorities, it remains somewhat preliminary. Despite these limitations, the EBA's true strength seems to lie in its ability to foster regulatory convergence and uphold the Single Market's integrity through collaboration. Instead of serving as a potential frontline supervisor, the effectiveness of the EBA lies in preserving the integrity of the Single Market through collaborative governance and fostering regulatory convergence between SSM and non-SSM states rather than direct intervention.[19] Article 26 emphasises the EBA's facilitative function, which aligns with its strengths and the tools under its current mandate, allowing it to issue regulatory technical standards and guidelines while synthesising information from national authorities. To enhance its impact, the EBA must address resource constraints and effectively mediate between diverse institutional actors,[20] a step that could significantly benefit NPLs governance.

---

15 The EBA has published policies on NPL-related issues, including Implementing Technical Standards on NPL transaction data templates, Guidelines on the management of non-performing and forborne exposures, Guidelines on loan origination and monitoring, and a Report on the Statutory Prudential Backstop. EBA (n 9), Opinion on the regulatory treatment of NPE securitization.

16 Guido Ferrarini, 'Single Supervision and the Governance of Banking Markets' (2015) European Corporate Governance Institute – Law Working Paper No. 294/2015, 11, http://dx.doi.org/10.2139/ssrn.2604074.

17 David Coen and John-Paul Salter, 'Multilevel Regulatory Governance: Establishing Bank-Regulator Relationships at the European Banking Authority' (2020) 22(1) *Business and Politics* 113, 122.

18 Valia Babis, 'The Single Rulebook and the European Banking Authority' in Federico Fabbrini and Marco Ventoruzzo (eds), *Research Handbook in European Economic Law* (Edward Elgar 2019) 262–263.

19 Eilís Ferran, 'The Existential Search of the European Banking Authority' (2016) 17 *European Business Organization Law Review* 285, 290 and 303.

20 Ibid., 288.

# TITLE VI

# AMENDMENTS

# ARTICLE 27

# AMENDMENTS TO DIRECTIVE 2008/48/EC

**Andrea Miglionico**

**Directive 2008/48/EC is amended as follows:**

**(1) the following article is inserted:**

**'Article 11a**

**Information regarding the modification of the terms and conditions of a credit agreement**

**Without prejudice to other obligations provided for in this Directive, Member States shall ensure that prior to modifying the terms and conditions of the credit agreement, the creditor communicates the following information to the consumer:**

**(a) a clear description of the proposed changes and, where applicable, of the need for consumer consent or of the changes introduced by operation of law;**

**(b) the timescale for the implementation of the changes referred to in point (a);**

**(c) the means for complaint available to the consumer regarding the changes referred to in point (a);**

**(d) the time period available for lodging any such complaint;**

**(e) the name and address of the competent authority to which the consumer can submit that complaint';**

**(2) the following article is inserted:**

**'Article 16a**

**Arrears and enforcement**

**1. Member States shall require creditors to have adequate policies and procedures so that they make efforts to exercise, where appropriate, reasonable forbearance before enforcement proceedings are initiated. Such forbearance measures shall take into account, among other elements, the consumer's circumstances and may consist of, among other possibilities:**

**(a) a total or partial refinancing of a credit agreement;**

**(b) a modification of the existing terms and conditions of a credit agreement, which may include among others:**

**(i) extending the term of the credit agreement;**

**(ii) changing the type of credit agreement;**

**(iii) deferring payment of all or part of the instalment repayment for a period;**
**(iv) changing the interest rate;**
**(v) offering a payment holiday;**
**(vi) partial repayments;**
**(vii) currency conversions;**
**(viii) partial forgiveness and debt consolidation.**

**2. The list of potential forbearance measures set out in point (b) of paragraph 1 is without prejudice to rules set out in national law and does not require Member States to provide for all of those measures in their national law.**

**3. Member States may require that, where the creditor is permitted to define and impose charges on the consumer arising from the default, those charges are no greater than is necessary to compensate the creditor for costs it has incurred as a result of the default.**

**4. Member States may allow creditors to impose additional charges on the consumer in the event of default. In that case, Member States shall place a cap on those charges'**

**(3) Article 22(1) is replaced by the following:**

**'Insofar as this Directive contains harmonised provisions, Member States may not maintain or introduce in their national law provisions diverging from those laid down in this Directive. However, Article 16a(3) and (4) shall not preclude Member States from maintaining or introducing more stringent provisions in order to protect consumers'**



## A. INTRODUCTION

27.01 The article regulates specific amendments to Directive 2008/48/EC on credit agreements for consumers – the Consumer Credit Directive (CCD)[1] by amending the Consumer Code and in particular by providing for the communication of information to consumers in the event of changes to the terms and conditions of agreements, as well as new provisions on late payment and

1 The directive harmonises EU rules regarding credit granted to consumers who borrow to finance purchases of goods and services (holidays, goods, new cars, etc.). It aims to open up the EU's consumer loan market, whilst improving the transparency of contract terms and the level of consumer protection. The directive was replaced by Directive (EU) 2023/2225 – which applies to credit agreements whereby consumers borrow money to buy goods and services – although it will remain valid until 20 November 2026.

late performance.[2] The Consumer Code sets out certain requirements for lenders relating notably to (i) the obligation to provide certain information prior to the amendment of the terms and conditions of a credit agreement and (ii) the exercise, where appropriate, of reasonable forbearance before enforcement proceedings are initiated. According to these amendments, a new Article 11a has been added stating that prior to modifying the terms and conditions of the credit agreement, the creditor must communicate information to the consumer on the proposed changes, the complaint option and the respective competent authority details. Article 11a regulates complaint procedures for consumers which should align with the European Banking Authority (EBA) Guidelines on complaints handling by credit servicers under CSD.[3] The Guidelines suggest applying to credit servicers the requirements of the existing Joint Committee Guidelines on complaints-handling. Those requirements include complaints management policy, complaints management function, registration, reporting, internal follow-up, provision of information and procedures for responding to complaints. Another amendment to the CCD is the addition of a new Article 16a which requires creditors to have adequate policies and procedures to exercise reasonable forbearance before any foreclosure proceedings are initiated. Moreover, such forbearance measures would need to consider a series of options such as the refinancing of the credit agreement or the modification of the existing terms.

**27.02** The article provides amendments to the Consumer Credit Directive to address the transparency of credit agreement modifications and the effective functioning of the forbearance framework. Article 11a of the CCD will require that creditors communicate specific information to a consumer before modifying the terms and conditions of a credit agreement. The set of information includes: a clear and comprehensive description of the proposed changes; a timescale for the implementation of the changes; and mechanisms by which the consumer may make a complaint relating to the changes. The new Article 16a of the CCD will require creditors (i.e., credit purchasers) to have adequate policies and procedures so they can exercise, where appropriate, reasonable forbearance before initiating enforcement proceedings. This article provides additional requirements regarding forbearance measures before enforcement proceedings with particular focus on the consumer's circumstances. Specifically, it requires creditors to balance policies and procedures

2 Consumer credit is a loan instrument which allows consumers to purchase consumer goods and services for which they do not have the funds.

3 See 'Final Report on EBA Guidelines Amending Joint Committee Guidelines on Complaints Handling for the Securities (ESMA) and Banking (EBA) Sectors' (24 July 2024), EBA/GL/2024/12.

with respect to the terms and conditions of a credit agreement. It has been noted that 'the improved protection that strikes a new balance in the creditor-consumer relationship is expected to foster the establishment of a trans-border credit market'.[4] Creditors need to exercise reasonable forbearance and take into consideration conditions of vulnerability which may affect consumers in the credit agreement.[5] Forbearance measures should aim to return the borrower to a sustainable performing repayment status, taking into account the amount due and minimising expected losses. When deciding on which steps or forbearance measures to take, credit institutions should take into account the interests of consumers and comply with consumer protection requirements, including those set out in Article 28 of Directive 2014/17/EU and in the EBA Guidelines on arrears and foreclosure.[6] Credit institutions should monitor the efficiency and effectiveness of forbearance activities.

## B. THE AMENDMENTS TO THE CONSUMER CREDIT DIRECTIVE

A consumer credit contract is an agreement between an individual (the debtor) **27.03** and any other person (the creditor) by which the creditor provides the debtor with credit of any amount. A creditor grants or promises to grant credit to a consumer in the form of a loan or other financial accommodation. Forms of consumer credit include credit card, charge card, personal loan, overdraft, high-cost, short-term loan, credit linked to the acquisition of a new good or service, leasing and hire purchase. Consumer credit agreements (where credit is granted to an individual) include unsecured loans, credit cards and hire purchase. The EU rules on consumer credit strengthen consumers' rights and support them in making informed decisions. The legislation was introduced to prevent irresponsible lending by introducing an obligation on creditors to perform an assessment of the creditworthiness of the consumer before issuing credit. The CCD 2008 was replaced by the CCD II 2023, which strengthened rules for consumer protection such as reasonable forbearance measures and

4 Marie-Astrid Huemer, 'Revision of Directive 2008/48/EC on Credit Agreements for Consumers' (June 2021) European Parliamentary Research Service https://www.europarl.europa.eu/RegData/etudes/BRIE/2021/694204/EPRS_BRI(2021)694204_EN.pdf.

5 Sara Fernández-López, Marcos Álvarez-Espiño, Lucía Rey-Ares and Sandra Castro-González, 'Consumer Financial Vulnerability: Review, Synthesis, and Future Research Agenda' (2024) 38(4) *Journal of Economic Surveys* 1045.

6 EBA, 'Final Report on Guidelines Amending Guidelines EBA/GL/2015/12 on Arrears and Foreclosure' (28 June 2024) EBA/GL/2024/10, https://eba.europa.eu/activities/single-rulebook/regulatory-activities/consumer-protection-and-financial-innovation/guidelines-arrears-and-foreclosure.

revised provisions on enforcement.[7] The CCD II aims to enhance responsible consumer lending and credit products to reduce potential risks of detriment for borrowers. Consumer lending practices should determine whether the borrower is likely to be able to repay without incurring substantial financial harm. Responsible lender indicators are to define what is an acceptable default rate within a risk pool for all credit providers and set up a mechanism to monitor default rates across the industry and identify statistical outliers which may indicate predatory lending practices.[8] In this context, Member States shall introduce measures to effectively prevent abuse and to ensure that consumers cannot be charged with excessively high borrowing rates. They may adopt prohibitions or limitations regarding specific charges or fees applied by creditors on their territory. Forbearance measures and enforcement procedures should not discriminate against consumers in the credit agreements. The borrower has the right to be informed of the eventual assignment of the credit, the consequent change in the creditor and the legal effects of the assignment prior to the conclusion of the contract.[9] This right extends to the precontractual information the creditor must provide before the conclusion of the contract.

**27.04** Given the significant consequences of enforcement proceedings for creditors and consumers, the CCD requires creditors to proactively deal with emerging credit risk at an early stage and to put in place necessary measures to ensure they exercise reasonable forbearance and make reasonable attempts to resolve the situation through other means before enforcement proceedings are initiated.[10] Enforcement proceedings should be seen as a last resort for both creditors and consumers and against this backdrop, the CCD requires creditors to exercise reasonable forbearance measures and make attempts to resolve the situation through other means. Forbearance may include extending the term of the credit agreement, changing the type of the credit agreement, partially

---

7 Olha O. Cherednychenko and Jesse M. Meindertsma, 'Irresponsible Lending in the Post-Crisis Era: Is the EU Consumer Credit Directive Fit for Its Purpose?' (2019) 42(4) *Journal of Consumer Policy* 483.

8 See Financial Services User Group, 'Responsible Consumer Credit Lending' (April 2029), FSUG opinion and recommendations for the review of the Consumer Credit Directive, https://finance.ec.europa.eu/system/files/2019-04/fsug-opinions-190408-responsible-consumer-credit-lending_en.pdf.

9 Héctor Simón-Moreno and Padraic Kenna, 'Protecting Homeloan Borrowers in the Emerging EU Secondary Market for Non-performing Loans' (2025) 17(1) *Journal of Property, Planning and Environmental Law*, https://doi.org/10.1108/JPPEL-07-2024–0028.

10 Forbearance is an exceptional arrangement between a lender and a borrower to postpone any enforcement proceedings. In a forbearance agreement, lenders and borrowers agree on forbearance measures to help borrowers, especially vulnerable ones, get back on track. Forbearance measures are a total or partial refinancing of a credit agreement, extending the term of the credit agreement or changing the type of the credit agreement. See Peter Norwood and Rita Antar, 'Tackling Causes of Over-indebtedness in the EU Consumer Credit Market' (March 2022) Finance Watch Policy Brief, p. 24.

or totally deferring payments of instalments for a period, reducing the borrowing rate or the total or partial refinancing of the credit agreement. In addition, Member States may allow creditors to impose charges on consumers who default on payment and in doing so they may also require that such charges are no greater than necessary to compensate the creditor for costs which it has incurred due to the default. The national legislator is also given discretion to decide whether to allow creditors to impose additional charges on the consumer in the event of default. However, if such a practice is allowed, Member States must necessarily put in place caps on those charges. Ample discretion is given to the Member States to shape their laws relating to arrears, default and forbearance and creditors also have considerable discretion; creditors will arguably need to revisit their forbearance policies as well as their practices vis-à-vis a defaulting consumer.[11]

11 Catherine Formosa and Kelly Cini, 'The Consumer Credit Directive Revamped' (3 January 2024), https://chambers.com/articles/the-consumer-credit-directive-revamped.

# ARTICLE 28

# AMENDMENTS TO DIRECTIVE 2014/17/EU

**Andrea Miglionico**

**Directive 2014/17/EU is amended as follows:**

**(1) the following article is inserted:**

**'Article 27a**

**Information regarding the modification of the terms and conditions of a credit agreement**

**Without prejudice to other obligations provided for in this Directive, Member States shall ensure that, prior to modifying the terms and conditions of the credit agreement, the creditor communicates the following information to the consumer:**

**(a) a clear description of the proposed changes and, where applicable, of the need for consumer consent or of the changes introduced by operation of law;**

**(b) the timescale for the implementation of the changes referred to in point (a);**

**(c) the means for complaint available to the consumer regarding the changes referred to in point (a);**

**(d) the time period available for lodging any such complaint;**

**(e) the name and address of the competent authority to which the consumer can submit that complaint';**

**(2) Article 28 is amended as follows:**

**(a) paragraph 1 is replaced by the following:**

**'1. Member States shall require creditors to have adequate policies and procedures so that they make efforts to exercise, where appropriate, reasonable forbearance before foreclosure proceedings are initiated. Such forbearance measures shall take into account, among other elements, the consumer's circumstances and may consist of, among other possibilities:**

**(a) a total or partial refinancing of a credit agreement;**

**(b) a modification of the existing terms and conditions of a credit agreement, which may include among others:**

**(i) extending the term of the credit agreement;**

**(ii) changing the type of credit agreement;**

**(iii) deferring payment of all or part of the instalment repayment for a period;**

**(iv) changing the interest rate;**
**(v) offering a payment holiday;**
**(vi) partial repayments;**
**(vii) currency conversions;**
**(viii) partial forgiveness and debt consolidation';**

**(b) the following paragraph is inserted:**

**'1. The list of potential forbearance measures set out in point (b) of paragraph 1 is without prejudice to the rules set out in national law and does not require Member States to provide for all of those measures in their national law';**

**(3) the following article is inserted:**

**'Article 28a**

**Assignment of the creditor's rights or of the credit agreement itself**

**1. In the event of an assignment to a third party of the creditor's rights under a credit agreement, or of the credit agreement itself, the consumer shall be entitled to plead against the assignee any defence which was available to the consumer as against the original creditor, including set-off where the latter is permitted in the Member State concerned.**

**2. The consumer shall be informed of an assignment referred to in paragraph 1, except where the original creditor, by agreement with the assignee, continues to service the credit vis-à-vis the consumer'**



## A. INTRODUCTION

This article provides relevant amendments to the EU Mortgage Credit Directive (MCD).[1] Specifically, the NPLs Directive makes revisions to Article 27 of the MCD, introducing a new Article 27a which requires that creditors communicate specific information to a consumer before modifying the terms and conditions of a credit agreement. This information includes: a clear and comprehensive description of the proposed changes; a timescale for the implementation of the changes; and mechanisms by which the consumer may make **28.01**

1 Directive 2014/17/EU of the European Parliament and of the Council of 4 February 2014 on credit agreements for consumers relating to residential immovable property and amending Directives 2008/48/EC and 2013/36/EU and Regulation (EU) No 1093/2010. The MCD was adopted on 4 February 2014 as part of the EU's efforts to create a single market for mortgages, and against the background of the global financial crisis. The Directive was amended by Regulation 2016/1011/EU on indices used as benchmarks in financial instruments and financial contracts or to measure the performance of investment funds.

a complaint relating to the changes. The NPLs Directive also amends Article 28 of the MCD, which requires creditors (i.e., credit purchasers) to have adequate policies and procedures so they can exercise, where appropriate, reasonable forbearance before initiating enforcement proceedings. A new Article 28a of the MCD is inserted which provides that, where there is an assignment to a third party of the creditor's rights under an agreement covered by the MCD, the consumer is entitled to plead against the credit purchaser any defence that was available to them against the original creditor. It also creates an obligation for the consumer to be informed about an assignment. According to the EU Commission Report, consumers are considered the weakest party of transactions with service providers in terms of access to relevant information on products and services.[2] This position is often exacerbated by behavioural issues such as cognitive bias relating to systematic errors in processing and interpreting information which affect consumers' decisions. The MCD aims to address this by ensuring that consumers receive appropriate information enabling them to make informed decisions. The MCD provides clear direction as to the granting or not of the loan depending on the outcome of the creditworthiness assessment, which represents a valuable tool to ensure responsible lending and consumer protection.[3]

**28.02** The MCD regulates arrears and foreclosures to encourage creditors to deal with emerging credit risk at an early stage and to make reasonable attempts to resolve the situation before initiating foreclosure proceedings. The economic impact of COVID-19 posed a risk that an increasing number of consumers would be unable to meet their financial commitments and might become over-indebted.[4] The MCD has contributed to raising the overall level of consumer protection in the EU, in particular by establishing a minimal level of protection in all Member States.[5] The MCD promotes cross-border trade in mortgage credits and a single market by providing a degree of harmonisation in the requirements for mortgage services.[6] It also increases customer mobility, unhindered access to databases in the creditworthiness assessment, the

---

2 EU Commission, 'Report from the Commission to the European Parliament and the Council on the Review of the Directive 2014/17/EU of the European Parliament and of the Council on Credit Agreements for Consumers Relating to Residential Immovable Property' COM(2021) 229 final, p. 4.

3 Christina K. Livada, 'Assessment of Consumers' Creditworthiness' (2019) 20(2) *ERA Forum* 225–226.

4 Arien van 't Hof, 'The First Years of the Creditworthiness Assessment Under the Mortgage Credit Directive: Is it Enough?' (2021) 10(1) *Journal of European Consumer and Market Law* 4–5.

5 Commission (note 2) 8.

6 Tatjana Josipović, 'Consumer Protection in EU Residential Mortgage Markets: Common EU Rules on Mortgage Credit in the Mortgage Credit Directive' (2017) 16 *Cambridge Yearbook of European Legal Studies* 223–224.

guarantee of responsible lending by credit providers, intermediaries and non-credit institutions and effective enforcement.[7] Article 27 of the MCD aims at predictability and transparency of the credit intermediaries. The creditor shall inform the consumer of any change in the borrowing rate, on paper or another durable medium, before the change takes effect. The information shall at least state the amount of the payments to be made after the new borrowing rate takes effect and, in cases where the number or frequency of the payments changes. If this is not possible because changes in the borrowing rate are determined by way of auction on the capital markets, the creditor shall, in good time before the auction, inform the consumer on paper or on another durable medium of the upcoming procedure and provide an indication of how the borrowing rate could be affected.[8]

## B. AMENDMENTS TO THE MORTGAGE CREDIT DIRECTIVE

The MCD defined the EU's framework of conduct rules for mortgage firms:[9] it applies to first and second charge mortgages. The MCD achieved three main policy objectives. Firstly, the MCD expanded the territorial scope of the regulatory regime for mortgage lending to consumers so that it includes lending secured by a mortgage on residential property in other European Economic Area states as well as in the UK. Secondly, charge mortgages allow the borrower to use any equity they may have in their home as security against another loan. The MCD moved second charge mortgage lending into the same regulatory regime as first charge mortgage lending. Thirdly, the MCD allows EU Member States to exempt buy-to-let lending from the conduct rules of the Directive; however, it requires that Member States exercising this derogation put in place an appropriate regulatory framework at a national level regulating consumer buy-to-let lending. **28.03**

The MCD contains mandatory rules on arrears, foreclosure and enforcement of claims. There are no strict rules applying to charges imposed on consumers in default. Member States may limit those charges to the amount that is necessary to compensate the creditor for costs it has incurred as a result of the default. However, they may allow creditors to impose additional charges on **28.04**

7 Vanessa Mak, 'Stretching the Borders of EU Law? – Full Harmonisation in the Consumer Credit Directive and Mortgage Credit' (2013) 2(1) *Journal of European Consumer and Market Law* 37–38.

8 Diederik Bruloot, Evariest Callens and Michiel De Muynck, 'Credit Intermediation and the European Internal Market for Mortgage Credit' (2019) 13(1) *Law and Financial Markets Review* 41–42.

9 Jorge Morais Carvalho and Kristin Nemeth, 'Implementation of the Mortgage Credit Directive in the EU Member States' (2017) 6(3) *European Consumer and Market Law* 131.

the consumer in the event of default but shall place a cap on those charges if they do so. Further, Member States shall not prevent the parties to a credit agreement from expressly agreeing that the return or transfer to the creditor of the security or proceeds from the sale of the security is sufficient to repay the credit. Regarding forbearance, Member States shall adopt measures to encourage creditors to exercise reasonable forbearance before foreclosure proceedings are initiated. According to Article 28(5), where the price obtained for the immovable property affects the amount owed by the consumer, Member States shall have procedures or measures to enable the best efforts price for the foreclosed immovable property to be obtained.

**28.05** Forbearance is considered the restructuring of troubled loans.[10] The International Financial Reporting Standards (IFRS) 9 ('Financial Instruments'), which replaced the International Accounting Standard (IAS) principle 39, regulates the recognition of expected credit losses.[11] According to the IFRS 9, forbearance should not lead to avoiding or postponing the recognition of impairment or obscuring the level of credit risk resulting from forborne assets. The IAS 39 made clear that restructuring is a credit event that might lead to impairment, and impairments have to be calculated based on the difference between the original and modified conditions. The standard does not rule out the possibility that restructuring might not involve impairment and there is ambiguity about whether a loan that has been restructured should forever be identified as impaired.[12] Consequently, lenders can choose to extend or otherwise modify the terms of loans that show evidence of financial stress. These loans might avoid arrears and as such might not be identified as impaired (or non-performing), despite underlying credit deterioration of the borrower. The existence of large-scale avoidance of arrears through forbearance (sometimes known as "extend and pretend") therefore might be invisible to regulators, investors and other users of financial statements. In 2014, the

---

10 In 2011 the UK Financial Services Authority (FSA) issued a guidance document on loan forbearance, noting that "we have concerns that certain accounting practices can have the effect of concealing the full effect of impairment and forbearance and thus may not present the true nature of credit risk within retail portfolios". See Financial Services Authority, 'Forbearance and Impairment Provisions – Mortgages. FSA Finalised Guidance' (October 2011), https://www.fca.org.uk/publication/finalised-guidance/fg11_15.pdf. Similar concerns were raised the same year in the US when the accounting standard-setter clarified its guidance around the definition of troubled debt restructurings (incidentally a term used only in US accounting), with the aim of developing more consistent standards in determining whether a modification of a loan receivable constitutes a concession to a borrower that is experiencing financial difficulty.

11 See https://www.ifrs.org/content/dam/ifrs/publications/pdf-standards/english/2021/issued/part-a/ifrs-9-financial-instruments.pdf.

12 See https://www.ifrs.org/content/dam/ifrs/publications/pdf-standards/english/2021/issued/part-a/ias-39-financial-instruments-recognition-and-measurement.pdf.

European Banking Authority (EBA) published technical standards for the reporting of non-performing loans and forbearance at an EU-level.[13] The EBA document provides the definition of "exposure", "non-performing exposures" and "forborne exposures". The European Central Bank (ECB) produced draft guidance on non-performing loans that build on the EBA criteria, including consideration of how the "unlikely to pay" criterion should be applied in practice, and how banks should manage and monitor forbearance, write-offs and collateral valuation.[14] In 2016, the Basel Committee on Banking Supervision provides a definition of forbearance as "a concession granted by a bank to a counterparty for reasons of financial difficulties that would not be otherwise considered by the lender".[15] Specifically, forbearance comprises concessions extended to any exposures in the form of a loan, a debt security or an off-balance-sheet item due to the position of the counterparty. This definition covers exposures of performing and non-performing status before the granting of forbearance measures. The main purpose is to ensure a harmonised approach to the disclosure of modified loans and debt securities due to the case of the borrower's financial difficulties.

13 EBA, 'FINAL Draft Implementing Technical Standards on Supervisory Reporting on Forbearance and Non-performing Exposures under Article 99(4) of Regulation (EU) No 575/2013' (2014), https://eba.europa.eu/implementing-technical-standard-supervisory-reporting-forbearance-and-non-performing-exposures.

14 ECB, 'Guidance to Banks on Non-performing Loans' (March 2017), https://www.bankingsupervision.europa.eu/ecb/pub/pdf/guidance_on_npl.en.pdf.

15 Basel Committee on Banking Supervision, 'Guidelines for Prudential Treatment of Problem Assets – Definitions of Non-performing Exposures and Forbearance' (2016) Consultative Document, http://www.bis.org/bcbs/publ/d367.htm.

# TITLE VII

# FINAL PROVISIONS

# ARTICLE 29

# COMMITTEE

**Andrea Miglionico**

1. **The Commission shall be assisted by a committee. That committee shall be a committee within the meaning of Regulation (EU) No 182/2011 of the European Parliament and of the Council.[1]**
2. **Where reference is made to this paragraph, Article 4 of Regulation (EU) No 182/2011 shall apply.**



## A. COMMITTEES' ROLE IN EUROPEAN COMMISSION'S IMPLEMENTING POWERS

This article refers to rules and general principles concerning mechanisms for control by Member States of the Commission's exercise of implementing powers (the so-called comitology regulation).[2] Before adopting implementing acts, the European Commission has to consult a committee comprising representatives of each of the EU countries on the draft that it is proposing. Comitology applies when the Commission has been granted implementing powers in the text of a law.[3] The Commission needs to be assisted by a committee **29.01**

1 Regulation (EU) No 182/2011 of the European Parliament and of the Council of 16 February 2011 laying down the rules and general principles concerning mechanisms for control by Member States of the Commission's exercise of implementing powers (OJ L 55, 28.2.2011, p. 13).

2 Christos Gortsos, 'The "Comitology Procedure" Under the European Parliament and Council Regulation (EU) No 182/2011 and its Importance for EU Banking Law' (2016) ECEFIL Working Paper Series No 2016/14, p. 16, https://ssrn.com/abstract=2716026.

3 Alexander H. Türk, 'Comitology' in Damian Chalmers and Anthony Arnull (eds), *The Oxford Handbook of European Union Law* (Oxford: Oxford University Press 2015) 327–328.

when defining the measures contained in the resulting implementing act.[4] Comitology committees are set up by the Council and European Parliament (or Council alone): they include one representative from every EU country and are chaired by a Commission official. Each committee decides its operating procedures, based on standard committee rules of procedure. Commission departments submit draft implementing acts to the responsible committees for an opinion. Most committees meet several times a year in Commission premises. Before each meeting, the Commission sends national authorities the invitation, agenda and draft implementing act. After the meeting, the Commission publishes the voting results and the summary record of the meeting in the comitology register. The Commission publishes an annual report on the work of the comitology committees, which details their activities in each policy sector. If the Commission is prevented from adopting a proposed implementing act (particularly where the comitology committee voted against it), it can refer the case to the appeal committee. The appeal committee functions in a similar way to the other comitology committees: it is made up of EU countries' representatives but at a higher level of representation. It is chaired by the Commission and follows the same voting rules. It gives EU countries the opportunity to have a second discussion. If the appeal committee rules against the Commission's proposed implementing act, the Commission must abide by its decision. In addition to EU member countries through the comitology committees, the Commission's implementing powers are also subject to supplementary checks by the European Parliament and EU Council, which have a right of information – all proposed Commission actions discussed in the committees are simultaneously disclosed to Parliament and Council; right of scrutiny – where Commission actions relate to a legislative act passed by the ordinary legislative procedure, Parliament and Council can object to the proposed implementing act if it exceeds the Commission's powers defined in the initial act. The Commission is then obliged to review its proposed act in the light of this input and decide whether to maintain, amend or withdraw it.

**29.02** Paragraph 2 of the provision refers to Article 4 of the Regulation No. 182/2011, which regulates the 'advisory procedure'. A comitology committee that comprises representatives of all member states and which must be consulted by the European Commission on proposals for implementing acts to be adopted using the advisory procedure. According to this procedure, votes are taken by

4 Paul P. Craig, 'Delegated Acts, Implementing Acts and the New Comitology Regulation' (2011) 36(5) *European Law Review* 671.

simple majority (i.e. 14 out of 27 Member States). The committee's opinion is not binding on the Commission, although it is obliged to take the 'utmost account' of the opinion and conclusions of the discussions in committee.[5] At this stage, the Council could have decided on the basis of non-binding criteria which committee proceedings had to be applied, but the advisory procedure is set as the rule. Having this procedure as a general rule, it would be easier to adopt implementing measures. As argued, 'Member States are put at a disadvantage, as under this procedure they have no relevant impact on the adoption of implementing measures and cannot prevent them, in the other hand the Commission has gained an unjustified power'.[6] The European Parliament and the Council have a right of scrutiny. Where the basic act has been adopted under the co-decision procedure, the European Parliament or the Council may at any time inform the European Commission that it considers the proposed implementing act to exceed the powers conferred on it. In such a case, the European Commission must review the draft act and decide whether to maintain, amend or withdraw it. The advisory procedure applies as a general rule to the adoption of implementing acts in other fields (such as individual measures in the field of culture).[7] The advisory procedure is used for any implementing act that is not subject to the examination procedure. This procedure is used when policy matters considered are not very sensitive politically. The advisory committee is chaired by a Commission official. The advisory procedure should be used with respect to any objections to harmonised standards and where the references to the harmonised standard concerned have not yet been published in the Official Journal of the European Union.

### B. PROCEDURES FOR CONTROL BY MEMBER STATES OF THE COMMISSION'S EXERCISE OF IMPLEMENTING POWERS

The regulation lays down the rules for the control by EU countries of the exer- **29.03**
cise by the Commission of its implementing powers (Article 291 of the Treaty

5 The advisory committee's opinion is not decisive. See Rafał Mańko, 'Reform of the Comitology Regulation' (March 2021) European Parliamentary Research Service, https://www.europarl.europa.eu/RegData/etudes/BRIE/2021/689360/EPRS_BRI(2021)689360_EN.pdf.

6 European Foundation, 'Reformed "Comitology", the Route to a Dominating EC' (10 January 2011), https://europeanfoundation.org/the-reform-of-the-comitology-procedure-has-given-more-powers-to-the-european-commission/.

7 European Parliament, 'Mechanisms for Control by Member States of the Commission's Exercise of Implementing Powers, "Comitology Regulation"' (16 February 2011), https://oeil.secure.europarl.europa.eu/oeil/en/document-summary?id=1143972.

on the Functioning of the European Union (TFEU)).[8] This control is known as 'comitology' procedures, i.e. the Commission must submit each draft implementing act to committees consisting of EU countries' representatives and chaired by the Commission. The regulation lays down two procedures for controlling the Commission's exercise of its implementing powers (granted by the legislator). The examination procedure, which is mainly used for: (i) measures of general scope and (ii) measures in certain policy fields (for example, agriculture, fisheries, environment, health, trade and taxation). Commission implementing acts must receive the support of a qualified majority of the committee.[9] If the committee gives an unfavourable opinion, the Commission may submit the draft act to an appeal committee to see whether the examination of the measure should continue or amend the text. If the outcome of the committee discussions is a 'no opinion', the Commission may adopt the draft act under certain conditions. The advisory procedure is generally used for all other implementing measures. When the basic legislative act has been adopted under the ordinary legislative procedure (the most common decision-making procedure, covering the majority of policy areas, and in which the European Parliament and the Council have equal weight), the European Parliament or the Council may at any time inform the Commission that it considers the proposed implementing act to exceed the powers conferred on the Commission. In such cases, the Commission must review the draft act and decide to maintain, amend or withdraw it.

**29.04** A comitology committee that comprises representatives of all member states and which must give an opinion on European Commission proposals for

---

8 According to Article 291(2) of the TFEU, if legally binding EU acts need uniform conditions to implement them across the EU, the act must empower the Commission (or the Council, in certain, limited circumstances) to adopt implementing acts. The act that empowers the Commission (or occasionally the Council) to adopt implementing acts is known as the 'parent act' or sometimes the 'basic act' or 'framework act'. The adoption of implementing acts is driven by the Commission. The Commission's powers are controlled by member states giving opinions on draft implementing acts prepared by the Commission in formal committees, rather than by representatives in the Council or the European Parliament. See Gijs Jan Brandsma and Jens Blom-Hansen, 'Controlling Delegated Powers in the Post-Lisbon European Union' (2016) 23(4) *Journal of European Public Policy* 531.

9 If a qualified majority (55% of EU countries representing at least 65% of the total EU population) votes in favour of the proposed implementing act, the Commission must adopt it. If a qualified majority votes against the proposed act, the Commission may not adopt it. If there is no qualified majority either for or against the proposed act, the Commission can either adopt it or submit a new, amended version. Three scenarios can be identified in that regard: (1) adoption of a positive opinion by the committee (endorsing the draft implementing act); (2) adoption of a negative opinion by the committee (rejecting the draft implementing act); (3) no-opinion scenario (lack of a qualified majority to support a negative or positive opinion within the deadline set). See Katrijn Siderius and Gijs Jan Brandsma, 'The Effect of Removing Voting Rules: Consultation Practices in the Commission's Delegated Act Expert Groups and Comitology Committees' (2016) 54(6) *Journal of Common Market Studies* 1265.

implementing acts to be adopted using the examination procedure, as set out in Article 5 of the Comitology Regulation.[10] According to this procedure, a committee is called upon for a binding opinion on a draft implementing act acting by qualified majority. If the committee delivers a positive opinion (a qualified majority of the committee votes in favour of the draft) the Commission can adopt the act. In case of a negative opinion (a qualified majority of the committee votes against the draft), the Commission cannot adopt the act, but can amend its proposal, or submit it to an appeal committee, where final voting takes place. Where the committee fails to deliver either a positive or a negative opinion, the Commission, subject to certain exceptions, may adopt the act. The examination committee is chaired by a Commission official. Draft implementing acts are often approved by consensus. If needed, examination committees give their opinion by qualified majority voting. In certain circumstances, the Commission can refer the opinion of the examination committee to the appeal committee. It has been noted that the comitology system works well for the large majority of decisions. However, in a number of high-profile and sensitive cases in recent years, Member States have been unable to find the necessary majorities to either vote in favour or against certain draft acts, a so-called 'no opinion' scenario. In these cases, the responsibility to take a final decision falls upon the Commission, obliging a decision to be taken without clear political backing from Member States.[11]

10 Daniel Finke and Jens Blom Hansen, 'Contested Comitology? The Overlooked Importance of the EU Commission' (2022) 29(6) *Journal of European Public Policy* 891.

11 European Commission, 'Comitology: Commission Proposes More Transparency and Accountability in Procedures for Implementing EU Law' (2017), https://ec.europa.eu/commission/presscorner/detail/en/ip_17_264.

# ARTICLE 30

# EVALUATION

**Andrea Miglionico**

1. **By 29 December 2026, the Commission shall carry out an evaluation of this Directive and present a report on the main findings to the European Parliament, the Council and the European Economic and Social Committee. The evaluation shall consist of at least the following:**
   (a) **the number of authorised credit servicers in the Union and the number of credit servicers providing their services in a host Member State;**
   (b) **the number of creditors' rights under non-performing credit agreements or of non-performing credit agreements purchased from credit institutions by credit purchasers domiciled or having their registered office or, if under their national law they have no registered office, their head office, in the same Member State as the credit institution, or in a different Member State than the credit institution, or outside of the Union;**
   (c) **an assessment of the existing money laundering and terrorist financing risk associated with the activities performed by credit servicers and credit purchasers;**
   (d) **an assessment of the cooperation between competent authorities under Article 26.**
2. **Where the evaluation identifies significant problems with the functioning of this Directive, the report shall outline how the Commission intends to address the identified problems, including steps and timings of the potential revision.**



## A. INTRODUCTION

30.01 This article regulates a common policy in EU law: the evaluation procedure of legislative acts. Specifically, the Commission is mandated to conduct an evaluation of the Directive and present a report by 29 December 2026. This evaluation will consider: the number of authorised credit servicers in the EU and the number of credit servicers providing their services in a host Member State; the number of creditors' rights under non-performing credit agreements or of the non-performing credit agreements purchased from credit institutions by credit purchasers domiciled or established in the same Member State as the credit institution, in a different Member State than the credit institution, or outside of the EU; the assessment of the existing money laundering and terrorist financing risk associated with the activities performed by the credit servicers and credit purchasers; and the cooperation between competent authorities. Paragraph 2 of the article states that if the evaluation report identifies significant issues with the application of the Directive, the Commission is mandated to intervene and find solutions to address the problems in a timely manner. This is an investigatory power of the Commission which conducts an assessment on the practical implementation of the Directive and its functioning among Member States.

As part of its better regulation agenda, the European Commission actively evaluates whether existing EU laws are meeting the needs of citizens and business.[1] The purpose of better regulation is to make European Union laws and policies simpler, more targeted and easier to comply with.[2] As noted, 'better regulation is not just about the process of law-making. It is also about the substance, implementation, and enforcement of EU laws. Laws need to be targeted, proportionate, predictable and clear – as does their enforcement and implementation'.[3] The Commission evaluates if specific laws, policies, and spending activities are fit for purpose and have delivered, at minimum cost, the desired changes to European businesses and citizens.[4] Fitness checks and evaluations inform political priority setting and contribute to strategic planning, **30.02**

1 The better regulation agenda helps the EU deliver evidence-based policies and laws that achieve their objectives in the most efficient way, while being tailormade to the needs of EU citizens, businesses, and civil society. The Better Regulation Guidelines and Toolbox provide concrete guidance to Commission services involved in preparing new initiatives and proposals, or managing and evaluating existing legislation. See European Commission, 'Better Regulation', https://commission.europa.eu/law/law-making-process/better-regulation_en.

2 Better regulation ensures that EU laws and policies are prepared in an open and transparent manner, informed by the best available evidence, and backed by comprehensive stakeholder involvement. See Marie Lecerf, 'Better Regulation: Joining Forces to Make Better Laws' (June 2022), European Parliamentary Research Service, https://www.europarl.europa.eu/RegData/etudes/ATAG/2022/733556/EPRS_ATA(2022)733556_EN.pdf.

3 Zach Meyers, 'Better Regulation in Europe: An Action Plan for the Next Commission' (March 2024), Centre for European Reform, p. 2, https://www.cer.eu/publications/archive/policy-brief/2024/better-regulation-europe-action-plan.

4 Giulia Listorti, Egle Basyte-Ferrari, Szvetlana Acs and Paul Smits, 'Towards an Evidence-Based and Integrated Policy Cycle in the EU: A Review of the Debate on the Better Regulation Agenda' (2020) 58(6) *Journal of Common Market Studies* 1558.

as well as to the revision of existing policies and legislation.[5] While evaluations and fitness checks are ex-post assessments of existing policies, their goal is to provide input to future revisions of the policy or legislation, if deemed necessary. They contribute to the process of structured screening of the EU acquis (stress-testing) aiming to ensure that it remains relevant, proportionate and fit to achieve its objectives in the most cost-efficient way.

## B. THE EVALUATION PROCEDURE AND BETTER REGULATION POLICY

**30.03** An evaluation is an evidence-based assessment of the extent to which a specific EU law, policy, or funding programme is: effective – in fulfilling expectations and meeting its objectives; efficient – in terms of cost-effectiveness and proportionality of actual costs to benefits; relevant – to current and emerging stakeholders' needs; coherent – internally and externally with other EU interventions or international agreements; and has EU added value (i.e. produces results beyond what would have been achieved by Member States acting alone).[6] A fitness check is a type of evaluation that assesses several related actions. It focuses on identifying how different laws, policies, and programmes interact, and their collective impact. The Better Regulation Guidelines and Toolbox provide common standards when the Commission evaluates the performance of its actions. All evaluations respect the principles outlined therein.[7] The Regulatory Scrutiny Board examines and issues opinions on the quality of selected evaluations and all fitness checks.[8] All evaluations and fitness checks are reported on in an evaluation report, which takes the form of a Commission staff working document.

**30.04** Commission evaluations and fitness checks analyse the performance of existing policies, programmes, and legislation. Based on evidence, evaluations assess how an existing policy or legislation is effective, relevant, coherent, and has an EU added value. These evaluations then inform the preparation of reviews or new initiatives. Impact assessments examine whether there is a need for

---

5 Paul J. Stephenson and Jonas J. Schoenefeld, 'The Role and Functioning of Evaluation in the European Union' in Frédéric Varone, Steve Jacob and Pirmin Bundi (eds), *Handbook of Public Policy Evaluation* (Cheltenham: Edward Elgar 2023) ch.17.

6 European Commission, 'Evaluating Laws, Policies and Funding Programmes', https://commission.europa.eu/law/law-making-process/evaluating-and-improving-existing-laws/evaluating-laws_en.

7 European Commission, 'Better Regulation: Guidelines and Toolbox', https://commission.europa.eu/law/law-making-process/better-regulation/better-regulation-guidelines-and-toolbox_en.

8 The Regulatory Scrutiny Board, an independent body of Commission officials and experts from outside the Commission, reviews impact assessments and selected evaluations. The Board publishes annual reports on what it has done to deliver on its mission.

EU action, analyse the possible impacts of available solutions, and guide the Commission's choice and preparation of the proposal. This analysis is carried out during the preparation phase, before the Commission finalises a proposal for a new or revised law. In addition, strategic foresight is an important tool for creating future-proof and coherent policies in all sectors. Strategic foresight explores different possible futures, alongside the opportunities and challenges they might present. Strategic foresight is set to become an integral part of the Better Regulation agenda. It will be embedded in policy-making across all policy areas to add a longer-term perspective, in particular in areas that are subject to rapid change.[9] Ultimately, it helps policymakers to act in the present to shape the future. In its Better Regulation Guidelines and Toolbox,[10] the Commission stresses that the guidelines are 'internal instructions for the Commission staff in order to deliver the objectives of better regulation', insisting they are not binding the Commission vis-à-vis other EU institutions.[11] The toolbox is intended to provide 'practical, hands-on guidance and operational details'; as a Commission internal document, the toolbox contains references to internal procedures and intranet pages that are not publicly available. Both the guidelines and the toolbox set out the methodology to be applied by the Commission for policy initiatives along the policy cycle. All future Commission initiatives and proposals are expected to be prepared in accordance with the updated guidelines and toolbox, although there will be a certain transition until their full implementation.

9 Foresight aspects, and notably major trends, will be considered in impact assessments, fitness checks, and major evaluations. See Stefano Vettorazzi and Irmgard Anglmayer, 'What is New in the Commission's 2021 Better Regulation Guidelines?' (February 2022), European Parliamentary Research Service, https://www.europarl.europa.eu/RegData/etudes/BRIE/2022/699463/EPRS_BRI(2022)699463_EN.pdf.

10 European Commission, 'Better Regulation Guidelines' (November 2021) SWD(2021) 305 final, https://commission.europa.eu/system/files/2021-11/swd2021_305_en.pdf.

11 Felice Simonelli and Nadina Iacob, 'Can We Better the European Union Better Regulation Agenda?' (2021) 12(4) *European Journal of Risk Regulation* 849.

# ARTICLE 31

# REVIEW CLAUSE

**Andrea Miglionico**

**Without prejudice to the legislative prerogatives of the European Parliament and the Council, by 29 December 2023, the Commission shall submit to the European Parliament and to the Council a report on:**

**(a) the adequacy of the regulatory framework regarding a potential introduction of caps on charges arising from the event of default applicable to credit agreements concluded with:**
  - **(i) natural persons for purposes related to the trade, business or profession of those natural persons;**
  - **(ii) SMEs, as defined in Article 2 of the Annex to Recommendation 2003/361/EC;**
  - **(iii) any borrower, provided that the credit is guaranteed by a natural person or is secured by assets or property belonging to that natural person;**

**(b) relevant aspects, including potential forbearance measures, of credit agreements concluded with:**
  - **(i) natural persons for purposes related to the trade, business or profession of those natural persons;**
  - **(ii) SMEs, as defined in Article 2 of the Annex to Recommendation 2003/361/EC;**
  - **(iii) any borrower, provided that the credit is guaranteed by a natural person or is secured by assets or property belonging to that natural person;**

**(c) the need for, and feasibility of, developing implementing or regulatory technical standards or other appropriate means to introduce common reporting formats for communications to borrowers under Article 10(2) and on forbearance measures.**

**Where appropriate, the report referred to in the first paragraph shall be accompanied by a legislative proposal.**

## A. INTRODUCTION

This article refers to the review procedure of the Directive. The review of legislation is part of the EU better regulation agenda[1] and responds to the obligation of the legislators to keep the existing body of legislation up to date.[2] The Commission was required to submit a report to the European Parliament and the Council, accompanied by a legislative proposal if appropriate, by 29 December 2023. This report should cover the adequacy of the regulatory framework regarding a potential introduction of caps on charges arising from the default applicable to credit agreements concluded with natural persons for purposes related with trade, business, or profession of that persons; micro, small, or medium-sized enterprises (SMEs); and any borrower, provided that the credit is guaranteed by a natural person or is secured by assets or property belonging to that person. The review also covers relevant aspects, including potential forbearance measures, of credit agreements concluded with natural persons for purposes related with trade, business, or profession of that persons; SMEs; and any borrower, provided that the credit is guaranteed by a natural person or is secured by assets or property belonging to that person. Finally, it addresses the need and feasibility to develop implementing or regulatory technical standards or other appropriate means to introduce common reporting formats for communication to borrowers under Article 10 and on forbearance measures. This is a relevant procedure which demands of the Commission the authority to inform the European Parliament and the Council about the effectiveness of the Directive on specific aspects such as the credit agreements concluded between market participants. The monitoring function of the Commission represents one of the key instruments of better regulation: evaluations,[3] fitness checks,[4] and impact assessments.[5] **31.01**

---

1 Better Regulation refers to a set of principles for designing EU policy and laws in a transparent, evidence-based manner with citizen and stakeholder involvement, covering the whole policy cycle from design to implementation, as well as evaluation and possible revision. See European Court of Auditors, 'Law-making in the European Union after almost 20 Years of Better Regulation' (2020) Review No 02, https://www.eca.europa.eu/lists/ecadocuments/rw20_02/rw_better_regulation_en.pdf.

2 Martin Weber, Nicholas Edwards and Stephan Huber, 'EU Review Clauses in Need of Review? An Analysis of Review Clauses in EU Legislation in the Context of Better Lawmaking' (2017) 8 *European Journal of Risk Regulation* 121–122.

3 Evaluation is an evidence-based assessment, undertaken by or on behalf of the Commission, of the extent to which an EU action has been effective, efficient, relevant to needs, and achieved EU added value.

4 Fitness Check is a comprehensive evaluation of a group of actions related in some way (usually through a common set of objectives) to identify and quantify any synergies or inefficiencies between actions, and their cumulative impact in terms of costs and benefits.

5 Impact assessment is a detailed analysis of a problem, including its underlying causes, the need for EU action and the advantages and disadvantages of potential solutions.

**31.02** Reviews of existing legislation provide an evidence-based assessment of the performance of policies and legislation.[6] Review findings support political decision-making and inform the design of possible future revisions. The systematic review of legislation has become a key policy-making tool at the EU level, most notably in the context of the EU's better regulation agenda. The European Parliament is strongly committed to the principles of better law-making, and particularly to the effective use of ex-ante impact assessment and ex-post evaluation throughout the legislative cycle. Accordingly, Parliament has a particular interest in following the transposition, implementation and enforcement of EU law and EU programmes and, more generally, monitoring the impact, operation, effectiveness, and delivery of policies and programmes in practice. Under Article 14 of the Treaty on European Union (TEU), the European Parliament is mandated to 'exercise functions of political control' of the Commission throughout the policy cycle. In the area of ex-post evaluation, Parliament scrutinises, inter alia, Commission action that is required to assess and review EU legislation after its adoption under the so-called 'review clauses'. The European Commission reviews, evaluates and reports on the implementation of a particular act after a certain number of years. While Parliament carries out its oversight duties in numerous ways, it does so in the area of ex-post evaluation by, among other things, scrutinising Commission action that is required to assess and review EU legislation after its adoption, as set out in the 'review clauses'.[7]

## B. THE REVIEW PROCESS

**31.03** There is no accepted common definition of 'review clause' in EU legislation. In most cases, the terminology reflects the evaluation procedure carried out by the EU institutions in order to monitor the correct implementation and transposition of legislative acts. Similarly, there is no 'typical' review clause in EU legislative acts and programmes. The review clauses vary in terms of their requirements, formulation, level of complexity, and detail. Specifically, review clauses: may have different requirements (from regular monitoring and reporting, including provision of data, on the one side, to reviews and evaluations of a legislative act or programme, on the other; some review clauses might call

6 Ex-post review of legislation is a key part of the EU Better Regulation policy, which aims at facilitating the achievement of public policy objectives at minimum cost and improving the added value of EU interventions.

7 Mark Dawson, 'Better Regulation and the Future of EU Regulatory Law and Politics' (2016) 53(5) *Common Market Law Review* 1209.

for the submission of a legislative proposal jointly with a review report, but this is not always the case); come in different forms (from regular, often annual, reports, to interim, mid-term, and final reports, to reviews and ex-post evaluations, sometimes including provisions for external evaluation); have different levels of complexity (from simple review provisions to complex, multiple provisions); might call for a single review at a certain point in the future or for repetitive reviews; and might be general or specific – review clauses might concern a legislative act or programme in its entirety, calling, for example, for a review of the legislative act itself, or they might concern only one or several specific articles of that act.[8] Review clauses also vary in terms of their formulation, level of complexity, and detail. While some are detailed and specific, others are quite general and/or vague and could potentially lead to a different follow-up. Despite the fact that review clauses are widely used in EU legislation, there are no common interinstitutional definitions of the different types of ex-post review. This can lead to 'situations where the content of a review clause, and correspondingly, its expected output is not always clear'.[9] The lack of common definitions of the different types of review possible leads to a myriad of terms or combinations thereof, notably regarding the ex-post reviews referred to as 'reviews' (e.g. 'review', 'review of the functioning and effectiveness', or 'review of all elements'). Other terms used are 'report on the results of the application', 'evaluation of the implementation', and 'report on the implementation and impact'. This lack of common definitions of the different types of ex-post review creates uncertainty as to what the Commission is required to look into and what kind of product it will produce.[10]

These review and monitoring clauses are usually included in individual provi- **31.04**
sions of the agreement with a title such as 'review', 'review clause', or 'evaluation'. They are usually included in the final provisions and cover the whole agreement. Special review clauses are not normally given a specific heading – such as 'special review', also their placement within the agreement is not always clear. These clauses very often require the review of a specific part of the agreement or a specific article. Commission evaluations and fitness checks

---

8 Ivana Kiendl Krišto with Vagia Poutouroudi, 'Review Clauses in EU Legislation. A Rolling Check-List' (July 2018), European Parliamentary Research Service.

9 European Court of Auditors, 'Press Release' (12 June 2018), https://www.eca.europa.eu/Lists/ECADocuments/INSR18_16/INSR_BETTER_REGULATION_EN.pdf.

10 European Court of Auditors, 'Ex-post Review of EU Legislation: A Well-established System, but Incomplete' (2018) Special Report No 16, https://www.eca.europa.eu/Lists/ECADocuments/SR18_16/SR_BETTER_REGULATION_EN.pdf.

analyse the performance of existing policies, programmes, and legislation.[11] Based on evidence, evaluations assess how an existing policy or legislation is effective, relevant, coherent, and has an EU added value.[12] These evaluations then inform preparation of reviews or new initiatives. Impact assessments examine whether there is a need for EU action, analyse the possible impacts of available solutions and guide Commission choice and preparation of the proposal. This analysis is carried out during the preparation phase, before the Commission finalises a proposal for a new or revised law. In addition, strategic foresight is an important tool for creating future-proof and coherent policies in all sectors. Strategic foresight explores different possible futures, alongside the opportunities and challenges they might present. Ultimately, it helps policymakers to act in the present to shape the future. Building on the regulatory fitness and performance programme (REFIT),[13] the Commission is moving into a higher gear to make EU laws simpler and to reduce unnecessary costs of regulation while still achieving intended objectives. By stress-testing the EU acquis through evaluations and fitness checks, the Commission's resulting simplification proposals will ultimately simplify EU laws and reduce regulatory burdens.

11 European Commission, 'Better Regulation', https://commission.europa.eu/law/law-making-process/better-regulation_en.

12 Policy tool resulting in a document or set of documents presenting a retrospective stocktaking of one or all aspects of an EU regulatory intervention (be it one or more legislative acts), with or without evaluative elements.

13 REFIT is the Commission's regulatory fitness and performance programme, which reviews existing legislation and measures to ensure they deliver the expected results at minimum cost and regulatory burden.

# ARTICLE 32

# TRANSPOSITION

**Andrea Miglionico**

**1. Member States shall adopt and publish, by 29 December 2023, the laws, regulations and administrative provisions necessary to comply with this Directive. They shall immediately communicate the text of those measures to the Commission.**

**2. They shall apply the measures referred to in paragraph 1 from 30 December 2023. By way of derogation from the first subparagraph, entities already carrying out in accordance with national law credit servicing activities on 30 December 2023 shall be allowed to continue carrying out those credit servicing activities in their home Member State until 29 June 2024 or until the date on which they obtain an authorisation in accordance with this Directive, whichever is the earlier. Member States that already have in place regimes that are equivalent to, or stricter than, those established in this Directive for credit servicing activities may allow entities already carrying out credit servicing activities under those regimes on 30 December 2023 to be automatically recognised as authorised credit servicers by the national provisions transposing this Directive.**

**3. When Member States adopt the measures referred to in paragraph 1, they shall contain a reference to this Directive or be accompanied by such a reference on the occasion of their official publication. Member States shall determine how such reference is to be made.**

**4. Member States shall communicate to the Commission the text of the main provisions of national law which they adopt in the field covered by this Directive.**



## A. INTRODUCTION

This article refers to the transposition of the Directive by Member States. It is a closure provision which indicates the timeline of adoption and publication **32.01** of the legislation into national law. Member States were expected to transpose the Directive into national legislation and regulation by 29 December 2023.[1] Member States were expected to apply those implementing measures from 30 December 2023, although entities already carrying out credit servicing activities on 30 December 2023 were allowed to continue carrying out those activities in their home Member State until the earlier of either 29 June 2024 or the date on which they obtain an authorisation under the Directive.[2] The scope of the Directive is limited to NPLs originated by EU credit institutions transferred or sold after 29 December 2023. The transposition of the Directive is crucial for the single market as it facilitates the cross-border sale and servicing of non-performing loans, increasing market liquidity and efficiency. It also helps to create a level playing field for credit purchasers and credit servicers across the EU. Specifically, the strengthened consumer protection measures assist in safeguarding borrowers' rights, reduce the risk of financial hardship and promote a more stable and trustworthy financial environment. The transposition of the Directive will provide legal certainty to stakeholders, creating a 'level playing field' in the EU countries.

**32.02** The NPLs Directive contains a number of discretions which Member States may exercise when transposing the provisions into national law. The deadline for the transposition of the Directive was 29 December 2023.[3] These rules apply from 30 December 2023. In this interim situation, the Directive states that entities in any EU Member State that carry out services pursuant to national law servicing activities after 30 December 2023 were allowed to continue carrying out such servicing activities until 29 June 2024 or until such entities obtain the relevant authorisation pursuant to the NPL Directive, whichever came first. In addition, any Member State that already has an equivalent or stricter legal framework for servicing activities than the one set forth in the NPL Directive may allow entities already carrying out servicing activities under such legal frameworks on 30 December 2023 to be automatically recognised as authorised servicers by the national provisions transposing the NPL Directive. The European Commission has adopted an implementing regulation dated 26 September 2023, laying down implementing technical standards

1 Although the deadline for transposing the NPL Directive was 29 December 2023, several EU countries have extensively delayed the transposition of the Directive into national law.

2 Member States were required to transpose this Directive by 29 December 2023. In February 2025, the Commission announced that it had decided to refer Bulgaria, Spain, Hungary, the Netherlands, Austria, Portugal and Finland to the Court of Justice of the EU (ECJ) for failing to transpose the Directive. See https://ec.europa.eu/commission/presscorner/detail/en/ip_25_405.

3 European Commission, 'Transposition Status – Credit Servicers and Credit Purchasers Directive', https://finance.ec.europa.eu/credit-servicers-and-credit-purchasers-directive_en.

(ITS) for the application of Article 16(1) of the NPL Directive with regard to the templates to be used by credit institutions for the provision to buyers of information on their credit exposures in the banking book. The Regulation is based on draft ITS submitted to the Commission by the European Banking Authority. The aim of the ITS is to provide a common standard for NPL transactions across the EU, enabling cross-country comparison and reducing information asymmetries between the sellers and buyers of NPLs. The Commission Implementing Regulation ((EU) 2023/2083)[4] sets out the templates to be used by credit institutions for providing information on certain in-scope NPLs (issued on or after 1 July 2018 that became non-performing after 28 December 2021) to credit purchasers. The templates will be used by credit institutions to provide detailed information on their credit exposures in the banking book to credit purchasers for the analysis, financial due diligence and valuation of a creditor's rights under a non-performing credit agreement or the non-performing credit agreement itself. The European Commission adopted the Implementing Regulation on 26 September 2023.

## B. PROCEDURAL MATTERS

Transposition of EU law is the procedure by which EU Member States incorporate EU directives into their national law in order to make their objectives, requirements and deadlines directly applicable.[5] Member States transposing directives into national law can choose the form and methods for doing so, but are bound by the terms of the Directive as to the result to be achieved and the deadline by which transposition should take place.[6] With regard to EU legislation and legislative procedures, Member States are obliged to transpose directives into their legislation within the prescribed deadline and to apply EU law correctly and effectively.[7] They are also obliged to report to the **32.03**

4 Commission Implementing Regulation (EU) 2023/2083 of 26 September 2023 laying down implementing technical standards for the application of Article 16(1) of Directive (EU) 2021/2167 of the European Parliament and of the Council with regard to the templates to be used by credit institutions for the provision to buyers of information on their credit exposures in the banking book.

5 https://www.europarl.europa.eu/cmsdata/226403/EPRS_ATAG_627141_Transposition_implementation_and_enforcement_of_EU_law-FINAL.pdf.

6 Directives must be incorporated by EU countries into their national legislation. Each directive contains a deadline by which EU countries must incorporate its provisions into their national legislation and inform the Commission to that effect. Member States play a key role in ensuring EU law is implemented correctly and in a timely manner. This is essential for people and businesses to optimally benefit from commonly agreed rules.

7 Andreas Witte, 'When does National Law Transpose a Directive?' (January 2017), ESCB Legal Conference 2016, 6–7 October 2016, p. 247, https://www.ecb.europa.eu/press/legconf/pdf/escblegalconference2016_201702.cs.pdf#page=249.

Commission on the transposition of directives into their national legislation, and on the performance of the legislation. Last, but not least, Member States are responsible for the enforcement of EU law (whether transposed or directly applicable) in their national legal systems. When the Commission uncovers a potential infringement of EU law, it launches a formal infringement procedure (Articles 258–260 TFEU).[8] The procedure begins when, for example, a Member State fails to communicate the measures transposing a directive's provisions, transposes a directive after the deadline, fails to transpose a directive at all or applies EU law incorrectly. Infringement proceedings can also be started by a Member State (Article 259 TFEU). The transposition of the NPL Directive establishes a structured legal framework for the management and transfer of NPLs, balancing the reduction of risks for credit institutions with borrower protection. The new framework enhances transparency and accountability in the secondary market for NPLs. Stakeholders are encouraged to review their internal procedures and authorisation requirements to ensure compliance.

**32.04** Directives need to be incorporated in Member States' national legislation. Each directive contains a deadline for transposition. By that date, EU countries must send the Commission the text of the national implementing measures, which incorporate the provisions of the Directive into their legislation. Delays in transposing EU law prevent citizens and businesses from enjoying the laws' benefits, create uncertainty as to what rules apply and negatively affect the functioning of the EU's internal market.[9] The Commission checks whether these national transposition measures are complete and meet the objectives set by the directive. If this is not the case, the Commission opens an infringement procedure for 'non communication'. The Commission may also initiate an infringement procedure in the case of incorrect transposition of directives. In some cases, where the Commission identifies a possible breach of EU law, it may decide to use a pre-infringement process, known as EU Pilot, instead of the infringement procedure. This is a tool that can be used where it is likely to lead to swifter compliance than a formal infringement procedure. It allows the Commission to resolve a number of cases without the need to move to an infringement procedure. This may be the case, for example, if the issues at stake are of a technical nature. It can also prove useful in cases where the

---

8 European Parliament, 'Monitoring the Implementation of EU Law: Tools and Challenges' (January 2025), https://www.europarl.europa.eu/cmsdata/292639/Study%20Monitoring%20implementation%20of%20EU%20law_Final.pdf.

9 European Commission, 'Implementing EU Law', https://commission.europa.eu/law/application-eu-law/implementing-eu-law_en.

Commission wishes to collect factual or legal information needed to carry out its assessment. It is not used where the breach of EU law is well-evidenced, obvious or self-acknowledged, nor is it used for more sensitive issues where discussions at a technical level are less likely to lead to a successful outcome. If national authorities fail to properly implement EU laws, the Commission may launch a formal infringement procedure against the country in question. If the issue is still not settled, the Commission may eventually refer the case to the Court of Justice of the European Union. In some cases, the Commission may request the Court to impose financial sanctions on the Member State concerned. The main purpose of an infringement procedure is to ensure that Member States apply EU law in the general interest. They therefore focus on systemic issues affecting many people or businesses. In isolated instances of possible wrongful application of EU law, issues may be best addressed via the national redress system.

On 21 December 2023, the Loan Market Association (LMA) published **32.05**
a guidance note on the Directive.[10] The LMA's guidance note provides an overview of new EU rules on NPLs contained in the Directive and the ITS. Together with the guidance note, the LMA also published a series of template notices required to be delivered under the Directive.[11] These can be adapted by market participants to help them meet the Directive's disclosure and reporting requirements.[12] The set of template notices comprises: a notice to be provided to a borrower, under Article 10(2) of the Directive, by a credit purchaser (that is, to a non-EU bank); a notice to be provided to a competent authority, under Article 15(2), by an EU bank selling NPLs to a credit purchaser; a notice to be provided to a competent authority, under Article 18(1), by a credit purchaser which appoints an EU bank, an EU supervised consumer credit or mortgage creditor or a credit servicer to perform credit servicing activities in relation to NPLs transferred to the credit purchaser; and a notice to be provided to a competent authority, under Article 20(1), by a credit purchaser selling NPLs to a new credit purchaser.

10 LMA, 'Loan Market Association Produces Reporting Templates to Help Market Participants Navigate the New EU Directive on Non-performing Loans' (11 January 2024), https://www.lma.eu.com/news-publications/press-releases?id=212&search_str=NPLs.

11 Both the guidance note and the templates were produced in consultation with a working group of sell-side banks and buy-side investors in the market.

12 The LMA published, in addition to a detailed guidance note on the Directive itself, a series of template notices which can be adapted by sellers and buyers to help them satisfy the various disclosure and reporting requirements. See https://www.lma.eu.com/npl.

# ARTICLE 33

# ENTRY INTO FORCE

**Andrea Miglionico**

**This Directive shall enter into force on the twentieth day following that of its publication in the Official Journal of the European Union.**



## A. INTRODUCTION

**33.01** This article refers to the date of entry into force of the Directive following the publication of act in the Official Journal of the European Union.[1] It is the date on which an EU act takes effect, which is the date specified in it or, in the absence of such date, the twentieth day following that of its official publication or notification. Adequate and timely publication of legislation provides legal certainty, which is a fundamental principle of European Union law.[2] EU legislation is unenforceable against individuals unless it has been published in that manner in the Official Journal.[3] According to Article 297 TFEU, legislative acts shall enter into force on the date specified in them or, in the absence thereof, on the twentieth day following that of their

1 The Official Journal of the European Union is the official publication (gazette) for EU legal acts, other acts and official information from EU institutions, bodies, offices and agencies. See https://eur-lex.europa.eu/oj/direct-access.html. The Official Journal, published by the EU's Publications Office and more commonly referred to as the OJ, is the core part of EU law.

2 A measure adopted by the public authorities cannot be enforced against individuals before they have an opportunity to acquaint themselves with it through its proper publication in the Official Journal of the European Union. See Case C-98/78 Racke v Hauptzollamt Mainz [1979] ECR 69 at para 15, ECJ; Case C-161/06 Skoma-Lux v Celní Reditelství Olomouc [2007] ECR I-10841 at para 37, ECJ (see para 34 on the meaning of 'proper publication'); Case C-146/11 Pimix ECLI:EU:C:2012:450 at para 33, ECJ.

3 Case C-161/06 Skoma-Lux sro v Celní Reditelství Olomouc [2007] ECR I-10841 at para 37, ECJ. See also Case C-146/11 Pimix ECLI:EU:C:2012:450 at para 34, ECJ.

publication.[4] Non-legislative acts adopted in the form of regulations and directives which are addressed to all Member States, as well as decisions which do not specify to whom they are addressed, shall enter into force on the date specified in them or, in the absence thereof, on the twentieth day following that of their publication.[5] Other directives, and decisions which specify to whom they are addressed, shall be notified to those to whom they are addressed and shall take effect upon such notification. The deadline for implementation of the NPL Directive into domestic legislation has passed, though many Member States are yet to comply, the rules may still be enforceable in defaulting Member States.[6] The entry into force is commonly associated with the transposition deadline, which is the date of the last day of the period that EU legal acts, mainly EU Directives, grant to Member States to adopt the necessary measures to comply with their provisions.[7] The transposition deadline is the date on which the EU provisions that require implementation need to be part of the national legal systems of the Member States. The transposition period is the time that runs from the entry into force of a Directive, the moment on which the obligation to implement is originated and the date on which the national implementing legislation needs to be adopted and in force in the Member States addressed by the EU legal act (transposition and applicability of the implementing legislation occurs).[8] Member States must issue implementing measures on or before the implementation deadline is met or risk the commencement of infringement proceedings by the EU Commission over failure to fulfil obligations under the Treaties.

## B. THE APPLICABILITY OF LEGISLATION

The entry into force of an EU legislation represents the date when the legisla- **33.02**
tion has legal existence in the EU legal order and in the national legal order of each Member State. It is common practice that the Directive enters into force 20 days after its publication in the Official Journal of the EU. Sometimes the date of entry into force is also the date of applicability of a Directive, meaning

4 See https://eur-lex.europa.eu/eli/treaty/tfeu_2016/art_297/oj/eng.

5 Julie Dickson, 'Directives in EU Legal Systems: Whose Norms Are They Anyway?' (2011) 17(2) *European Law Journal* 190.

6 Miranda Campbell, 'Q&As on the EU Non-Performing Loan Directive' (2024) 17(2) *Corporate Rescue and Insolvency* 64.

7 Bernard Steunenberg and Mark Rhinard, 'The Transposition of European Law in EU Member States: Between Process and Politics' (2010) 2(3) *European Political Science Review* 495.

8 Asya Zhelyazkova, 'Complying with EU Directives' Requirements: The Link between EU Decision-making and the Correct Transposition of EU Provisions' (2013) 20(5) *Journal of European Public Policy* 702.

that from the date when it enters into force, the Directive is also applicable; it can be fully invoked by its addressees and is fully enforceable. However, due to the complexity of the domains that are regulated, a period of time may be needed between the date the Directive enters into force, i.e. it legally exists, and the date it can actually be applied, i.e. the date when it is enforceable and the legal rights and obligations can be effectively exercised. This period of time (*vacatio legis*) is introduced for Member States, competent authorities, operators, organisations, licence holders and any other addressees or beneficiaries of the Directive to prepare their systems, processes, procedures, documentation, etc. for compliance with the new rules.[9] It is common practice of the legislator to establish two different dates under the article on entry into force. One date establishes the legal existence of the act (entry into force)[10] while the second date establishes the term when it becomes applicable (applicability).[11] The date of applicability therefore represents the date from which the Directive can produce rights and obligations on the addressees and can be directly enforced towards the courts, administrations, national governments, etc. This means that before the date of applicability, obligations or privileges can neither be exercised nor enforced. Member States cannot start delivering authorisations, approvals, certificates, etc. issued in accordance with the new regulations and at the same time producing all the legal effects of the Directive from the date of entry into force of the Directive, but only from the date of its applicability. However, during the gap period existing between the date of entry into force and the date of applicability, Member States and competent authorities can prepare the process towards the issuance of such authorisations, approvals and any other certificates in accordance with the new provisions. In addition, during the period of vacatio legis, an option that Member States and competent authorities can consider, in order to avoid issuing certificates on the last day before the date of applicability, is to issue the new certificates in accordance with the new regulation while clearly indicating in those certificates that they

9 Vacatio legis is a period given for the recipients of the legislation to adapt to the upcoming rights and obligations and take the necessary measures to benefit from the legal effects of the Directive, namely for the purposes of mutual recognition of approvals in the credit servicers market.

10 At this date, a regulation becomes part of the EU legislation. However, often provisions are not applicable by this date, but later. In many cases, entry into force is the 20th day following the publication date. In other cases, an absolute date is specified.

11 Date where provisions of the regulation must be followed and can be enforced by Member States. Not all requirements specified in a regulation necessarily must apply at the same date. Differences concerning the date of application are specified in the Directive.

are only valid as of a certain date that would coincide with the date of applicability of the Directive. This means that new procedures and authorisations may be issued, but are not yet effective and cannot be mutually recognised among Member States until the common date of applicability established by the Directive.

# ARTICLE 34

# ADDRESSEES

**Andrea Miglionico**

**This Directive is addressed to the Member States.**



## A. THE ADDRESSEES OF THE DIRECTIVE

**34.01** This article refers to the addressees of the Directive, which are the Member States. It is a standard clause in directives that indicates that the provisions of the Directive are valid in the EU countries' legal order. It is usually placed as the last Article of the legislative act to make clear that the Directive is addressed to the Member States (unless other parties are indicated), placing the responsibility for its implementation on national governments. A directive can be addressed to and is binding upon Member States alone and cannot be addressed to subjects of EU law other than the Member States. Although directives may be directed to one Member State or to a certain number of Member States, in practice, they are usually addressed to all of them.[1] The specification of the addressees signifies the last provision of the Directive and is placed before the closing formula of the legislative act, setting the place and date of adoption of the legislation.[2] This article should be read in conjunction with provisions that establish the rules for the transposition of the Directive.

1 Sacha Prechal, *Directives in EC Law* (2nd edn., Oxford: Oxford University Press 2005) 55.

2 Eleni Kosta, 'Article 65 Addressees' in Eleni Kosta and Franziska Boehm (eds), *The EU Law Enforcement Directive (LED): A Commentary* (Oxford: Oxford University Press 2024) 846.

## B. LEGAL ANALYSIS

The NPLs Directive is addressed to the Member States, meaning it is their responsibility to incorporate the legislative act into national law. Each country is obliged to create enforcement mechanisms, designate competent authorities, and ensure businesses comply with the new rules. While organisations must meet security and reporting obligations, it is the governments that set the legal framework. The Directive is implemented through national laws, which define how organisations must comply. While Member States must follow the core requirements of the Directive, they have some flexibility in defining enforcement mechanisms, penalties, and specific compliance processes. However, they cannot weaken the Directive's minimum security standards or reporting obligations. If a Member State fails to implement the Directive correctly, the Commission can take legal action, including referring the country to the Court of Justice of the European Union. This could result in fines or other measures to force compliance, ensuring a uniform approach across all EU countries. Under primary law, the EU has only limited powers of enforcement, as EU law is usually enforced by the Member States. Furthermore, Article 291(1) TFEU adds that 'Member States shall adopt all measures of national law necessary to implement legally binding Union acts'. Where uniform conditions for implementing legally binding Union acts are needed, the Commission exercises its implementing powers (Article 291(2) TFEU). As pointed out, the addressees of the law ascertain their rights and duties in their own language, and may, however, rather paradoxically, also lead to interpretation disputes in case of alleged or real linguistic discrepancies between the language versions.[3] Further, the accessibility of the Directive should be public and accessible to all addressees. Failure to transpose the language of the Directive into the national legal systems within a given time limit makes Member States responsible to the Commission and leads to an infringement procedure.[4] Article 260(3) TFEU was not solely to encourage Member States to transpose directives efficiently **34.02**

3 Stefaan van der Jeught, 'Current Practices with Regard to the Interpretation of Multilingual EU Law: How to Deal with Diverging Language Versions?' (2018) 11(1) *European Journal of Legal Studies* 9.

4 Klen Teder, 'Failure of a Member State to Fulfil Obligations: Case C-577/23 Commission v Estonia (Directive ECN +)' (2025) *Journal of European Competition Law & Practice*, https://doi.org/10.1093/jeclap/lpaf036.

and within the applicable timeframe.[5] Member States should provide a list of those provisions under domestic law which transpose the equivalent provisions under the Directive. This would allow the Commission to assess if there are any manifest lacunas in these measures when determining whether to impose the penalty.

5 According to Article 260(3) TFEU, the Commission can propose financial sanctions when a Member State fails to transpose a directive into national law on time and fails to communicate the missing transposition.

# INDEX